WHO RUNS THE CHURCH?

Books in the Counterpoints Series

Church Life

Exploring Theology

WHO RUNS THE CHURCH?

4 VIEWS
ON CHURCH GOVERNMENT

· **Peter Toon**
· **L. Roy Taylor**
· **Paige Patterson**
· **Samuel E. Waldron**

· **Paul E. Engle** *series editor*
· **Steven B. Cowan** *general editor*

GRAND RAPIDS, MICHIGAN 49530 USA

We want to hear from you. Please send your comments about this book to us in care of zreview@zondervan.com. Thank you.

ZONDERVAN™

Who Runs the Church?
Copyright © 2004 by Steven B. Cowan

Requests for information should be addressed to:

Zondervan, *Grand Rapids, Michigan 49530*

Library of Congress Cataloging-in-Publication Data

Who runs the church? : four views on church government / Peter Toon ... [et al.] ; Steven B. Cowan, general editor.
    p. cm.—(Counterpoints)
    Includes bibliographical references and index.
    ISBN 0-310-24607-5
    1. Church polity. 2. Protestant churches—Government. I. Toon, Peter, 1939-
II. Cowan, Steven B., 1962- III. Series : Counterpoints (Grand Rapids, Mich.)
BV647.3.W48 2004
262—dc22   2004008341

Peter Toon: Unless otherwise noted, Scripture taken from the King James Version. Other Scripture taken from the *Holy Bible: New International Version*®. NIV®. Copyright © 1973, 1978, 1984 by International Bible Society. Used by permission of Zondervan. All rights reserved. **L. Roy Taylor:** Scripture taken from *The Holy Bible: English Standard Version,* copyright © 2001 by Good News Publishers. Used by permission. All rights reserved. **Paige Patterson:** Bible text from *The New King James Version.* Copyright © 1979, 1980, 1982, Thomas Nelson, Inc. **Samuel E. Waldron:** Scripture taken from the *New American Standard Bible.* Copyright © 1960, 1962, 1963, 1968, 1971, 1972, 1973, 1975, 1977, 1995 by The Lockman Foundation. Used by permission.

Printed in the United States of America

---

04 05 06 07 08 09 10 /❖ DC/ 10 9 8 7 6 5 4 3 2

CONTENTS

5. CLOSING REMARKS

INTRODUCTION

Steven B. Cowan

"But we've never done things that way."

The woman with whom I was speaking was a member of the church I pastored. She was objecting to my proposal that we modify our church polity in light of what I and others took to be the biblical teaching on church government. I replied, "But the question has to do with what the Bible teaches on the matter, doesn't it?"

"But it's not Baptist." The church was a Baptist church, and the proposal for changing church government required that we adopt a view most contemporary Baptists do not hold.

"Well, many of the *earliest* Baptists did things this way," I explained. "So, even though modern Baptists follow a different pattern, this form of church government is not unheard of among Baptists. And, again, the real issue is biblical teaching."

"But it's not practical," she retorted.

After explaining why the proposal might be more practical than she thought, I said, "Again, the real issue is what the Bible teaches about church government."

"But we've never done things that way."[1]

Though the church eventually adopted the proposal, this woman remained unconvinced. Her response to my arguments reflects what I take to be the general and common approach to questions of church government among Christians today. There is a familiar and traditional way that individual churches (and denominations) conduct their polity, but there is little or no theological reflection on that tradition. Things are done a certain way because that's the way they have always been done.

I am not sure that I can prove that this is how most Christians approach such issues, but my own personal experience provides me with much anecdotal evidence. I never recall, for example, ever hearing any discussions of biblical teaching on church government as I grew up among Southern Baptists (though there was the occasional accusation that Presbyterians and Methodists had it all wrong). And even when I went to seminary (a large Southern Baptist seminary), neither my classes in systematic theology nor in pastoral ministry offered so much as one lecture on forms of church government and the rationale that we Baptists have for doing things our way. I do not think that my experience is unique.

Thus the central question addressed in this book: *How (and by whom) should the church be governed?* In this brief introduction, I will seek to explain why this question is important, what answers may be and have been given to the question, and what other questions arise in relation to it.

THE IMPORTANCE OF THE QUESTION

As the book's subtitle suggests, there is a variety of answers to our central question (at least four!). This variety underscores the importance of the question in more than one way. For one thing, the question is surely important *historically*. Disagreements over matters of ecclesiology, including forms of church government, have been the source of numerous schisms in church history. For example, in seventeenth-century England, ecclesiological debates led to the formation of three major Protestant traditions. The Presbyterians and Congregationalists separated from the Church of England and from each other in part over the nature of church government. Baptists parted ways with all of the above over disagreements involving either infant baptism or church government. So, the question of this book is clearly relevant to explaining the visible disunity of the body of Christ.

For this reason, the question of church government also has great *practical* significance for the contemporary church. There is much discussion today of Christian unity, including strong appeals to look beyond our traditional differences and present a united front in our mission to reach the world with the gospel of Jesus Christ. It would, therefore, seem apropos for Christians to revisit the ancient debate over forms of church government. If disagreements on this topic lie at the root of Christian disunity, then what could be more germane to promoting unity than to engage in serious theological dialogue over the nature of church government and other related ecclesiological issues?

Sadly, such dialogue these days is rare. Of course, the major systematic theologies published recently still contain the required chapter on church government for the sake of completeness.[2] And denominational presses no doubt publish books and pamphlets on such ecclesiological issues for their constituencies. Yet, despite the historical and practical significance of church government for church unity, there has been a dearth of books and articles written in venues and for audiences designed to engender serious dialogue among dissenting parties.[3] And my own experience as a pastor and teacher tells me that the average evangelical Christian, no less than the scholar, has not so much as considered that "the way we do things in church" might actually be wrong. Writing in a slightly earlier generation, but with words clearly applicable for today, Thomas Witherow once remarked that

> the majority of Christians contrive to pass through life without ever giving an hour's thought to this most interesting theme. Most people are content to let their ancestors [today it would be their felt needs] choose a church for them, and every Sabbath walk to Divine worship in the footsteps of their great-grandfathers—they know not why, and care not wherefore. . . . The result is, that vast masses of men and women live in utter ignorance, not only of the Scriptural facts bearing on the case, but even their own denominational peculiarities; they are Prelatists, Independents, or Presbyterians by birth [or self-interest], not conviction; they view all forms of Church Government as equally true, which is the same thing as to count them worthless; they have no definite ideas on the subject; and thus, in the absence of public instruction, they are . . . prepared to fall in with any system or no system, as may best suit their private convenience or promote their worldly ambition.[4]

There may be explanations for the neglect of the study of church government. On the one hand, much of the contemporary call for unity among Christians is decidedly atheological. The call is for Christians to achieve visible unity by ignoring or de-emphasizing theology. "Doctrine divides" is the slogan. And the proposed solution is to set aside doctrine and unite around shared religious experiences or a common love for Jesus. In such a climate, "denominational differences" (i.e., matters of ecclesiology) will be thought to be the most unimportant and unnecessary of theological pursuits.

On the other hand, even among those who take theology seriously, the question of church government may seem unworthy of deep thought and discussion. As Robert Reymond has pointed out, "It has become a commonplace in many church circles to say that Scripture requires no particular form of church government. The form a given church employs, it is said, may be determined on an *ad hoc* or pragmatic basis."[5] This perspective may be found even among theologians. For example, Millard Erickson has written that "churches are not commanded to adopt a particular form of church order" and that "[t]here may well have been rather wide varieties of governmental arrangements [among New Testament churches]. Each church adopted a pattern which fit its individual situation."[6]

David L. Smith echoes the same view. He writes:

> The ministry of governance of the church is an important one. Yet Scripture never sets forth one form of governance as the one, God-ordained model. At most, the Bible advances certain principles that suggest a representative role—principles best served by the congregational form. But, nothing prohibits other forms which would work effectively while allowing the members a major voice in the making of decisions.[7]

Smith and Erickson both claim that the New Testament can offer at least some support for any of the three historical forms of church government—episcopal, presbyterian, or congregational. This, of course, is an exegetical issue that would properly occupy part of any theological discussion on church government (and one of the authors of this book—Peter Toon—would likely agree with this point). Yet the apparent implication that these authors would draw from their assessment of the biblical data is that the form of church government adopted by any given church is largely a matter of indifference as long as certain basic and broad principles are maintained. Another evangelical theologian, Wayne Grudem, argues a bit more explicitly for this conclusion. Though claiming the New Testament *does* exhibit a particular form of church government, he says nevertheless that "a number of different types of church government systems seem to work *fairly well*."[8] He adds that

> the form of church government is not a major doctrine like the Trinity, the deity of Christ, substitutionary atonement, or the authority of Scripture. . . . It seems to me, then, that there ought to be room for evangelical Christians to differ amicably over this question in the hope that further understanding may be gained. And it also seems that individual Christians—while they may have a preference for one system or another, and while they may wish at appropriate times to argue forcefully for one system or another—should nevertheless be willing to live and minister within any of several different Protestant systems of church government in which they may find themselves from time to time.[9]

The authors of the present book disagree. Certainly, Christians ought to "differ amicably." And no doubt the form of church government is not an *essential* doctrine of the Christian faith (like the Trinity and the deity of Christ) which determines someone's eternal destiny. Nevertheless, despite our profound disagreements, we are all united in the conviction that the form of church government is not a matter of indifference. As Thomas Witherow says, "Though we may not regard the polity of the New Testament Church as essential to human salvation, we do not feel at liberty to undervalue its importance."[10] In other words, the issue of church government may not be a doctrine crucial to the *esse* (being) of the church, but it is a doctrine crucial to the *bene esse* (well-being) of the church, vital to its spiritual health.

For one thing, some of the contributors herein will contend that the Bible is *not* silent or unclear on the form of church government. They will argue that the Bible clearly sets forth a particular form of church government (though, of course, they will disagree on what that form is!). And even if the Bible by itself turns out to be ambiguous on this matter, it may be (as one of our authors will argue) that a combination of scriptural principal and church tradition will clearly set apart one form of church government as the most prudent and providentially ordained model. We do not, of course, expect you, the reader, to take our word for any of this, but we do ask your indulgence long enough to consider the arguments on all sides. And we ask you to keep in mind that the position which denies one best or biblically mandated form of church government is itself a view that can and has been disputed. Clearly, it is important for both the health and unity of the church that Christians discuss and debate this issue.

THE MAJOR OPTIONS IN CHURCH GOVERNMENT

Historically, there have been three major models of church government: episcopalianism, presbyterianism, and congregationalism. In this section, I will provide a brief sketch of these three models.

Episcopalianism

Though various episcopal bodies will differ on important details, they all share the characteristic of having an episcopate (office of bishop) distinct from and superior to the officers of local churches. Episcopal government is thus, in some sense, hierarchical, with the bishop ordaining and governing the leaders (often called priests or rectors) of several local parish churches. The territory and churches over which the bishop rules is called a "diocese." In many episcopal denominations, an archbishop has authority over many (or all) the other bishops (see Figure 1).

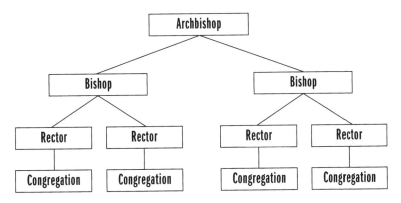

Figure 1

The Roman Catholic Church is perhaps the most well-known and straightforward episcopal system.[11] The governments of the Eastern Orthodox churches are also episcopal in nature. Among Protestants, the Anglican Church, the Episcopalian Church in the United States, the United Methodist Church, and some Lutheran groups all practice versions of episcopalianism. In this book, the Reverend Dr. Peter Toon, a rector in the Church of England, defends a moderate version of episcopalianism common among Protestants.

Presbyterianism

This system can be said to be a "representative" form of church government (see Figure 2). In presbyterianism, the local church is ruled by a group of elders (called a "session" by most groups) who are chosen by the congregation. Members of the sessions from several local churches in a geographical region are also members of the *presbytery* which has ruling authority over their several churches. In turn, at least some members of each presbytery are also members of a general assembly which governs the entire denominational body.

In addition to this general structure, presbyterians also distinguish two types of elders. Some elders are *ruling* elders who provide leadership in setting policy and supervising various church ministries, but do not necessarily preach and teach. *Teaching* elders are given the responsibility to preach and teach in the church.

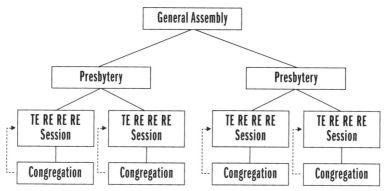

Figure 2

There are many groups that practice presbyterianism, including the Presbyterian Church (USA), the Presbyterian Church in America, the Christian Reformed Church, and (somewhat more loosely) the Assemblies of God. Dr. L. Roy Taylor, the stated clerk of the Presbyterian Church in America, provides a defense of the presbyterian model in this book.

Congregationalism

What most clearly distinguishes the congregational system from the others is the doctrine of *the autonomy of the local church* (sometimes called *independency*). What is meant by this is that each local church, under the authority of Christ, governs itself. For congregationalists, no ecclesiastical authority exists outside or above the local assembly of believers.

As one might expect, within these autonomous local churches is a great variety of internal structures and operations. In fact, Wayne Grudem has identified at least five distinct systems of internal congregational government.[12] Not all of these are widely practiced, however. So, for the purposes of this book, I have chosen to include what seem to me to be the two most significant and prominent of the congregationalist models.

Single-Elder Congregationalism. In this model—probably the most widely used—the local church is overseen by one elder or pastor chosen by the congregation and clearly distinguished as its spiritual leader. The single elder is usually assisted by (or in some cases *supervised* by) a group of deacons (see Figure 3). Under the term "single-elder congregationalism," I also include those churches which have additional pastoral staff-persons (e.g., associate pastors, youth pastors, etc.), but which clearly set apart one pastor as *the* (senior) pastor.

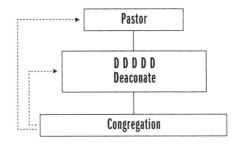

Figure 3

Plural-Elder Congregationalism. Similar to presbyterianism, those who follow this model see the local church as governed, by biblical design, by a *plurality* of elders or pastors (see Figure 4). It is distinguished from presbyterianism, however, in that (1) the elders have no authority or jurisdiction outside their own local church, and (2) there is no distinction made between ruling and teaching elders. For plural-elder congregationalists, all elders/pastors both teach and rule.

Plural-elder congregationalism is demarcated from single-elder congregationalism in that (1) a church with only one pastor is considered deficient, and (2) all the pastors/elders are considered to be equal in authority. The plural-elder congregationalist strongly rejects the idea of a *senior* or *primary* pastor in the church. Rather, the pastors of the local church work together as a team to lead and teach the church.

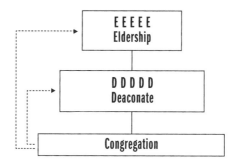

Figure 4

Congregationalism in its various forms is practiced by many denominations, including Southern Baptists, General Baptists, and all other Baptists, as well as Churches of Christ, Bible churches, and all other independent churches. In this volume, Dr. Paige Patterson, president of Southwestern Baptist Theological Seminary and former president of the Southern Baptist Convention, writes in defense of single-elder congregationalism. Samuel E. Waldron, a Baptist pastor and Ph.D. candidate in theology at Southern Baptist Theological Seminary, defends plural-elder congregationalism.

ISSUES IN CHURCH GOVERNMENT

Several interrelated issues must be addressed to answer the question of how the church should be governed. In order to be as thorough as possible, I have asked each of our four contributors to discuss the following matters (though each in his own preferred style and order).

1. *The structure of church government.* As outlined in the previous section, each form of church government reflects a distinctive pattern of organization. Each author, therefore, will explain in some detail how he believes the church (whether local or denominational) should be structured.

2. *The number and nature of church officers.* Are the officers of the church limited to the pastors and deacons of the local church, or should there be bishops and archbishops holding ecclesiastical offices beyond the local church? What authority do these church officers have? How do they relate to each other—is there a senior pastor who supervises the other church staff or are all pastors on par regarding their office and authority? Is there a distinction between ruling and teaching elders? What is the role of deacons?

3. *The historical development of church government.* Though this book is primarily concerned with systematic and not historical theology, I thought it would be helpful to the readers to put each model of church government in historical context. The history of doctrinal beliefs and practices can aid us in both understanding and evaluating them. For example, as the reader will soon discover, one objection raised about the episcopal system is that it cannot be found in Scripture, but makes its appearances in the early post-apostolic church. On the other hand, some episcopalians (e.g., Peter Toon) believe the fact that this system appears so early in church history is a powerful argument for its legitimacy.

4. *Hermeneutical assumptions.* Where one comes down on the issue of church government will depend to some degree on the principles of interpretation with which one approaches the biblical text. In particular, it will clearly matter whether one believes that church practices should be limited to what the Scriptures explicitly teach or command, or whether one believes that churches are free to adopt any practice that the Scriptures do not forbid. The reader will discern that this question sharply distin-

guishes the Anglican Peter Toon (who rejects a strict *sola Scriptura* approach) from the other authors.

5. *The biblical data relevant to church government.* The Bible does have something to say about church polity, even if it is not decisive or clear. Each author was asked to discuss what he takes to be the relevant biblical texts and draw whatever conclusions he thinks are warranted given his hermeneutical assumptions. Taylor, Patterson, and Waldron all believe that the biblical data are decisive for their respective views on church government. Toon disagrees, arguing that whatever may be gleaned from Scripture regarding church government is insufficient, and that it is God's providential guidance of the church in its first five centuries—which resulted in the episcopacy—that must decide the issue.

6. *The practical implications of church government.* Doctrine almost always has practical implications. It is evident that the form of church government a church adopts will have a direct impact on the lives of church members and the course of the church's life and ministry. How a church is structured and what officers it ordains (and who ordains them) impacts who does what in the ministry of the church as well as how it is done. Moreover, the form of church government determines what problems a church will face and how they will be solved. For example, the episcopal system (at least in principle) has the potential to settle disagreements in the church relatively easily by having the leadership make authoritative pronouncements.[13] Single-elder congregationalists have to be concerned more than others about one person having too much power and "lording it over" the flock, while plural-elder congregationalists must avoid the potential of a deadlocked leadership when equal pastors disagree on the right course of action.

These are the issues most relevant to adjudicating the centuries-long disagreements over forms of church government. This book's contributors have endeavored with God's help to present the best possible case for their respective views in an effort to promote understanding and unity in the body of Christ. It is hoped as well that this book will contribute, in God's grace and providence, to the *bene esse* not only of local churches whose members read it, but also of the glorious church universal.

Introduction Notes

[1]This conversation is not verbatim, though it does reflect the gist of what was discussed at the time.

[2]Three recent and widely used systematic theologies that "keep the tradition" are Millard J. Erickson, *Christian Theology* (Grand Rapids: Baker, 1985); Wayne Grudem, *Systematic Theology: An Introduction to Biblical Doctrine* (Grand Rapids: Zondervan, 1994); and Robert L. Reymond, *A New Systematic Theology of the Christian Faith* (Nashville: Thomas Nelson, 1998).

[3]For example, a survey of articles appearing from 1970 to 2002 in a major arm of evangelical interdenominational scholarship, *The Journal of the Evangelical Theological Society*, turned up thirty-one articles related to any topic in ecclesiology. The great majority of these dealt with the role of women in the church, only two addressed issues related to the sacraments, and only two addressed issues directly related to church government. The latter were W. Harold Mare, "Church Functionaries: The Witness in the Literature and Archaeology of the New Testament and Church Periods," *JETS* 13:4 (Fall 1970): 229–39; and Gordon D. Fee, "Reflections on Church Order in the Pastoral Epistles, with Further Reflection on the Hermeneutics of Ad Hoc Documents," *JETS* 28:2 (June 1985): 141–51.

[4]Thomas Witherow, *The Apostolic Church: Which Is It?* 5th ed. (originally published in 1881; reprinted in Korea), 16–17.

[5]Reymond, *A New Systematic Theology*, 896.

[6]Erickson, *Christian Theology*, 1084. In fairness, I should add that Erickson does believe that there are biblical principles that are best fulfilled by the congregational form of church government (see pp. 1085–87).

[7]David L. Smith, *All God's People* (Wheaton, Ill.: Victor, 1996), 375.

[8]Grudem, *Systematic Theology*, 936 (emphasis his).

[9]Ibid., 904.

[10]Witherow, *The Apostolic Church*, 14.

[11]The Roman Catholic Church is the one episcopal church that can clearly be said to be hierarchical. There is an archbishop (the pope) who rules authoritatively over all the bishops, who in turn govern dioceses each with several parishes overseen by priests. By contrast, the Church of England, though structured similarly, gives less authority to the archbishop and bishops. The Archbishop of Canterbury serves in more of an advisory role and functions as the president of the general synod of bishops.

[12]See Grudem, *Systematic Theology*, 928–36.

[13]In practice, however, things do not work so easily in episcopal churches (especially those less rigidly structured than Roman Catholicism) because leaders are often reluctant to be heavy-handed.

Chapter One

EPISCOPALIANISM

EPISCOPALIANISM

Peter Toon

While those who hold to an episcopal church polity encompass a wide theological spectrum, what unites them is the use of the term "bishop" (Greek, *episcopos*) to describe a subgroup within the totality of all of its ordained pastors or ministers.

For some, "bishop" is used of the pastor who, in the hierarchy of clergy, is above the deacon and the presbyter (= priest) and constitutes an altogether different and higher order of ministry. In this understanding bishops are seen as belonging to the historical episcopate and of being "in apostolic succession." The Roman Catholic, Orthodox, Eastern, Old Catholic, United (e.g., Church of South India), and Anglican churches, as well as a few national Lutheran churches (e.g., in Scandinavia) ascribe to this view.

In other denominations, including those of a Methodist and Lutheran origin, "bishop" is used of the clergyperson who is the superintendent of a given area wherein are multiple parishes and pastors. However, as bishop-superintendent, he or she is not considered above other clergy in terms of holy hierarchy, divine order/appointment, or unique relation to the apostles and the apostolic age.

Because Anglican Christians are called Episcopalians in America, because I worked among them within the Protestant Episcopal Church of the United States for eleven years, and because I have worked within the Church of England for a much longer period, I shall focus my discussion on episcopalianism with special reference to the Anglican Communion of Churches, of which the American Episcopal Church and the established Church of England are members. In doing so, I must note that the noun "episcopalianism" is seldom used by members of the Anglican Communion of Churches, which trace their origins to the Church of England (*ecclesia anglicana*). Instead, Episcopalians in America and Anglicans worldwide usually speak of the historic episcopate to indicate that the order of bishops is found through time and across space since the early centuries of the Christian church.

Thus in this presentation I shall take "episcopalianism" specifically to mean "the church government/polity of the thirty-eight member churches of the international Anglican Communion of Churches," noting that the names of these member churches vary from "Anglican" to "Episcopal" to "the Church of [a country]." To put it another way "episcopalianism" is used as an alternative to speaking of "the Anglican Way." As I proceed, I shall make contrasts between the Anglican Way and other Ways that come under the general heading of episcopalianism.[1]

I proceed by making four basic and preliminary points.

PRELIMINARIES

The first point: in this Anglican jurisdiction of the one, holy, catholic, and apostolic church, bishops are not solely in charge. Certainly they have responsibilities and duties which are uniquely theirs—e.g., ordaining presbyters and deacons, caring pastorally for them, and defending the faith from error—but the dioceses and provinces are governed by synods, and the parishes by vestries/local councils. Thus it is preferable to speak of *synodical* government rather than episcopal government. A synod consists of a house of bishops, a house of clergy (presbyters and deacons), and a house of laity. Major decisions—e.g., a change in rules for church marriages—have to be supported by all of these houses. In contrast, lower clergy and laity do not have the same full participation in church government in either the Orthodox or the Roman Catholic churches where a synod consists only of bishops.

The second point: by virtue of the Threefold Ministry of bishops, priests, and deacons, the Anglican Way has definite similarities to the Orthodox Way (of Constantinople, Antioch, Moscow, etc.) and the Roman Catholic Way (of the Vatican in Rome). However, in the Anglican Way, while archbishops serve as the titular heads (= presidents) of the college of bishops in a given province, there are no patriarchs or popes. The Archbishop of Canterbury is the first among equals, not the patriarch of the Anglican Communion of Churches or the head of the Church of England. In fact, the Anglican Way claims to be "reformed Catholic" as against Eastern Catholic or Western/Roman Catholic or Medieval Catholic.

The third point: each of the member provinces of the Anglican Communion of Churches is an independent entity which freely chooses to be within the Communion. The Anglican Church of Uganda does not take orders from the Anglican Church of Canada and vice versa. Yet instruments of unity are in place to seek to keep the Communion stable and walking together. Obviously, these instruments of unity do not always work well, especially when some member churches in the West seek to embrace modern sexual innovations and do so without full consultation with their partners abroad. For that reason, the instruments of unity—the See of Canterbury, the Anglican Consultative Council, the Lambeth Conference of Bishops, and the Primates' (or Archbishops') Meeting—have major problems to solve and healing work to accomplish in this new millennium.

Indeed, much of the turmoil within the Anglican world over the past thirty or so years has been the product of imbalances in the episcopal form of government, usually due to one of the partners (bishops, clergy, or laity) attempting to overmaster the other two. By analogy, the situation is rather like what happens in marriage when the husband or wife decides to move beyond the theological order of the home (as envisioned, say, by the Book of Common Prayer) to a simple dominance by power over the other. These struggles for power are not reflections of the underlying polity, but only of fallen human nature.

The fourth point: since the Reformation of the sixteenth century, the Anglican approach to doctrine, worship, discipline, and polity has been deeply influenced by the commitment to norms found in the patristic period of the early church. This commitment has been put simply in terms of 1, 2, 3, 4, and 5. The Anglican Way rests upon *one* canon of Scripture with *two* testaments, *three* creeds (Apostles', Nicene, and Athanasian, summarizing the essentials of the catholic faith as found in Holy Scripture), *four* ecumenical councils (from Nicea in AD 325 to Chalcedon in 451, setting forth dogma, doctrine, and canon law), and *five* centuries of historical development (of polity, canon law, liturgy, etc.)[2] Thus any exposition of Anglican polity or church government is always an exercise in the use of Scripture *and* tradition. The full authority of Scripture is not in question or doubt, but the way in which it is received and interpreted is significant.

In contrast, the Roman Catholic and Orthodox churches, while embracing the patristic era, also give equal or semi-equal weight to the developing tradition of the following centuries in West and East; the Methodist and Lutheran churches give much less weight to the tradition of the first five centuries.

PATRISTIC ORIGINS

Those churches which maintain the historical episcopate claim that their polity is based upon that which developed in the providential guidance of God from the apostolic age through the first few centuries of the Christian church. For them, this means that it is both wholly in accord with apostolic teaching and takes into account the practical results of the evangelization, church planting, and teaching of the apostles, their fellow workers, and their successors.

Thus the Anglican form of church government is an attempt to conform in general terms to the pattern in place in the early church in the third, fourth, and fifth centuries.[3] That is the church which actually decided, under God, the content of the canon of the New Testament; established the first day of the week as the festival of the Resurrection or the Lord's Day; created major feasts/festivals (Easter, Pentecost, etc.); and set forth the dogmas of the blessed, holy, and undivided trinity of the Father, Son, and Holy Ghost and of the one person of Jesus Christ, made known in two natures, divine and human. In contrast, the "episcopalian-ism"of the Roman Catholic and Orthodox churches took much longer to develop, needing more time for their special character-istics to become explicit (e.g., the emergence of the papacy and its claim to be the successor of Peter, the head of the college of bishops and the vicar of Christ on earth).[4]

Returning to the patristic era, we have to accept that our knowledge of the church and how it was actually organized locally is minimal from the apostolic age until the end of the second century. In the *Letters* of St. Ignatius of Antioch, written early in the second century, a clear differentiation is evident among bishop, presbyter, and deacon, but this distinction may not have existed in all city churches. Apparently, however, by circa AD 200 such hierarchy was in place virtually everywhere. In the scope of the Threefold Ministry of bishops, presbyters, and deacons, the bishop was the chief pastor and teacher of the flock as well as president of the college/meeting of presbyters. Elected by the church membership, the bishop was usually ordained/consecrated by existing bishops. (Records exist that show lists of bishops for each church were kept, including the names of bishops by whom they were ordained and consecrated.) And as city churches (with their one bishop and several presbyters) established missions in nearby towns, presbyters went to the smaller churches to serve as pastors, and so it was that bishops came to have multiple churches in their care and presbyters came to be pastors of individual churches. From this process developed the diocese.

Naturally the larger congregations in the major cities exercised greater influence because of their resources and strategic position in the Roman Empire. The bishop of such churches was likely to be given the title of *archbishop* or *metropolitan* or, in a few cases, *patriarch*, and to function as president of the meetings of bishops in a given area.

To be more specific, we may say the following in terms of the developing concept of "apostolic succession." For Ignatius of Antioch (circa 105), the bishop was the center of the Christian congregation, its true celebrant of the Eucharist, and the guarantee of its apostolicity. For Irenaeus of Lyons (died c. 200), some six or seven decades later, the primary emphasis was upon the bishop as holder of an apostolic see and thus the sign of continuity in apostolic faith and teaching. Crucial to his understanding as he faced a vast array of Gnostic sects was the publicly known succession from an apostle of Jesus Christ. Thus he included in his writing a list of those apostolic men who had held the major sees. Fifty years after the death of Irenaeus, the chief concern of Cyprian of Carthage (who engaged in controversies with Decians and Novatians) was the unity of the catholic church. For him, succession to the office of bishop was central.

From the first part of the third century we possess in *The Apostolic Tradition*, usually ascribed to Hippolytus (died c. 236), copies of the ordination services used at Rome and elsewhere. The

Threefold Ministry is the norm and all ordinations are performed by bishops. Only bishops ordain a bishop; a bishop ordains presbyters, with presbyters assisting; and only a bishop ordains deacons. It is to be noted that the consent of the congregation was essential to the ordinations. And ordination is seen both as giving authority to act as the minister of Christ and of giving the power/gift of the Holy Spirit for particular tasks of ministry.

It may be useful to note that "episcopacy" as used theologically, and not as a form of ecclesiastical organization, refers to the office of oversight within the body of Christ, the household of God, the seat of authority, and the fount of ministry. That the *episcope* of the church in the earliest times should have settled in the form of monoepiscopacy (rather than in the form of presbyteral episcopacy) is a fact that one cannot set aside. As a minimum we surely have to say that it was allowed, if not directed, by the Holy Ghost.

From the second century on, church governance was chiefly through bishops' decretals (disciplinary letters), local regional councils, and (from 325) general councils. The latter expressed their determinations and rules for public conduct of clergy and laity in the church in terms of "canons."[5] These were then enforced by the local bishops. In time these canons were gathered together (e.g., the *Dionysiana* of 514 by Dionysius Exiguus and then the *Decretum* of Gratian in the mid-twelfth century).

To commend and defend the emerging polity of the early church, as classical Anglicans do, is not to claim an infallibility for the church in the third, fourth, and fifth centuries. Obviously, the church erred and was imperfect in many matters, as *The Articles of Religion* makes clear. Yet it is difficult to believe that Almighty God, the Father of our Lord Jesus Christ, would have allowed the church in its formative years of growth and expansion in Europe, Africa, and Asia to go so seriously wrong as to make a major mistake in terms of its general polity and church government.

Obviously there were weak and bad bishops (just as there were many holy, wise, and learned ones) and obviously there were theological developments in the late patristic period concerning the role of certain bishops—especially that of the bishop of Rome—which seemed to go way beyond that which is in harmony with both the letter and the ethos of the New Testament. Even so, the general institution of the Threefold Ministry and of the principle of one bishop with one diocese seems to have been specifically what God in his providence both purposed and allowed.

THE SCRIPTURES AND THE FATHERS

In the preface to the Ordinal ("The Form and Manner of Making, Ordaining, and Consecrating Bishops, Priests, and Deacons") are these words:

> It is evident unto all men, diligently reading Holy Scriptures and ancient Authors, that from the Apostles' time there had been these Orders of Ministers in Christ's Church—Bishops, Priests and Deacons. Which Offices were evermore held in such reverend estimation, that no man might presume to execute any of them, except he were first called, tried, examined and known to have such qualities as are requisite for the same; and also by public Prayer, with Imposition of Hands, were approved and admitted thereunto by lawful Authority.

So let us visit the "Holy Scriptures and ancient Authors" to verify this claim.

The New Testament (against the background of holy hierarchy in the Old Covenant) suggests the seed if not the full flower, the principle if not the full concept, of the differentiation of ordained ministers. Consider: the Lord Jesus Christ commissioned and sent out not only the Twelve but also the Seventy (Luke 9–10); the relation of the apostle Paul to those who assisted him (e.g., Timothy and Titus); and the relation between Timothy and Titus and those whom they ordained and appointed. Note also the intriguing references to "them that have the rule over you" (Heb. 13:17), to them who "are over you in the Lord" (1 Thess. 5:12), and to "such as these" [the household of Stephanas] (1 Cor. 16:15–16, NIV). Further, it is possible that James, the Lord's brother, was (what was later called) a monarchical bishop in Jerusalem (see Acts 21:18). It is not hard to see the Threefold Ministry in its infancy.

While noting such, one also readily concedes that the well-known passage, Titus 1:5–7, identifies the terms *presbyteros* and *episcopos* (cf. also Acts 20:17, 28; 1 Peter 5:1–2). Yet, when these words were written in the first century, all the churches acknowledged that the visiting apostle or evangelist or representative of the apostle had an authority in certain matters "above" that of the local presbyters/bishops and the local congregation of Christ's flock.

It is important to recognize that the modern Anglican, unlike some of his seventeenth-century ancestors, does *not* see any blueprint for the polity and government of the church written in Scripture.[6] He is too well aware that biblical studies have shown that there is no one form of ordained ministry and church government found in the books of the New Testament. Rather, there are several forms and types. He is conscious that the development of monoepiscopacy has been much studied and various theories have been advanced as to why this particular form became dominant and then universal.

As to the meeting of the church leadership in local, national, and international synods/councils, the Anglican again sees the seeds and justification of this in such passages as Acts 15:28 and Matthew 18:20. In 1930 a committee of the Lambeth Conference of Bishops expressed the general view of Anglicans as to the emergence of the episcopate:

> The Episcopate occupies a position which is, in point of historical development, analogous to that of the Canon of Scripture and the Creeds.... If the Episcopate ... was the result of a ... process of adaptation and growth in the organism of the Church, that would be no evidence that it lacked divine authority, but rather that the life of the Spirit within the Church had found it to be the most appropriate organ for the functions it discharged.[7]

The case of the emergence of the canon of Scripture is illuminatory. The church of God the Father was wholly based on the gospel concerning his Son, our Lord Jesus Christ, from the beginning but it was that church which collected, sifted, and gave its approval to those documents now a part of the Canon. That is, the church recognized which documents were inspired by the Holy Ghost and had the authority of an apostle behind them and then decided that these were the books of sacred Scripture. So the church witnessed and recognized the emergence and growth of the historical episcopate.

Examining the biblical basis of ordained ministry, the Roman Catholic biblical scholar Raymond E. Brown comments:

The fact that the episcopate is seen as a structure that gradually developed in the Church rather than as something that was within the expressed direction of Jesus does not, in my opinion, reduce the episcopate to just another possible form of church government. Episcopacy is intimately related to apostolicity which is an essential note of the Church. In its basic meaning apostolicity expresses the Church's fidelity to the apostles' proclamation of the Gospel and its continuation of their mission to bring men under God's rule (kingdom) heralded by Jesus. An episcopacy that, at least in a limited way, is traceable to the apostolic period can function as a clear sign of apostolicity and as an effective means of preserving the continuity of apostolic proclamation and mission. Acts 20:28–30 and Titus 1:9–11 indicate that even in NT times one of the principal tasks of the episcopate was to preserve the apostolic teaching free from heresy. The lists of bishops that appeared in the late 2nd century (in particular the lists of the Roman bishops) were intended to demonstrate a line of legitimate teachers as a guarantee that the teaching of the churches faithfully represented the teaching of the apostles. The formalizing of ordination at the hands of the bishops served to make clearly recognizable those whom the Church had delegated to celebrate the Eucharist and thus keep the sacramental tradition pure.[8]

THE ANGLICAN COMMUNION OF CHURCHES

The history of the Anglican Communion of Churches begins in England, the land of the Angles, with the church that was known and is described (e.g., in the Magna Carta) as *Ecclesia Anglicana*. With the arrival of the Roman Empire in Britain came those with the Christian gospel and soon followed churches and martyrs (e.g., St. Alban, the first British martyr of either 209 or 305). The Celtic church, as it is known, was sufficiently well organized to send bishops to the Synod of Arles in 314 and to the Council of Ariminum. After the arrival of Bishop Augustine (sent from Rome in 597) and the establishment of the See of Canterbury, the Celtic and Roman branches of the church united and the whole land began to organize into dioceses. This is the period of the Anglo-Saxon church and lasted until the Norman conquest.

The resulting *Ecclesia Anglicana* was in communion with the Bishop of Rome and the catholic church of West and East. She also was a missionary province, sending missionaries to evangelize the pagans of Britain and of northern Europe (see, e.g., the work of St. Boniface [680–754], the "apostle of Germany").

In the following centuries, *Ecclesia Anglicana* used a liturgy in Latin for its public worship as did its forebears in Rome and continental Europe. Also she came more and more under the influence of the Bishop of Rome, who claimed the right to appoint bishops for the English dioceses and receive taxes. During the Middle Ages, English kings often strongly protested and resisted this papal power.

Therefore, when in 1533–36, Henry VIII broke all relations between his kingdom and the Bishop of Rome, he was left with a nation organized into provinces, dioceses, and parishes administered by archbishops and bishops, priests and deacons, and communities of monks and nuns. At first, the public religion remained exactly what it had been for centuries. But gradually and then quickly under Henry's son, Edward, reforms arising from the influence of the Renaissance and the Protestant Reformation in Germany and Switzerland began to make their way into the *Ecclesia Anglicana*, now called in the vernacular "the Church of England."[9] With the King, acting alone or through Parliament, assuming the place previously occupied by the Pope, the Church of England adopted a reformed Catholicism. Under Queen Elizabeth I in 1559 this adoption was solidified and defended against Roman Catholics abroad and Puritans at home.

Those who complain about the interference of the civil government in the Church of England may need to be reminded of the role that Constantine played in the calling of the Council of Nicea and the production of the Nicene Creed in AD 325. The Reformation Church of England claimed and accepted the same imperial authority for Henry VIII, Edward VI, and Elizabeth I. What people often miss, however, is that the civil ruler in such a conception of polity remains a representative—a double representative, in fact—of God, through the vocation as ruler, and of the people, as their constitutional head. This system was not an invention of Constantine or Henry, but only an application of Paul's and Peter's teaching about civil governors in the New Testament, with the background stretching to the role of kings in Israel and Judah, especially such models as David, Solomon, and Josiah.

In terms of the Church of England's church government, the inherited organization of provinces, dioceses, and parishes remained intact. So too did the ancient gatherings of clergy in convocation, where changes in church practice and law were approved. Further, the Threefold Ministry of bishop, priest (presbyter), and deacon was retained. But to replace the variety of Latin service books of the medieval period, Archbishop Thomas Cranmer produced the Book of Common Prayer in English, which included all the services the parishes needed for daily worship, funerals, weddings, and baptisms. He also produced the Ordinal, which included the public services for the making of deacons, the ordaining of priests, and the consecrating of bishops. What went by the wayside were the monasteries and convents. What changed were the language and doctrine of the church—not the basic dogmas of the faith as set forth in the creed—but the teaching on sacraments, the way of salvation, and the relation of Scripture to tradition. The revised doctrine is highlighted and set forth in the Thirty-Nine Articles of Religion.

As for canon law, the English Reformation required not only new laws but a new basis for lawmaking. The massive medieval law code from the fifteenth century, the *Corpus Juris Canonici*, was not relevant in many particulars. In a 1534 convocation the clergy resolved that "the Bishop of Rome has not in Scripture any greater jurisdiction in the kingdom of England than any other foreign bishop," and thus the Church of England removed herself from the principal lawmaking authority in the Western church. And so she drew up her own revised canon law, a process which came to its completion with *The Canons of 1604.*

To guide the work of reformation and renewal, the reformed Catholic (= Protestant) leaders of the Church of England in both Parliament and convocation looked to the church of the Fathers, the early church before it was divided into East and West. Thus was adopted the commitment stated above in terms of 1, 2, 3, 4, and 5. And from this basis of God-inspired Scripture and providence-guided tradition, the position of the Church of England as a church that had retained the episcopate, the liturgy, and traditional canon law was defended by such writers as John Jewel in *An Apology for the Church of England*

(1562) and Richard Hooker in *The Laws of Ecclesiastical Polity* (1594–97). The latter specifically defended the polity of the Church of England against Puritan (presbyterian) calls for major changes in the Church of England in a Genevan direction, changes to remove the order of bishops and radically change the liturgy and canon law.

In opposing the Puritan call for the parity of all ministers/pastors, Hooker wrote:

> A Bishop is a Minister of God, unto whom with permanent continuance, there is given not only power of administering the Word and Sacraments, which power other presbyters have; but also a further power to ordain Ecclesiastical persons, and a power of Chiefty in Government over Presbyters as well as Lay men, a power to be by way of jurisdiction a pastor even to Pastors themselves.[10]

For Hooker, the presbyter is a full minister of Word and sacraments but his "authority to do these things is derived from the Bishops which did ordain him thereunto, so that even in the things that are common unto both, yet the power of the one, is as it were certain light borrowed from the other's lamp."[11]

John Jewel was wholly committed to the final authority of the Scriptures for the church but in the use of and interpretation of the Bible he saw clearly the need for help from the ancient church. "In this conference and judgement of the Holy Scriptures, we need oftentimes the discretion and wisdom of learned fathers." And he continued, "We for our part have learned of Christ, of the Apostles, of the devout fathers" and thus "verily in the judgement of the godly five hundred of those first years are worth more than the whole thousand years that followed afterward."[12]

In 1654 Archbishop John Bramhall looked back over a century of the history of the Church of England as a catholic and reformed church and wrote: "We do not arrogate to ourselves either a new Church, or a new religion or new Holy Orders....Our religion is the same as it was, our Church the same as it was, our Holy Orders the same as they were, in substance; differing only from what they were formerly, as a garden weeded from a garden unweeded."[13] *Ecclesia Anglicana* of 1400 was thus the same Church as *Ecclesia Anglicana* of 1600. One of the major weeds that had been expelled from the garden was, of course, "popery"!

In the Thirty-Nine Articles, Article XXXVII makes it clear that the Bishop of Rome has no jurisdiction in the realm of England (other Articles reject Roman doctrines of the Mass, purgatory, innovation of saints, and justification). The presumption is that the Roman Catholic Church requires the kind of reformation that the Church of England has experienced.

The polity of the Reformed (Evangelical) and Catholic Church of England (and churches that originated from her) may be described as "mixed"—a combination of episcopal, presbyterial, and congregational authorities, expressed in a representational system. The King and Parliament represented the laity, the bishops exercised their authority under law, and the presbyters (even before the reintroduction of convocations, etc.) had both the protection of law and the "parson's freehold" to permit their free operation, again under the same law that governs all. At the parish level the churchwardens as laymen had great responsibility for the upkeep of the church, the maintenance of its services, and the relief of the poor and needy.

As mentioned earlier, in the Roman Catholic Church, and to a great degree in the Orthodox churches, the presbyters (priests) and laity only have a limited authority at the parish level in terms of the implementation of what is decided "above" them. However, the Lutheran and the Methodist churches allow for the full participation of laity in decision-making at the national as well as the local level.

Anglican polity was in the sixteenth century, and has remained into the twenty-first century, a purposely cumbersome system, since it is meant to frustrate the immediate demands of fallen men for quick action to be imposed on all. These quick impositions are almost always wrong, given human nature. The current distortions in Anglican polity, much visible in the American Anglican Church (ECUSA), for example, are all essentially the result of demands for quick action and the denial of the traditional consultation and harmonization of the partners in a mixed polity. One example of the distortion is the development of the office of bishop as the chief executive officer of the diocese and thus also its chief liturgical officer. This produces a very different atmosphere and relations than when a bishop is understood as a pastor and shepherd intended to provide godly teaching, help, and guidance.

It is worth recalling that the American Episcopal Church's adaptation of the Anglican system within a republican form of government, known as the compromise of 1789, removed all temporal/prelatical power from the bishops, leaving them only spiritual/sacramental authority. (In England at that time, bishops still were thought of as prelates.) Thus the Protestant Episcopal Church of the newly created United States of America did a fine thing in making bishops primarily shepherds and teachers of the flock. Regrettably this proper understanding was seriously eroded during the second half of the twentieth century, the result being a complete departure from the original and wise American Anglican polity. That departure has been the engine of disunity in America ever since, including within the small Anglican continuing churches (formed since the 1970s by secession from the Episcopal Church) to the extent that they have imitated the radically changed polity of the contemporary ECUSA.

The Anglican Way was exported to countries around the world both by British colonists, for their own spiritual welfare, and by dedicated missionaries for the salvation of souls.[14] At first, the churches overseas were merely extensions of the Church of England, but later they became independent Anglican churches without the special relation to the state that applied and still applies in England. The result is that in the third millennium there are many more active Anglican Christians outside than within England. And making allowances for local culture and customs, all these independent Anglican churches, whether in the West Indies of East Africa, Malaysia or Canada, have essentially the same polity as the mother church.

In each national church or province there are dioceses with their bishops; within the dioceses are parishes with their pastors (priests and deacons). In each diocese there is a diocesan synod chaired by the bishop and within each national church or province there is a national/provincial synod chaired by the presiding bishop/archbishop of the province. In all these synods are representatives of clergy and laity so that decisions truly include the whole body and not merely the bishop(s) or clergy. And at the parish level there is the parish council or the vestry. Obviously, differences in details are numerous in such a large global Communion which embraces so many races and cultures.[15]

The laity's representation is almost never a direct democracy. It really can't be, unless the episcopate and the lesser clergy are to be excluded from government. The closest Anglicans come to direct democracy would be the annual parish meeting, but even there the chief authority is the election of representatives to serve on the vestry. And, until quite recently, the rules in many provinces governing the authority to vote at parish meetings excluded women, not out of misogynism, but to place the authority in the heads of households (as representatives of them) and to avoid sowing dissension within households (by creating the circumstances in which a husband and a wife might be able to vote against one another in a parish meeting).

BISHOPS AND THEIR PLACE IN EPISCOPALIANISM

Like the Orthodox churches, the Eastern churches, and the Roman Catholic Church, the Church of England and the Anglican Communion have always accepted the need and usefulness of bishops as the chief pastors. To these bishops is given the care of the whole church, clergy, and laity, as well as the responsibility to teach and defend the faith, supervise worship, administer the sacraments, ordain priests and deacons, and maintain discipline. This role and the distinction between bishops and presbyters was simply a given of the English Reformation under Henry VIII and Edward VI.

But as the Church of England matured in her reflections on how she differed from continental Protestantism and Romanism, her divines came to hold common certain convictions about episcopacy/the historical episcopate.

The first may be expressed in terms of order or ordered government in the Church of God. Only those who have been rightly ordered/ordained by those who have the authority to ordain are allowed to function as pastors and ministers of Word and sacrament in the national church. (The details of this ordering are supplied by the Ordinal.) The Lambeth Conference of 1958 stated:

> Ordination must be performed by those who have received authority to exercise *episcope* in the Body, and to admit others to share in the ministry. This acknowledgement by the Body of the authority of the ordaining member means that his own ordination to the ministry of

episcope must be recognized and accepted. From this arises the principle of continuity by succession, which appears to be indispensable, at least from a human point of view.[16]

The second commonly held conviction is that the office of bishop in the church of God represents a partial (not total) continuation of the office of an apostle. Of course, the apostles had and could have no successors in their capacity as eyewitnesses of the resurrected Lord, with a direct commission from him. What the historical episcopate continued was the ministry of oversight of the church of God in matters of worship, doctrine, evangelization, and discipline.

As in the Orthodox and Roman Catholic churches, the diocesan bishop may be assisted in a large diocese by other bishops who are subordinate to him and who are called by such names as suffragans, auxiliaries, coadjutors, and assistants; however, there are serious questions as to the wisdom of having multiple bishops in one diocese, even if only one is in charge. Unlike bishops of the Orthodox and Roman Catholic churches, Anglican bishops are allowed to marry.

The Church of England's third conviction relates to the papacy. It holds that while the Bishop of Rome is certainly to be regarded and honored as the bishop of the historic church in that ancient and great city and may be accorded the honor of "Patriarch of the West," he is *not* to be given any further titles, especially the excessive ones that emerged in the medieval period. For Anglicans, the pope has no authority in any other diocese than his own and any others which may call for his specific help and intervention. (For more on the papacy, see the conclusion below.)

While there is full agreement on the fact of bishops in the Anglican Way, there are various views of the relation of the historical episcopate to the whole church. These views have often been stated in terms of the *esse* or the *bene esse* or the *plene esse*.

The Esse

The claim that the historical episcopate is of the *esse* (true being) of the one, holy, catholic, and apostolic church is made by a minority, specifically Anglo-Catholics or very high churchmen. Proponents claim that the episcopate *guarantees* the church. Thus the church derives all her authority from the Lord Jesus Christ

through the divinely ordained means of the historical episcopate. Only bishops, who are in this apostolic succession of persons and doctrine, and the priests whom they ordain, have
authority and grace to celebrate the Eucharist as an effectual
sacrament of grace. As such, denominations that do not possess
the historical episcopate cannot be sure that the sacraments they
offer are genuinely and truly means of conveying the presence
of the Lord Jesus Christ and the grace of God the Father.

The Bene Esse

The claim that the historical episcopate is of the *bene esse*
(well-being) of the one, holy, catholic, and apostolic church is made
by evangelical churchmen or liberal churchmen alike. Proponents
recognize that the church has a variety of branches and that many
of these branches do not maintain the historical episcopate.
Nonetheless, they accept that these branches, be they of sixteenth-
or nineteenth-century vintage, Presbyterians or Southern Baptists,
constitute Christian societies where the gospel is preached and the
Lord obeyed. Thus, their arguments in favor of the historical episcopate tend to be utilitarian: the value of an ancient and long succession of persons and doctrine in time and through space;
focusing local leadership in one person, not a group; making a
bishop a shepherd of his flock and father in God to his clergy. In
short, they hold that episcopacy is the best as well as the most natural method of church government, for it brings the greatest good
to the church of God in terms of value and usefulness.

The Plene Esse

The claim that the historical episcopate is of the *plene esse*
(fullness of being) of the church is made by those who believe
that the high claim of *esse* is erroneous and that the low claim of
bene esse is inadequate. This is the position that I would take. Our
doctrine of the historical episcopate as the *plene esse* of the church
proceeds from the position that the church is called to be one
and holy and catholic and apostolic. We acknowledge that none
of the branches or denominations of the church contain and
reflect fully all four marks. All are in some ways deficient, be
they churches with bishops or without.

But in this view the historical episcopate is seen as providing the embodiment of the gospel in church order in two ways. First, it provides the effectual sign of unity, the biblical proclamation that the church of Jesus Christ is one. Second, it includes the principle of apostolicity. The episcopally ordained ministry is sent to represent Christ to his church and is representative of his church. It provides the guardianship of the Word and sacraments, of the faith, and of the flock of Christ. The historical episcopate is thus an effectual sign of the relation of Christ to his church, for it shows forth his authority within his church.

That said, it will be a fully expressive and instrumental sign *only* in a future, reunited, visible church on earth. Thus it belongs to the *plene esse* and not the *esse* of the church. Episcopal orders are necessary not for the *existence* of the church but for the *fullness* or perfection of being of the church.

At this point I need to comment on the expression "apostolic succession," which can be used in several ways. Here are two. It may refer to the succession of bishops in a given see or bishopric *or* it can point to a succession of bishops and ministers in the church through space and time through the means of episcopal ordination and consecration.

As used in the second sense, it is the God-given focus of unity in the church through space and time. The episcopal office is best understood as a whole, one and indivisible, with the individual bishops sharing in it. In this corporate or collective episcopate, each bishop forms a living link both between the church of his place and other local churches as well as between the church of today and that of generations past and generations to come. Obviously, the historical episcopate cannot guarantee unity any more than it can guarantee orthodoxy in a sinful world where people can exercise freedom to disagree and do their own thing. But to accept these present realities in no way negates the episcopate as a God-given unity that one day will be perfected.

Unlike the Orthodox and Roman Catholic churches but like the Lutherans and Methodists, the Anglican Communion regards as true and genuine Christians those baptized in denominations that profess the Nicene Creed yet do not have the apostolic succession. However, in proposals for union with them, Anglicans ask that the historical episcopate become a part of the new unity. Ever since the Lambeth Conference of 1888, the

Anglican Communion has made it clear that the basis on which it will engage in a potential union in any part of the world is "the Lambeth Quadrilateral," which comprises these four statements:

1. The Holy Scriptures of the Old and New Testaments as containing all things necessary to salvation and as being the rule and ultimate standard of faith.
2. The Apostles' Creed as the Baptismal Symbol; and the Nicene Creed, as the sufficient statement of the Christian Faith.
3. The two Sacraments ordained by Christ himself—Baptism and the Supper of the Lord—ministered with unfailing use of Christ's words of Institution, and of the elements ordained by him.
4. The historical Episcopate, locally adapted to the methods of its administration to the varying needs of the nations and peoples called of God unto the Unity of his Church.

The Quadrilateral assumes that each church, on the one side the Anglican and on the other, say, the Lutheran, already has its own formularies and that the purpose of these four statements is to establish that there is a basis to begin discussions toward intercommunion and unity.

The recent agreements for intercommunion between the Evangelical Lutheran Church of America and the Episcopal Church of the U.S.A. include the ELA's receiving of the historical episcopate. Regrettably, however, both these churches are plagued by extreme liberalism in doctrine and ethics and do not provide a wholesome example of what the Lambeth Conference had in mind!

CONCLUSION

Because the Roman Catholic Church makes amazing claims about one particular *episcopos*, it is necessary to note them and make a comment.

In the recent and authoritative *Catechism of the Catholic Church*, the doctrine of the relation of the Bishop of Rome to the historic episcopate and the whole church of God on earth is stated very clearly.[17] The foundation of the doctrine is the claim that when Christ instituted the Twelve he constituted them in the form of a "college," at the head of which he placed Peter. As the successor of Peter, the Roman pontiff presides over the college of bishops, the successors of the apostles.

According to this view, the Lord Jesus appointed Simon alone, whom he named Peter, as the "rock" of his church, giving him the keys of the church and making him the shepherd of the whole flock. Thus the pope, as Peter's successor, "is the perpetual and visible source and foundation of the unity both of the bishops and of the whole company of the faithful."

The college or body of bishops has no authority unless it is united with the Roman pontiff as its head. But *with* the pope as its head, the college has supreme and full authority over the universal church and exercises this in various ways but chiefly in an ecumenical council (e.g., Vatican II).

As noted earlier, this perspective is rejected by all the Orthodox churches for whom the Bishop of Rome is the Patriarch of the West (as he was so recognized in the fourth and fifth centuries) but not the head of the whole college of bishops. It is further rejected by other churches that claim to have kept the historic episcopate in their ongoing life (e.g., the Anglican Communion of Churches). Having said this, it is only fair to state that the pope would not be an important figure in the world today if there were not, undergirding the papacy, the doctrinal development of the late patristic and early Middle Ages and the organization in the Vatican City based upon these theological claims!

Turning now to the general ecumenical scene, let's consider one final issue. When one church is commending to another the need for the historical episcopate or when one church is considering the adoption of the historical episcopate into its life and polity, inevitably the question arises, "What kind of bishop?"

Are we thinking of the monarchical bishop of the second and third centuries who, while being clearly distinguished from the presbyters, was the pastor of one congregation and the normal celebrant at the Eucharist on the Lord's Day? Or are we thinking of the bishop of the fourth century onward who rules over a diocese which may have dozens or even hundreds of distinct parishes, wherein presbyters are the pastors? Put another way, are we thinking of a pastor or a prelate, a local bishop-celebrant or a bishop-administrator?

Perhaps we should be thinking of the historical episcopate in terms of bishops in communion with one another but with small enough dioceses that they can be truly pastors and celebrants who are always accessible to their flock. In all the churches (Roman, Orthodox, Anglican) with the historical episcopate an urgent need exists for the reform and renewal of the office and work of diocesan bishops, so that they truly reflect their membership and function as apostolic ministers and pastors. Many dioceses are too big and and their bishops are primarily administrators who hand over their primary gospel duties to assistant and auxiliary bishops. Thus those who are in the apostolic succession often live and work in such a manner as to make a mockery of it, and, conversely, some ministers who are not in the historical episcopate, or who have not been ordained by it, live apostolic lives of godliness and fruitfulness.

However, if one is looking for a means to set forth the continuity through time and unity across space of the church of God (understood as a visible society wherein the Word of God is preached and the sacraments are administered), then the historical episcopate really has no competitor. Thus these churches bear a great responsibility to ensure that they function in a way that is according to its best doctrine and practice and not as reflecting an infirm or corrupt institution.

A PRESBYTERIAN'S RESPONSE

L. Roy Taylor

AREAS OF AGREEMENT

There is much that Dr. Toon advocates in his explanation of episcopacy with which Presbyterians could agree. All contributors to this volume hold to the Protestant principle of *sola scriptura*, that the Holy Scriptures alone are our supreme and final rule in faith and practice, what we believe and how we live. I affirm with him that ecclesiastical structure present in the New Testament was not as complex as in subsequent centuries and that church polity developed over several centuries. The monoepiscopacy[18] of the mid-second century evolved into the diocesan episcopacy[19] unquestionably evident by the third century. I acknowledge that a gradation of clergy appeared early in the history of the church with the Threefold Ministry described by Hippolytus in the third century.[20] I happily maintain that no one view and practice of church government is essential to the being or existence (*esse*) of the church.[21] Therefore, I agree with the position that the "historic episcopate" or any other one form of church order is essential to the validity of an ordination or the validity of sacraments.

I share as well a rejection of the claims of the papacy that the Bishop of Rome, the pope of the Roman Catholic Church, is the vicar of Christ, the successor to Peter, and supreme head of the church on earth. I agree that the church herself is not infallible, contrary to the claims of the Roman Catholic Church and the Eastern Orthodox churches. I concur with Toon that though tradition is not on par with Scripture, it is nevertheless valuable in helping us understand and appreciate Scripture, theology, and history.[22] I affirm as well the statement of the Nicene Creed that the church is one, holy, catholic, and apostolic. Presbyterianism and the episcopate emphasize the connectionalism of the visible church, an emphasis that tends to be secondary or neglected in independent churches. With Toon, I grieve over the loss of visible unity that has been absent in the church for almost a thousand years[23] and I pray for, yearn for, and work for greater visible unity of the church. As Toon sees a tendency toward doctrinal laxity, moral relativism, and authoritarian abuse of power among bishops, I would also note that those tendencies are present in presbyterian and independent churches as well. Depravity may be expressed through any system of church polity.

There are also several observations Toon made which I appreciate, though I would not fully agree with them. For example, his 1, 2, 3, 4, and 5 mnemonic device is both descriptive and helpful in understanding not only churches in the Anglican Communion, but also the Presbyterian-Reformed and Lutheran communions as well.

The Roman Catholic Church is the highest form of episcopacy. When Protestants think of episcopacy, they tend to think of the Roman Catholic Church with its authoritative clerical hierarchy of bishops, archbishops, cardinals, and the pope at the apex of the ecclesiastical pyramid. Toon points out that there are several varieties of ecclesiastical structures within the category of episcopal government, just as I have stated that there are varieties of ecclesiastical structure within the category of presbyterian church government. The Roman Catholic model has the strongest authority with the pope as the supreme head of all branches of the Roman Catholic Church in every nation. In the Anglican model, however, the Archbishop of Canterbury is regarded as the first among equals within the Anglican Communion worldwide, but he has no supreme authority over Anglican bishops worldwide. Toon contends that the polity of the churches in the Anglican Communion is not exclusively episcopal, but a "combination of episcopal, presbyterial, and congregational authorities, expressed in a representational system." In the Lutheran and Methodist versions of episcopacy, the bishop superintends parishes and pastors within a geographical area but is not regarded as being in apostolic succession. Moreover, the participation of the laity is more prominent in America in both episcopal- and presbyterian-governed denominations, in keeping with the American civil democratic-republic and the biblical norm.

While I disagree with the view that the historic episcopate is necessary for the *plene esse* (fullness of being) of the church, I appreciate our Anglican brother's emphasis that bishops are to be primarily pastors rather than chief executive officers. Having ancestral roots in the membership, clergy, and episcopacy of the Church of England, I appreciated Toon's account of its history.

Dr. Toon demonstrates that there are different views of apostolic succession. The Roman Catholic, Eastern Orthodox, and Anglo-Catholic view of apostolic succession emphasizes a supposedly unbroken chain of episcopal ordination of bishops from the laying on of hands by the apostles for their successors unto the present. Low church Anglicans, along with the Presbyterian and Reformed, agree with the statement that those ministers who are faithful to the apostolic doctrine, worship, evangelization, and discipline are in a *spiritual* apostolic succession.

AREAS OF DISAGREEMENT

Though I agree with Toon's account of the development of episcopacy, and though his distinction between the hierarchal episcopacy of the Roman Catholic Church and the synodal episcopacy of the Anglican churches is a step toward a more representative church government than Roman Catholicism, there are at least five significant matters on which I must respectfully disagree.

1. If one discounts the extravagant claims of the Roman Catholic Church to the primacy of Peter and the pope being the supreme head of the church, the argument for the "historical episcopacy" is primarily a historical argument rather than a biblical argument. Toon argues that "the modern Anglican, unlike some of his seventeenth-century ancestors, does not see any blueprint for the polity and government of the church written in the Scripture" and "there is no one form of ordained ministry and church government found in the books of the New Testament. Rather, there are several forms and types." Instead, the Anglican sees principles, doctrines, and seeds in the teaching of Jesus and in the teaching and work of the apostles (Luke 9–10

[commissioning of the Twelve and the Seventy]; Heb. 13:17; 1 Thess. 5:12; 1 Cor. 16:15–16; and Acts 21:18) that require a gradation of clergy and the leadership of the bishop over clergy and laity. Other passages cited are Acts 15:28 and Matthew 18:20 as justification for national and international meetings of the church.

Virtually all Christian communions see the apostles as holding a unique noncontinuing office. Through the apostles, the New Testament was written directly or indirectly.[24] Apostles were given powerful spiritual gifts to attest their ministry (Heb. 2:3–4; Mark 16:20). Through the apostles, the church began its expansion out of its Jewish roots into the Gentile world (Acts 1:8; Eph. 2:20). That Jesus commissioned the Seventy after he chose the twelve apostles does not establish the necessity of a gradation of clergy. Acts 15:28 and Matthew 18:20 certainly justify national or international ecclesiastical assemblies, but do not prove that such assemblies are to be episcopal synods. Presbyterians and congregationalists may cite the same passages to justify their own assemblies.

Toon cites the 1930 Lambeth Conference of Bishops and Roman Catholic scholar Raymond E. Brown to the effect that the episcopate is a "historical development, analogous to the Canon of Scripture and the Creeds . . . a structure that gradually developed in the Church rather than something that was within the expressed direction of Jesus." He concedes the presbyterian argument that "the well-known passage, Titus 1:5–7, identifies the terms *presbyteros* and *episcopos* (cf. also Acts 20:17, 28; 1 Peter 5:1–2)," but emphasizes that the apostles or their representatives had some authority in certain respects over the local presbyter/bishops. Due to the unique and temporary nature of the office of apostle, few would dispute that the apostles or their representatives had some authority in certain respects over the local presbyter/bishops. The unique role of the apostles does not negate the fact that the terms *presbyteros* and *episcopos* are used as synonyms in the New Testament and do not describe a gradation of clergy at that point in time.

There was unquestionably a development in church polity over a relatively short period of time: (1) an incipient presbyterian order in the first century evinced by the New Testament;[25] (2) monoepiscopacy, the monarchial bishop (senior pastor of a local church), bishops, and presbyters differentiated, early second century; (3) diocesan episcopacy, overseeing a group of churches in a geographical area, late second century; (4) presbyters regarded as sacrificial priests; Cyprian advocates supremacy of Bishop of Rome, mid-third century; (5) metropolitan episcopacy, urban archbishops gaining ascendancy over rural bishops, early fourth century; (6) five patriarchs given special honor,[26] late fourth century; and finally (7) the Roman papacy, Leo I claims authority over all other bishops, mid-fifth century. Anglicans, Roman Catholics, and the Eastern Orthodox may argue that this evolution of polity was providentially intended and guided.[27] A better explanation would be that there were several factors that caused the church to move toward a model of governance similar to that of the state, namely (1) persecution and the effort to maintain theological orthodoxy; (2) geographical and political factors (the five patriarchal cities, Rome as the first capital of the Empire, and Constantinople as the second); and (3) efficiency of operations.

2. Closely related to the episcopate being essentially a historical argument, I take issue with the role tradition plays in determining what form of church government is of divine institution (or at least intention) and therefore should be used today. As I indicated above, there are three perspectives on the role of tradition, closely tied to one's view of the church as infallible or fallible (see note 22). Like the Reformed and Lutheran position, Toon posits that the church is not infallible, and affirms that synods and councils are subject to error and do err. While acknowledging this, he seems to come close to the Roman Catholic position on tradition by proposing that the development of the episcopate is analogous to the development of the canon of Scripture and the ecumenical creeds of the church's first five centuries.

Yes, all things that occur are within the providence of God and he works all things together for the good of his people (Rom. 8:28), but some of those events that he allows or limits are evil. When a Protestant looks at Old Testament history and that of the early church, he or she notes a number of developments that were not divine intentions.[28] For example, God allowed ancient Israel to select Saul as a "king like all the nations" but it was not his best intention (1 Sam. 8). In fact, God warned Israel through the prophet Samuel of the dire consequences of choosing Saul.[29]

When the church of the first five centuries patterned its polity after the civil government, it did so under God's permission, but not necessarily with God's approval. While Roman Catholics and the Eastern Orthodox accept the decisions of all seven ecumenical councils, most Protestants (including Anglicans) do not accept the decisions of all seven (recall Dr. Toon's 1, 2, 3, 4 [ecumenical councils], 5 summary). The First Council of Nicea (325) produced the Nicene Creed, accepted by virtually all Christians. The Second Council of Nicea (787) declared the veneration of icons and statues to be legitimate, a concept Protestants reject. If one uses history to interpret the New Testament's references to church order, one may deduce that the New Testament teaches an incipient episcopacy. If, however, one uses the Bible (both Old and New Testaments) to interpret the history of the early church, one would legitimately conclude that the church deviated from the biblical pattern of church polity (presbyterian-representative) and modeled its church structure after the civil government.

3. I take issue with the concept of apostolic succession set forth as an essential of the historical episcopate. This concept arose in the late second century as a way to combat heresies and preserve and propagate the faith as taught by the apostles. Later the idea of Petrine supremacy was added to the earlier teaching. The Roman Catholic Church and the Eastern Orthodox churches (along with Anglo-Catholics) advocate a concept of apostolic succession in which there supposedly exists an unbroken chain of bishops from the original apostles, each ordained through the laying on of hands.[30] Bishops in this apostolic succession are to be faithful to the apostolic doctrine, worship, evangelization, and discipline.

However, there are problems with this high church view of apostolic succession. First, it is not possible, with absolute certainty, to compose a list of an unbroken chain of episcopal ordinations all the way back to the original apostles. Second, numerous instances could be cited of bishops, supposedly in apostolic succession, who held to heretical theological views, were personally immoral, were not pastoral, abused their authority, or failed to exercise ecclesiastical discipline. The qualification of such dishonorable bishops for apostolic succession would solely be their ordination.

It is better to understand apostolic succession in the spiritual sense; that those ministers who are faithful to the apostolic doctrine, worship, evangelization, and discipline are in a spiritual apostolic succession regardless of their status in a gradation of clergy or the form of church polity within which they were ordained. While Toon, on one hand, seems to concede that faithful ministers may be in apostolic succession in a spiritual sense (the low church Anglican, Reformed, and Lutheran view), he also appears to require that the historical episcopate (based on the high church view of apostolic succession) is indispensable for the *plene esse* of the church.

4. I question whether a historical episcopate is necessary for the visible unity of the church. Many Christians yearn for a return to a visibly united church, which has been absent since the Great Schism of 1046. From my perspective, three of the four statements of the "Lambeth Quadrilateral" of 1888 form a good starting point for interchurch discussions concerning unity. However, to require all churches to conform to the historical episcopate as a nonnegotiable condition for possible union is an insuperable barrier. If the historical episcopate is not essential to the *esse* (being or existence) of the church, why make it one of the few nonnegotiable conditions for discussions concerning the unity of the church?

5. Finally, and most importantly, we must address the question of whether the Bible does indeed teach a particular form of church government and, if so, what it is. Toon has expressed the opinion, held by many others, that the Bible does not teach a particular church order, but that it was given providentially through historical development rather than through biblical revelation. The historic episcopate is indeed historic, with roots traceable to the second century. But the question is, does the Bible teach episcopacy? Recognizing that the Scriptures do not give a detailed and complex plan for church government,[31] I respectfully disagree with the premise underlying the historical episcopate. Instead, I maintain that the Bible (both Old and New Testaments) teaches the principles of the presbyterian-representative form of church government through explicit statements, examples, and precedents. I refer the reader to chapter 2 for a full defense of that position.

A SINGLE-ELDER CONGREGATIONALIST'S RESPONSE

Paige Patterson

Peter Toon has provided a splendid statement of the position of Anglicanism or episcopalianism in ecclesiastical governance. The fact that I can agree with few of his conclusions should not cloud in any way the accurate and succinct manner in which he has stated the claims for Anglican church polity.

I do support Toon's avowal that the polity, canon law, and liturgy developed during the first five centuries made many of the churches at the end of that period look quite different from those pristine assemblies of the New Testament era. Also, I agree that church government in the Anglican format is "an exercise in the use of Scripture *and* tradition." Accordingly, I applaud Toon's forthrightness in acknowledging that "the Anglican form of church government is an attempt to conform in general terms to the pattern in place in the early church in the third, fourth, and fifth centuries."

Furthermore, I am grateful for Toon's awareness that Ignatius's distinctions among the words "bishop," "presbyter," and "deacon" "may not have existed in all city churches." Finally, Toon seems to acknowledge that ordinations proceeded only with "the consent of the congregation," a phrase that I interpret to mean the local assembly of believers in a given location.

WHAT IS THE AUTHORITY FOR CHURCH GOVERNMENT?

While areas of agreement with Toon are sparse, in one sense all the areas of disagreement can be reduced to one issue—namely, *authority for determining church government and polity*. Although I will attempt to flesh out various opposing perspectives, one must begin with this single issue that is determinative for all of the rest.

Sola scriptura vs. Scripture and Tradition

Simply stated, I believe that the contemporary church should be committed to the rediscovery and reimplementation of the apostolic pattern of church government found in the New Testament documents; whereas Toon is willing to embrace the result of five centuries of development in the post-apostolic church. To put the matter another way, I believe that churches should invoke the Bible alone for faith *and practice*. Toon certainly holds a high view of Scripture, but his allegiance to *tradition* pushes him to embrace a position, at least regarding ecclesiastical form, which elevates tradition to a level almost indistinguishable from Scripture. In fairness, I am confident that Toon will object, saying that the Scriptures are inspired of God in a sense that elevates them above tradition. In so saying, he, of course, will distinguish himself and Anglicanism from the Roman church, which regards Scripture as foundational but attributes similar authority to tradition.

While I respect Toon's view of the superiority of Scripture over tradition, I want to suggest that the mistake of Anglicanism is insufficient rigor in applying this distinction.

Two Problems with the Appeal to Tradition

Toon's view—his 1, 2, 3, 4, and 5 principle—encounters two insurmountable barriers in my estimation. First, sometimes there was not agreement even among orthodox Christians about the phrasing of the creeds. Here I do not have in mind the heterodoxy of Arius, Apollinarius, Nestorius, Eutyches, etc., but rather the centuries-long confrontation between East and West over the *filioque* clause, or even the description of Mary as the "mother of God" (*theotokos*). This is to say nothing at all of the disagreements in polity, canon law, and liturgy that developed by the fifth century.

Although many have alleged contradictions in the New Testament documents, such as supposed disagreements between the apostles Peter and Paul, evangelical Christians have found those allegations uniformly unconvincing. Most evangelicals argue that the Scriptures are preserved from such contradictions through the process of inspiration, whereby fallible men wrote what was vouchsafed to them by the infallible Holy Spirit who "bore them along" (*pheromenoi*) above the error to which they were by human nature prone (2 Peter 1:21). If this is the case, and if we admit to the fallibility of the post-apostolic writings and conclusions, then for evangelicals the matter of authority is decided. It is vested in Scripture alone, and it remains to debate hermeneutical issues in the attempt to decipher what precisely the Scriptures mean.

Toon's response to this is an appeal to conjecture. He writes, "Yet it is difficult to believe that Almighty God, the Father of our Lord Jesus Christ, would have allowed the church in its formative years of growth and expansion in Europe, Africa, and Asia to go so seriously wrong as to make a major mistake in terms of its general polity and church government." Or again, "As a minimum we surely have to say that it was allowed, if not directed, by the Holy Ghost." But this argument assumes that the conclusions of the church in the first five centuries were usually correct. Or, to put the best face on the matter, this way of thinking assumes that because the church of the first five centuries came to appropriate conclusions in some matters (Christology and the Trinity), all of its conclusions were either directed of the Holy Spirit or else at least allowed by God.

This assumption, in my persuasion, is of dubious merit. Toon, at least in this chapter, does not carry his confidence in tradition past the fifth century. But he does not tell us any good reason for taking the end of the fifth century as the *terminus ad quem* for authoritative tradition. However, since Anglicanism itself represents a significant rupture in Western Christianity, it strikes me that Toon has a need to establish why the first five centuries of tradition commend themselves in a way that subsequent centuries do not. If the response is that they were closer to the apostolic era, then we must ask why is the second century not of more value than the fifth century? And, more important, how can the break of Anglicanism from Rome find justification, assuming that Rome essentially inculcates the doctrines embraced by the church in the first five centuries?

In addition, we must also know how Toon "knows the mind of the Lord" on this matter. If God reveals himself, as in the Scriptures, then we are safe to claim understanding. But to assume that whatever God allows to take place is therefore right and good seems perilous to me. God obviously allowed the bloody reign of Idi Amin in Uganda, but I know of few who would venture the opinion that this reign had the *approval* of God. It would be an exercise in casuistry to try to argue that God *approved* of Amin's brutality. In other words, since some people got some things wrong in the first five centuries, what authority will help us distinguish between those who got it right and those who got it wrong? If the answer is an appeal to the Scriptures, then I rest my case.

Now we turn to the second mistake in this sort of reasoning. In developing his ecclesiology, Toon selected Ignatius as the appropriate tradition to follow. He is guarded in this assertion, acknowledging that the ecclesiology outlined in Ignatius was not everywhere endorsed or practiced. Nevertheless, he insists that by AD 200 "virtually everywhere" Ignatius's system was in place. However, in this same volume, Sam Waldron has shown that Ignatius, of all the extant literature of the earliest post-apostolic church, stands alone in his ecclesiology even though it must be admitted that the model of Ignatius eventually became that of most of the church East and West. Waldron's point is that Ignatius should not be viewed as normative for the second Christian century, a view that I too support. If this is correct, then it becomes clear that Toon's position does more than allow ecclesiastical tradition to trump the Bible. By selectively choosing the second century, he disregards the evidence favoring the predominance of other forms of early church government and, thereafter, rather uncritically buys into the ecclesiastical developments of succeeding centuries.

ADDITIONAL PROBLEMS

Episcopal Ordination and Sacramental Administration

Most other differences that I have with Toon are essentially further developments of the discussion above. For example, he says that the commissioning of the Twelve and then the Seventy suggests "the differentiation of ordained ministers." But surely there is nothing in the text to suggest ordination of any of these. Toon admits that this is only "the principle if not the full concept." But this, it seems to me, is still a bold leap with little evidential support.

Toon naturally argues that "only those who have been rightly ordered/ordained by those who have the authority to ordain are allowed to function as pastors and ministers of Word and sacrament in the national church." Predictably, as one coming from the free church tradition, I doubt that ordination in the New Testament bore any more than a distant resemblance to current Roman, Anglican, or even Protestant practice. Be that as it may, the doctrine that all believers are "priests" before God (1 Peter 2:5, 9; Rev. 1:6; 20:6) suggests that the limitation of "ordination" almost certainly did not apply to the earliest churches in their practices of evangelism, teaching, or the administration of the ordinances.

Toon also suggests the possibility that denominations that do not possess the historical episcopate "cannot be sure that the sacraments they offer are genuinely and truly means of conveying the presence of the Lord Jesus Christ and the grace of God the Father." This avowal brings to the surface ecclesiological differences of a more serious variety—namely, those that carry soteriological implications. To begin, I would deny that the sacraments are a means of conveying the presence of Christ or the grace of God in any way other than as gracious pictures or symbols that present the gospel in graphic depiction just as it is proclaimed in word through preaching.

Worse, Toon's endorsement of apostolic succession ties the administering of the ordinances and, at least by implication, the salvific grace of God to a line of succession that sometimes included reprobates (for example, the Avignon popes) who were themselves arguably not among the redeemed of God. No one would argue that the gospel, to be the gospel, needs to be given by a regenerate person. But surely the gospel is the gospel whenever one saved person shares it with another, whether part of the apostolic succession or not. And if no bishop is present and a "lay" believer immerses the new Christian in baptism, is that not New Testament baptism, wholly pleasing unto God? The burden of proof to say otherwise rests here upon Toon.

Magisterial Involvement in the Church

Toon attempts to find an acceptable matrix for magisterial involvement in church affairs by a reminder that Constantine essentially coerced the convening of the Council of Nicea. Looking for scriptural support Toon appeals to what the apostles Paul and Peter say about civil governors in the New Testament. But how can the recognition of the divine origin and authority for human government by the apostles Peter and Paul be construed as authority of government to impinge on the affairs of the church? Surely all one must do to answer this idea is to point out the incredible loss of life, property, and freedom that has been the hallmark of such "unions" in almost every era. The Inquisition, which in its punitive phase frequently turned to the state for the dirty work, the persecution of the Anabaptists by some of the magisterial Reformers, and even the sorrows visited upon Baptists by Anglicans in both England and the colonies provide just a few examples of the dangerous liaison between church and state.

Moving from the anecdotal to the hermeneutical, what possible justification can there be for interpreting passages that recognize a divine purpose in government and call on believers to be good citizens as meaning that the state has license to be involved in the affairs of the church? The church, after all, should consist of a fellowship of twice-born people ordered by the Holy Spirit in response to Jesus as sovereign. The state consisting at best of a mix of redeemed and unredeemed is in no position to know the mind of the Spirit or to ascribe suzerainty to Christ.

The Utilitarian Argument for Episcopalianism

Finally, I contest the idea that "episcopacy is the best as well as the most natural method of church government for it brings the greatest good to the church of God in terms of value and usefulness." This statement takes the form of an unsupported proclamation. Although with more space, Toon could probably defend this proposition, I doubt that it would be very convincing to me. I would admit that congregationalism has not been without its flaws, injustices, and errors. Further, I would even admit that a hierarchical or Anglican form of church government can certainly boast some legitimate utilitarian advantages. Even from the angle of the utilitarian, however, its long history of insensitivity and abuse is just too sad a chronicle to merit Toon's optimism. This is apparent as recently as the struggles of the American Catholic bishops in the face of allegations of pedophilia and homosexuality.

But the question of the utilitarian is not the ultimate issue. Even if it could be shown that episcopacy is finally the more useful form of ecclesiastical government, the issue remains: What has God revealed? This brings the matter full circle. For Toon's case for episcopacy to be convincing to me, he must show it to me in the New Testament. This does not mean that I am uninterested in the theology of the first five centuries or that I believe that the study of patristic thought is of limited value for the contemporary church. Profitable insights and understandings are found in abundance in such literature. But the question is not the value of such literature. The question is the authority or relative authority of these sources.

Consequently, I must dissent, as my ecclesiastical forefathers always did, from the position advocated by Toon, i.e., that Anglican church government and the concept that bishops are more than local church pastors is justified, much less mandated, by the development of these concepts in the first five centuries. For me, the Bible alone is the appropriate court of adjudication. This is the case first because of its inspiration, making the Scriptures the *logia tou theou*. The apostles wrote what God specifically intended and not mere ruminations about their own religious experiences. Because no subsequent generation of the church, theologians included, can state such a claim, all other views must be tried in a biblical court!

Second, the Bible certainly does not tell everything. For example, I can find no verse about the virtues or vices of asparagus. My experience of it suggests that if it tastes that bad, then it must be sinful; but I have no authority about this from the Bible. However, when the Bible speaks either by mandate or by precedent, it represents not only truth but also sufficient guidance for the ordering of life and church. And there are no bishops in the New Testament except local congregational pastors!

A PLURAL-ELDER CONGREGATIONALIST'S RESPONSE

Samuel E. Waldron

I begin my reply to Peter Toon's fine statement of episcopacy (perhaps he would prefer me to speak of Anglicanism) with a sense of significant appreciation. I surely appreciate the clarity with which he has distanced his understanding of episcopacy from Roman Catholicism. He has capably shown the lines of demarcation that separate his view from Romanism. I also appreciate the clear call to Anglican bishops to live up to their heritage by lives of godliness and fruitfulness. His evident desire to distance himself from what he calls "extreme liberalism" is also to be commended. Toon's labors elsewhere to emphasize the importance of the Puritan and Reformed heritage of evangelicals is also appreciated. It saddens me, of course, to see him in the present debate departing from that heritage. Nevertheless, Peter Toon has written a lucid defense of the classically Anglican view of church government.

Toon is also to be commended for the frank way in which he admits certain of the more difficult facets of his position. The very first sentence of his chapter makes clear that "what unites" the several ways in which episcopalianism is used "is the use of term 'bishop' (Greek, *episcopos*) to describe a subgroup within the totality of all its ordained pastors or ministers." Later he makes the telling admission that in three places in the New Testament there is an identification of the terms *presbyteros* and *episcopos*. In another place, Toon even admits that "early in the second century" the distinction between bishop and presbyter "may not have existed in all city churches." By making these admissions, Toon has conceded the substance of the biblical case against episcopacy. With these admissions before us, one might be tempted to wonder what else needs to be said.

A SUMMARY OF TOON'S CASE

But, of course, Toon does not see it that way and believes that much remains to be said. Indeed, such a response would miss the essence of the Anglican defense of episcopalianism. Our Anglican brother attempts to make a case for episcopacy right into the teeth of these seemingly fatal admissions. He argues, in the first place, that in the New Testament no one form of church government is revealed and that, hence, the New Testament cannot decide this issue. He then argues that, since all sides admit episcopacy did become the universal form of church government by no later than the third century of the Christian era, it is unlikely that this happened without the approval of divine providence. He also argues that the development of episcopacy was the necessary prolongation of those aspects of the apostolate needed by the living church. He argues as well that the tradition of the first five centuries of the Christian era must be allowed a certain authority in the church. He argues finally that the recognition of the Canon by the early church provides a telling illustration of why that tradition must necessarily be allowed such authority. Thus, the shape of Toon's argument is defined. In default of a clear, biblical witness on the issue of church government, it relies on what it sees as an indispensable early tradition in the living church to establish the case for episcopacy.

I view this denial of a clear, biblical blueprint for church government and its consequent appeal to the early tradition of the church as the most fundamental problem with Toon's (and Anglicanism's) position. Therefore, it is on this issue that I will concentrate my rebuttal. In my opinion, Toon's position is vulnerable to attack both in terms of what the New Testament teaches about the Democratic principle (congregational suffrage) and the Independent principle (the independence of each local church). However, one must show that there *is* a clear, biblical blueprint for church government and that the New Testament *is* a sufficient guide in these matters. Only then will it do much good to show the New Testament evidence for the democratic and independent principles of church government to one imbued with an Anglican mind-set.

NO BIBLICAL BLUEPRINT FOR CHURCH GOVERNMENT?

The foundation of Toon's defense of Anglicanism is stated in these two sentences taken from the heart of his article:

> It is important to recognize that the modern Anglican, unlike some of his seventeenth-century ancestors, does *not* see any blueprint for the polity and government of the church written in Scripture. He is too well aware that biblical studies have shown that there is no one form of ordained ministry and church government found in the books of the New Testament.

It is only the premise that Scripture contains no blueprint for church government that allows Toon to appeal to church tradition as decisive. The significance of these sentences for Toon's argument cannot be overestimated. These sentences compose its very foundation. However, a number of observations will show how shaky this foundation is.

First, Toon has assumed, rather than proven, the whole burden of his argument. He asserts that "biblical studies have shown that there is no one form of ... church government found in ... the New Testament." In a footnote he supports this assertion by referring the reader to unspecified, recent dictionaries of the New Testament and biblical theology. Perhaps Toon is right, but he will have to do better than this to prove his point. After all, this is the whole difference of opinion between Toon and the rest of us in this book, and between Anglicanism and the rest of the Reformed heritage.

Second, Toon's appeal to unspecified dictionaries of biblical theology in his note is suspect from another point of view. I do not dispute that a number of less orthodox forms of biblical theology have found multiformity in the ecclesiology of the New Testament, but then they have also found such multiformity in respect to other crucial doctrines of the New Testament. Does

Toon's acceptance of their assertion of multiformity with regard to ecclesiology obligate him to accept multiformity with regard to Christology, for example? What kind of theological premises is Toon accepting in order to have ecclesiological multiformity? Does he really want to accept such premises?

Third, there is, of course, an orthodox form of biblico-theological multiformity that I would be ready to accept. This view sees the different *theologies* of the New Testament not as contradictory, but as supplementary. Such a view of multiformity does Toon no good, however, because it does not lead to the conclusion Toon wants—that there is no divinely revealed form of church government. The different *theologies* of the New Testament on the orthodox view would conspire to provide a rich revelation of such a church government, rather than lead us to conclude that no such divinely revealed church government exists.

Fourth, how can an Anglican like Toon come to the same New Testament as the rest of us and not see a divinely revealed church government? I speculate the problem is that Anglicans are "looking for love in all the wrong places." What I mean is that they come to the New Testament with a number of unconscious assumptions about what a divinely revealed church government should look like, assumptions molded by the beloved, ecclesiological tradition in which they are immersed. When they read their New Testaments and see nothing remotely similar to these assumptions, they conclude that there is no divinely revealed church government. But another conclusion is equally possible: biblical church government looks nothing like Anglicanism. Perhaps Anglicans are unconsciously reasoning in a small circle and looking for all the wrong things.

PROVIDENTIAL GUIDANCE OF TRADITION?

Having proven to his own satisfaction that one cannot look to the New Testament for the church's government, Toon is ready to press upon us the necessity of giving the early tradition of the church its due.

It is commendable that Toon's appeal to tradition is carefully nuanced. He does not view this tradition as infallible. Furthermore, it is not all tradition, but the tradition of the third, fourth, and fifth centuries that he regards as most significant.

This tradition is viewed as providing consistent development to the apostolic teaching and is normative for the church. Toon attempts further to commend deference to early tradition in a number of ways.

For instance, he argues that the tradition of the early church "established the first day of the week as the festival of the Resurrection or the Lord's Day." I must disagree. With the Puritans I affirm that the first day of the week was appointed by divine authority through the apostles. The New Testament's frequent mention of the first day of the week as having religious significance for the church (Matt. 28:1; Mark 16:2, 9; Luke 24:1; John 20:1, 19; Acts 20:7; 1 Cor. 16:2) and its designation as the Lord's Day (Rev. 1:10) is sufficient to show this. The Lord's Day was not established by early tradition but by apostolic authority as recorded in the New Testament.

Toon also appeals to the fact that early tradition "created major ... festivals (Easter, Pentecost, etc.)" as showing its importance. I see no sin in allowing the cultural significance of Easter to impact our choice of hymnody and sermon topic on what is called Easter Sunday. Yet, neither do I regard the celebration of Easter (or any of the other religious festivals Toon has in mind) as having any divine mandate or practical necessity for the church.

The most frequentedly repeated of Toon's arguments to commend early tradition is his appeal to a directing providence in the early tradition of the church. Perhaps the strongest such appeal is this one:

> Yet it is difficult to believe that Almighty God, the Father of our Lord Jesus Christ, would have allowed the church in its formative years of growth and expansion in Europe, Africa, and Asia to go so seriously wrong as to make a major mistake in terms of its general polity and church government.

A number of responses to this passionate appeal come to mind. One is tempted to warn the unwary believer (and remind our brother) that Roman Catholicism did not spring out of thin air in the sixth century. Much of the externalism, legalism, and ceremonialism that Protestants associate with Roman Catholicism was already becoming visible in the earliest centuries of the church.[32]

Even granting Toon's premise that an overruling providence guarded the early church in its major developments, there is still a major problem with his argument. Toon assumes that the development of episcopal church government was of major importance to divine providence. Now if Toon were arguing about the development of the doctrine of the Trinity or the doctrine of the person of Christ, he might be on stronger ground. However, Anglicans including Toon himself insist that church government was of so little importance to the Holy Spirit that it was not even divinely revealed in the Scriptures. He cannot have it both ways. He cannot insist that a normative church government was so unimportant to God that he did not even bother to reveal it in the Bible, and then insist that it is so important to God that it is inconceivable that he would have allowed the early church to have erred on the subject.

THE CANON DEPENDENT ON TRADITION?

Perhaps the most significant of Toon's attempts to commend the early tradition of the church is his argument that the reception and interpretation of Scripture is inseparably tied to that tradition. He remarks: "Thus any exposition of Anglican polity or church government is always an exercise in the use of Scripture *and* tradition. The full authority of Scripture is not in question or doubt, but the way in which it is received and interpreted is significant." Later he argues that the early church "decided, under God, the content of the canon of the New Testament." This argument seems persuasive. If we would not even have a New Testament apart from the early church and its tradition, how can we ignore its interpretation of the New Testament when it comes to church government?

Here too Toon's house is built upon the sand and not upon the rock. Why? In the first place, even accepting the general idea that we should listen to the tradition of the church in the way we read our Bibles (and I do accept this idea), it does not follow that we should follow that tradition even when it contradicts the New Testament. When episcopacy declares that the bishop and the presbyter are two different offices, and does this in the face of the New Testament's clear teaching that they are the same office, it simply contradicts the New Testament. No amount of tradition or argumentation can change this. Furthermore, I have shown in my chapter that there is a tradition earlier than that chosen by Toon that does not so contradict the New Testament. Certainly, we are at liberty to choose the tradition that most clearly reflects the teaching of the New Testament.

Second, Toon has assumed substantially the same view of the Canon and its interpretation as that advocated by Rome against the early Reformers. Their argument was, according to Calvin, that since the Canon was church-authenticated, it must be church-interpreted. Thus, the Reformers were guilty of both presumption and folly in assuming to interpret the Bible contrary to the tradition of the church. When Toon argues, in spite of his care in distancing himself from Rome, that the early church "decided" the content of the Canon and, therefore, may decide the proper interpretation of the Bible and its teachings on church government, he is using substantially the same argument as Rome.

Calvin's argument holds against both Rome and Toon. The church did not "decide" even "under God" the content of the Canon. The Word of God is self-authenticating. It decided its own content by vindicating itself in the heart of the early church. The church decided nothing. It merely submitted to, accepted, and recognized the foundation upon which it had been built (Eph. 2:20). Since the Word of God is self-authenticating, it is also self-interpreting. The tradition of the early church may (and ought to) be treated as a trusted and respected adviser, but never anything more. I will let Calvin in *The Institutes of the Christian Religion* speak for himself, the other Reformers, and me:

> It is a very false notion, therefore, that the power of judging of the Scripture belongs to the Church, so as to make the certainty of it dependent on the Church's will. Wherefore, when the Church receives it, and seals it with her suffrage, she does not authenticate a thing otherwise dubious or controvertible; but, knowing it to be the truth of her God, performs a duty of piety, by treating it with immediate veneration. But, with regard to the question— How shall we be persuaded of its divine original, unless we have recourse to the decree of the Church? This is just as if any one should inquire, How shall we learn to distinguish light from darkness, white from black, sweet from bitter? For the Scripture exhibits as clear evidence

of its truth as white and black thing'
or sweet and bitter things do of the'

NEW TESTAMENT EVIDENC

Having shown what he believes to be
allowing the tradition of the early church to guiu.
standing of church government, Toon proceeds to tie ι.
and the Scriptures together.

Essentially, what Toon does is attempt to establish the idea
that the New Testament indicates a pattern of hierarchical oversight at different places. Toon appeals to (among other things)
the Twelve, the apostle Paul's primacy among his missionary
associates, the relation of Timothy and Titus to the churches and
eldership Paul appointed them to oversee, and to James, the
Lord's brother.[34] These are the same supposed evidences to which
other brethren appeal to prove that there should be a primary
elder, a senior pastor, or a minister distinct in office from the other
elders. Toon, however, appeals to these passages to prove episcopacy. This should make Patterson and Taylor stop and think!

Substantially the same problem may be discerned with each
of the evidences to which Toon appeals. Toon confuses the
unique ministry of apostles of Christ with the ordinary ministry
of the bishops or presbyters of local churches. The Twelve, Paul,
Timothy, Titus, and arguably James the Lord's brother all illustrate the working of apostolic authority in the first churches. The
Twelve, Paul, and James (arguably—cf. 1 Cor. 15:7; Gal. 1:19)
were all apostles of Christ. Timothy and Titus were apostolic delegates or representatives and, thus, exercised a kind of apostolic
ministry and authority. Such ministry could not long continue
after the deaths of the Lord's apostles. The New Testament certainly distinguishes the authority of apostles of Christ from that
of the overseers of local churches. (Contrast Matthew 10:1–4; Acts
1:15–26; 1 Corinthians 14:37; 2 Corinthians 12:12; Galatians 1:1,
11–17 with 1 Timothy 3:1–7 and Titus 1:5–9. Also note particularly Ephesians 4:11 and 1 Corinthians 12:28 where apostles are
clearly distinguished from pastor-teachers.) To speak of apostolic
succession (in the Anglican sense where bishops become those
successors) requires not only the distinguishing of bishops and
presbyters contrary to the New Testament, but also the clouding

...ear distinction between apostles of Christ and bishops ...ined by the New Testament.[35]

RESTATEMENT

Toon's argument amounts to a denial of the Puritan view of the regulative principle of the church. This is not surprising since Anglicans have historically been marked by a denial of the regulative principle and have adopted what has sometimes been called the normative principle. The twentieth of the Church of England's Thirty-Nine Articles states: "The Church hath power to decree rites or ceremonies and authority in the controversies of the Faith. And yet it is not lawful for the Church to ordain anything contrary to God's Word written."[36] James Bannerman helpfully contrasts the Puritan doctrine on this matter with the Anglican doctrine:

> In the case of the Church of England, its doctrine in regard to Church power in the worship of God is, that it has a right to decree everything, except what is forbidden in the Word of God. In the case of our own Church, its doctrine in reference to Church power in the worship of God is, that it has a right to decree nothing, except what expressly or by implication is enjoined by the Word of God.[37]

The difference between Puritans and Anglicans may be helpfully illustrated by means of two builders intent on building the temple of God. Mr. Anglican must use the materials of the Word of God, but has no blueprint and may use other materials. Mr. Puritan must use only materials of the Word of God and has a blueprint. Clearly, the two completed buildings will differ drastically.

There are, at least, four biblical arguments for the Puritan regulative principle of the church. First, the church is the house of God (1 Tim. 3:14–15) and it is the prerogative of God alone to order the affairs of his own house. Bannerman eloquently states this:

> The fundamental principle that lies at the basis of the whole argument is this, that in regard to the ordinance of public worship it is the province of God, and not the province of man, to determine both the terms and the manner of such worship.... The path of approach to God

was shut and barred in consequence of man's sin: it was impossible for man himself to renew the intercourse which had been so solemnly closed by the judicial sentence which excluded him from the presence and favour of his God. Could that path ever again be opened up, and the communion of God with man and of man with God ever again be renewed? This was a question for God alone to determine. If it could, on what terms was the renewal of intercourse to take place, and in what manner was fellowship of the creature with his Creator again to be maintained? This, too, was a question no less than the former for God alone to resolve.[38]

Not only does God possess this prerogative, the Bible shows that he exercises it (Gen. 4:1–5; Ex. 20:4–6). What insensitivity to their position before God it is for men to presume that they have the right to order the house of God!

Second, the introduction of extrabiblical elements into the house of God inevitably tends to nullify and undermine God's appointed order (Matt. 15:3, 8–9; 2 Kings 16:10–18). This tendency is amply illustrated in evangelical churches today.

Third, the wisdom of Christ and the sufficiency of the Scriptures are called into question by the addition of unappointed elements into the house of God. With all our weakness, sin, and folly, will Christ leave us without an adequate guide in the most important matter of the ordering of the house of God? Second Timothy 3:16–17 requires us to raise this question. Is ordering the church for the glory of God a good work which the man of God is peculiarly required to perform? Then, the Scriptures are able to thoroughly equip the man of God for this task.

Fourth, the Bible explicitly condemns all worship in the house of God that is not commanded by God (Lev. 10:1–3; Deut. 4:2; 12:29–32; 17:3; Josh. 1:7; 23:6–8; Matt. 15:13; Col. 2:20–23). Three of these passages deserve special comment. In its original context Deuteronomy 12:29–32 is addressed precisely to the question of how God should be worshipped (v. 30). The answer given here is very clear. "Whatever I command you, you shall be careful to do; you shall not add to nor take away from it" (v. 32). Colossians 2:23 condemns what may be literally translated as "will worship." Herbert Carson states the unavoidable implication of this phrase: "The words ... imply a form of worship which a man devises for himself."[39] Leviticus 10:1–3 is the frightening account of what happened to Nadab and Abihu when they displeased God in the way they worshiped him. What was it that brought upon them such a shocking judgment? Verse 1 is explicit. They "offered strange fire before the Lord." The meaning of the phrase, "strange fire," is expounded in the following clause. The Hebrew literally reads that it was fire "which He had not commanded them." The mere fact that they dared to bring unauthorized fire brought fiery death upon them.

The church is the house of God. It is unthinkable that God has left its government up to the traditions of men.

CONCLUSION

Toward the end of his chapter Toon affirms that the "succession of bishops and ministers in the church through space and time through the means of episcopal ordination and consecration . . . is the God-given focus of unity in the church through space and time." This is a truly remarkable conclusion for Toon to reach. He has admitted that episcopacy is so little the focus of biblical revelation that it is not even clearly taught in the Scriptures. Yet he asserts that it is still so important that it is the "God-given focus of unity in the church through space and time." With all due respect to our dear brother, it is difficult to believe that the Lord Jesus Christ would make this the focus of the unity of his church. Even leaving aside the deplorable spiritual and doctrinal condition of many individuals who now occupy such an episcopate, this is difficult to believe. Toon himself admits that the New Testament is not clear on the matter, that only the seed of episcopacy is found there, and that episcopacy must be learned from later tradition. Can this really be the focus of the unity of the church through space and time?

Chapter 1: Episcopalianism Notes

Peter Toon

[1]The articles on the early church, the Reformation, and the Anglican Way in the *Oxford Dictionary of the Christian Church*, eds. F. L. Cross and E. A. Livingston (New York: Oxford University Press, 1997) are a very good source to gain basic information and a book list for all the major topics covered in this chapter.

[2]The formularies of the Anglican Way (including the Thirty-Nine Articles and the Ordinal) are contained in the Book of Common Prayer (1662) which is still in use in English and in translation into other languages around the world.

[3]For the early church see W. H. C. Frend, *The Rise of Christianity* (London: Darton, Longman and Todd, 1984).

[4]However, for the rapid emergence of the Roman see as a preeminent center of leadership and juridical authority see Henry Chadwick, *The Early Church* (Pelican History of the Church, vol. 1, 1967), chapter 16.

[5]For canon law in the early church see Peter L'Huillier, *The Church of the Ancient Councils* (Crestwood, N.Y.: St. Vladimir's Seminary Press, 1996) and in the Anglican Communion see Norman Doe, *Canon Law in the Anglican Communion* (Oxford: Clarendon Press, 1998). And for the general theme of authority in the Anglican churches see Stephen W. Sykes, ed., *Authority in the Anglican Communion* (Toronto: Anglican Book Center, 1987).

[6]In order to consider carefully and rationally whether or not there is a single blueprint in the New Testament for any specific church polity and government, one can do no better than carefully read the learned articles on such words/themes as "apostle," "presbyter," "bishop" and "church" in recent dictionaries of the New Testament/biblical theology.

[7]*Report of the Lambeth Conferences 1867–1948* (London: SPCK), 218.

[8]Raymond E. Brown, *Priest and Bishop: Biblical Reflections* (New York: Paulist, 1970), 82.

[9]For the English Reformation see A. G. Dickens, *The English Reformation* (London: Batsford, 1989).

[10]Richard Hooker, *The Laws of Ecclesiastical Polity*, VII, ii, 3.

[11]Hooker, VII, vi, 3.

[12]John Jewel, *An Apology for the Church of England,* III.

[13]See his *Works* (1851), vol. 1, 199.

[14]For an overview of the development of the Anglican Communion from a national church to an international family of churches see William L. Sachs, *The Transformation of Anglicanism: From State Church to Global Communion* (Cambridge: Cambridge University Press, 1993).

[15]For an introduction to modern Anglicanism see *The Study of Anglicanism*, eds. Stephen Sykes, John Booty, and Jonathan Knight (Minneapolis: Fortress Press, 1998). I have an essay in this book on "The Articles of Religion."

[16]*Report of the Lambeth Conference 1958* (London: SPCK), 288.

[17]See *Catechism of the Catholic Church,* Part 1, Article 9, Paragraph 4.

L. Roy Taylor

[18]A senior pastor, usually of a local church located in a larger city, who presided over the administration of the sacraments and the preaching of the Word.

[19]A senior pastor of a larger church who had oversight of presbyters who served smaller and frequently rural churches within a given geographical area.

[20]Deacon had become the entry-level clergy position, presbyter the next, and bishop the highest.

[21]Some maintain that their particular form of ecclesiastical polity is essential to the existence of the true church. Examples include the Roman Catholic Church, the Eastern Orthodox churches with episcopal polity, churches stemming from nineteenth-century Landmark Baptist movement with congregational government, and the Restorationist movement (Churches of Christ) with plurality of elders in independent churches. Even *jure divino* presbyterians who hold that presbyterianism is by divine law have never asserted that presbyterianism is essential to the existence of the church or that the Presbyterian Church is the only true church.

[22]By "tradition" we mean the biblical and apostolic teachings of the church handed down from one generation to another. Since the Roman Catholic Church and the Eastern Orthodox churches hold that the church is infallible, tradition is put on par with Scripture. Conversely, the sixteenth-century Anabaptist view was that the church was infected with pagan synergistic teachings early in its history. Therefore, the church is not infallible and tradition and church history are virtually useless. Since the nineteenth century, dispensationalism, with its view that every dispensation ends in widespread apostasy and divine judgement, has reinforced the tendency of evangelicals to undervalue tradition and church history. In the Reformed and Lutheran perspective, the church is not infallible, but she is wise. Therefore, tradition, sifted through the grid of Scripture is of great value, though not on par with Scripture.

[23]The Great Schism of 1046 marked official division between the Western and Eastern branches of the church. Protestant denominations emanate from the Western branch from the sixteenth-century Protestant Reformation.

[24]Luke, author of Luke and Acts, was a missionary companion of Paul. John Mark, author of the gospel of Mark, accompanied Paul on part of his first missionary journey and was later discipled by Peter.

[25]See my discussion in chapter 2 of this book.

[26]The five patriarchal cities were Jerusalem, Antioch of Syria, Rome, Alexandria, and Constantinople.

[27]Of course, Anglicans and the Eastern Orthodox would omit the final stage, the Roman papacy, from the providential process. Low church Anglicans would not regard presbyters becoming sacrificing priests as a positive development.

[28]Few, if any Protestants, would say that events in the early church such as presbyters coming to be regarded as sacrificing priests, claims of Petrine-papal supremacy, praying for the dead, giving communion to the dead, a belief in the *perpetual* virginity of Mary, the assumption of the soul of Mary into heaven, and the veneration of Mary were what God intended for the church.

All of these developments were allowed by God to occur within the first five centuries of the church.

[29]One of my former seminary students quaintly said, "God answers prayer 'yes,' 'no,' 'wait,' or 'OK, but you will be sorry.'" God's allowing Israel to have a "king like all the nations" was an OK-but-you-will-be-sorry answer to their insistent request.

[30]The Roman Catholic Church has yet to officially recognize the bishops of the Anglican Communion as being in the line of true apostolic succession equal to the RCC.

[31]No one claims that the minute details of a Presbyterian *Book of Church Order*, the canon laws of an episcopally governed church, or the constitutions and by-laws of a congregationally governed independent church are found in Holy Writ.

Samuel E. Waldron

[32]This is not the place to give extended proof for this. Nor is it necessary to prove what ought to be clear on any Protestant's reading of the early fathers. The *Didache* (also known as *The Teaching of the Twelve Apostles*, though it is certainly not inspired) is one of the earliest Christian writings and one of the most respected. Nevertheless, it illustrates the kind of misunderstanding that gradually set in after the departure of the apostles of Christ and unconsciously manifests an externalism often associated with legalism. Referring to Jesus' warning in the gospels not to fast as the hypocrites do (Matt. 6:16; Luke 18:12), it remarks, "Your fasts must not be identical with those of the hypocrites. They fast on Mondays and Thursdays; but you should fast on Wednesdays and Fridays." *Early Christian Fathers*, trans. and ed. by Cyril C. Richardson (New York: Macmillan, 1970), 174. The quotation is from the *Didache* 8:1.

[33]John Calvin, *The Institutes of the Christian Religion*, trans. John Allen, 7th ed. (Philadelphia: Presbyterian Board of Christian Education, n.d.) 1:87. The whole of Calvin's treatment of the self-authentication of Scripture and the testimony of the Spirit in Book 1, chapter 7 of the *Institutes* confirms and expands the view epitomized in the quotation given and is worth careful attention.

[34]Toon also thinks that the Seventy sent out by Jesus, Hebrews 13:17, 1 Thessalonians 5:12, and 1 Corinthians 16:15–16 are suggestive of the differentiation of ordained ministers. The suggestion is so faint that I cannot see it and so do not know how to refute it.

[35]Since the cessation of the office of apostle of Christ is the crucial premise of the argument for the cessation of the miraculous gifts of the Spirit, the reader should be warned that to permit apostolic succession is also to leave oneself defenseless against the arguments of charismatics.

[36]Quoted in James Bannerman, *The Church of Christ* (Edinburgh: Banner of Truth, 1960), 1:339.

[37]Bannerman, 1:339–40.

[38]Bannerman, 1:340, 341.

[39]Herbert Carson, *Tyndale New Testament Commentaries: The Epistles of Paul to the Colossians and Philemon* (Grand Rapids: Eerdmans, 1976), 79.

Chapter Two

PRESBYTERIANISM

PRESBYTERIANISM

L. Roy Taylor

Various branches of the church have chosen names for themselves that denote what they regard as a distinctive and important doctrine or practice. Baptists have so denominated themselves because of their belief in believer's baptism by immersion. Charismatic and Pentecostal Christians use a name that underscores their experience with the Holy Spirit. Methodists were originally so designated because of their methodical approach to personal piety. Lutheran believers use the term "Lutheran" to describe their distinctive theology that follows the teachings of the pioneer German Protestant Reformer, Martin Luther. Many Christians in the Presbyterian and Reformed tradition use the designation "Presbyterian" because we Presbyterians believe that the system of church government taught in the Holy Scriptures, in both the Old and New Testaments, and employed in the church until the mid-second century AD, is a representative form of church government by elders elected by the people of God. "Presbyterian" is derived from the New Testament Greek term *presbyteros* that is usually translated as "elder." "Reformed" denotes a system of theology, while "presbyterian" denotes a form of church government.[1]

TYPES OF CHURCH GOVERNMENT

Using the analogy of civil government, episcopal church government is analogous to a monarchy, congregational church government is analogous to a pure democracy, and presbyterian church government is analogous to a representative republic. We must be quick to say that these are broad major categories. There are certainly variations within each category. For example, the strongest form of an episcopal church government is the Roman Catholic papacy. The pope of the Roman Catholic Church is regarded as the supreme bishop of the church. He has the strongest authority of any bishop in any branch of the church in the world. The Archbishop of Canterbury is the prime hierarch of the Church of England, but he does not have the level of authority that the pope has. On the other end of the continuum, congregational church government in its purest form is found in smaller congregations. As congregations grow larger, it becomes impractical to have the congregation vote on minute details of church ministry operations. Therefore, larger congregations that originate with congregational church government often develop a *de facto* presbyterian government whereby a representative group governs the church. That group may be a group of elders, a group of deacons,[2] or a combination of ordained and unordained leaders. Other larger congregations that originate with congregational church government often develop a *de facto* episcopal government whereby the senior pastor is the primary decision-maker on major issues. While some may regard this as novel, it is actually a replication of the older monoepiscopacy of the second century.[3]

There are also variations within presbyterian church government. Some presbyterian denominations have a more hierarchal system whereby ecclesiastical power flows from the higher courts of the church to the lower courts. Other presbyterian denominations hold to a more "grassroots" presbyterianism whereby ecclesiastical power flows from the lower courts of the church to the higher courts. The reader should understand that there is no presiding bishop or other hierarchal clergy or ministers in a presbyterian system. Churches, however, are not independent but interdependent. There is a gradation of church courts: at least two, usually three, and sometimes four courts, depending on the size of the denomination. These bodies are called courts rather than councils (a designation stemming from the tradition in the Church of Scotland), perhaps because they are responsible for church discipline. The representative leaders of a local church are the ministers and elders, called a "session" in the Presbyterian tradition or a "consistory" in the continental

Reformed tradition.[4] The *presbytery* is the church court consisting of ministers and ruling elders representing churches from a smaller geographical area. A *synod* is the church court consisting of ministers and ruling elders representing churches from a larger geographical area. The *general assembly* is the church court consisting of ministers and ruling elders representing churches from an entire denomination.[5]

The presbyterian system of church government is representative and connectional. The congregation elects the elders to the session of the church. The local church is governed by the session. The congregation votes on calling a pastor. The presbytery approves or disapproves of the establishment of a pastoral relationship between a minister and a particular church. Presbyterian churches also have deacons, who do not have a governing role, but rather a ministry of mercy. By "connectional" we mean that local churches see themselves as part of the larger church, that local churches are not independent but are accountable to the larger church, and that local churches do not minister alone but in cooperation with the larger church.

THE CASE FOR PRESBYTERIAN CHURCH GOVERNMENT

Not only do theories of church government fall into broad categories, but also advocates of various theories argue for their positions with varying degrees of certainty. Some argue that no form of church government is taught in the Bible.[6] Some argue that the Bible teaches only one broad theory of church government that must be adapted to every historical and cultural situation. Others argue that the Bible does not teach any one particular normative pattern for church government and that church government is to be determined largely by practical and circumstantial principles. For example, the Church of England and the Protestant Episcopal Church believe that the New Testament church was an episcopacy,[7] while the Reformed Episcopal Church teaches, "This Church recognizes and adheres to Episcopacy, not as of Divine Right, but as a very ancient and desirable form of Church Polity."[8] When we seek to determine what form of church government to adopt, most Christians would turn first to the Bible. But there are other factors to consider as well, such as common sense, culture, Christian wisdom, local circumstances, biblical precedents, and general biblical principles, not just biblical commands and prohibitions.[9]

BIBLICAL, NOT JUST NEW TESTAMENT, PRECEDENT

Presbyterians do not argue that the minute details of church government are to be found in the Bible, but that the general principles of ecclesiastical polity are to be derived from Scripture. Presbyterian church government is found in both the Old Testament and the New Testament. Presbyterians believe that the principle of representative church government by elders originated in the Old Testament, was continued into the New Testament, was practiced in the early church, fell in to disuse in the mid-second century, and reappeared in the church in the sixteenth century in the Protestant Reformation of the Western church in Europe. When presbyterians discuss church government we begin in the Old Testament because we believe that the church is composed of the people of God in both the Old and New Testaments. Presbyterians believe that the church is not exclusively a New Testament body of God's people, but that it spans testaments. That is, the church originated in the Old Testament and the New Testament church is directly connected to the Old Testament company of the people of God.[10] All systems of Christian theology recognize that there are similarities and dissimilarities, continuities and discontinuities, between the Old and New Testaments.[11] Presbyterian-Reformed Christians believe that the church includes believers of both the Old and New Testaments for several reasons: (1) they have the same Savior—the Lord Jesus Christ; (2) they have the same destiny—heaven; (3) they are saved on the same basis—the grace of God, and (4) they receive eternal life by the same instrumentality—faith.[12] Therefore, presbyterian ecclesiology (theology of the church) prefers the term "biblical church," not just the "New Testament church."

The Origin of the Office of Elder

The office of elder originated in the Old Testament. Old Testament Israel was a patriarchal society, as were most ancient Middle Eastern societies. Respect and deference were shown to older men. Wisdom gained through long life experience was honored. An inherent authority was concomitant with being an elder of a household, village, or tribe. After the Lord had appeared to Moses in the burning bush, he instructed Moses to gather the elders of Israel together to inform them that he was about to deliver Israel from Egyptian bondage and lead them into the Promised Land (Ex. 3:16; 4:29). The elders were to go with Moses to represent the people of Israel in their cause before Pharoah (3:18). After giving Moses the Law (Ex. 20–23), the Lord instructed him to bring seventy elders to the base of the mount that they might worship the Lord in confirmation of the covenant (24:1, 9–11).

Later this patriarchal cultural tradition was elevated to a spiritual office. When Moses had led the people of Israel out of Egypt and they had begun their second year of sojourn in the wilderness, he became overwhelmed with the burden of leadership. Though the Lord had led the people through the Red Sea on dry land and had miraculously provided them with water and manna, they had grown discontent and longed to return to Egypt (Num. 11:4–6). Dismayed by the people's fickleness and ingratitude, Moses cried to the Lord like a Monday-morning pastor, "I am not able to carry all this people alone; the burden is too heavy for me. If you will treat me like this, kill me at once, if I find favor in your sight, that I may not see my wretchedness" (vv. 14–15). The Lord did not grant Moses' petition, but instead instituted a system of shared spiritual leadership through a plurality of elders.[13] He instructed Moses to gather seventy men from the elders of Israel who were recognized and proven leaders (v. 16).[14] He then demonstrated his approval of the elders by sending his Spirit upon them (vv. 17, 24–25). When the Spirit rested upon them, "they prophesied. But they did not continue doing it" (v. 25). This visitation of the Holy Spirit served as evidence of God's hand being on them and was, in a sense, their ordination. God earlier had shown his favor to the Levites and Aaronic priests in their ordination (Num. 8; see also Lev. 8). It should be noted that the purpose of the plurality of elders was that spiritual leadership be a *shared* leadership. The second generation shared in Moses' authority to command the people of God (Deut. 27:1). Joshua continued the practice of shared spiritual leadership through the elders (Josh. 8:10).

The Influence of the Synagogue

Though the office of elder as spiritual leader was instituted in the days of Moses over 1,400 years before Christ, it did not blossom until the inauguration of the synagogue system in the sixth century BC. After the Babylonians destroyed the temple in Jerusalem in 586 BC and deported the people of Judah, the exiles began to gather for the reading of Scripture, worship, the exposition of Scripture, and prayer.[15] The exilic prophets Jeremiah (Jer. 29:1) and Ezekiel (Ezek. 8:1; 14:1; 20:1, 3) referred to elders as leaders among the people of God during that time. With the spread of the synagogue system, the prominence of elders grew. After the return from the Babylonian captivity, the rebuilding of the temple under Zerubbabel, and the resulting reinstitution of the levitical sacrificial system, synagogues continued to be established wherever Jews went in the Mediterranean world, and the rabbis (teachers) and elders grew in prominence.

The Office of Elder in the New Testament

By the time of Christ synagogues were virtually everywhere there was a Jewish community. The New Testament phase of the church was initially primarily Jewish, with the conversion of 3,000 on the Day of Pentecost (Acts 2) and the growth of the Jerusalem church to 5,000 (Acts 4:4), followed by further rapid growth (Acts 5:14; 6:7, et al.). The apostle Paul's missionary strategy involved preaching in synagogues, where there would be some conversions among Jews and Gentile proselytes to Judaism but a greater receptivity among the "God-fearers"[16] who often provided relational bridges into the pagan Gentile culture.[17] The Epistle of James, most likely one of the earliest books of the New Testament, refers to the assembly of Christians for worship as a "synagogue" (a more literal translation of James 2:2).[18] Of course, the New Testament phase of the church grew out of the matrix of Judaism. Though the church became increasingly Gentile as the gospel flourished among Gentiles, it rightly saw itself as the legitimate continuation and fulfillment of the religion revealed first through the Law and the Prophets, and brought to fruition by the life, death, resurrection, and ascension of the divine Messiah, Jesus of Nazareth. First-century Christians continued to use the Old Testament Scriptures and received the books of the New Testament as they were produced. The first-century church continued the practice of accepting a plurality of elders as spiritual leaders, a practice obviously endorsed by Christ's own apostles.

Indeed, the death of the apostle James (Acts 12:2) about AD 44 was a catalytic factor that marked a transition in the Jerusalem church.[19] Up to that point the church there had been under the direct spiritual leadership of the apostles who had remained even after the stoning of Stephen around AD 35 or 36. However, about the time of the persecution by Herod Agrippa I (and James's execution), Luke's record begins to regularly mention *elders* in the Jerusalem church. Barnabas and Saul delivered the famine relief offering from the Gentile churches to the *elders* of Jerusalem (Acts 11:30). *Elders* sat with the apostles in the council at Jerusalem (15:2, 4, 6, 22–23; 16:4). A number of years later, it was to the *elders* of Jerusalem that Paul gave a report of his missionary endeavors (21:18). It is natural and logical that those who occupied the temporary office of apostle would turn the leadership over to those who held the office of elder, given its historic and respected origins.

THE BIBLICAL PRACTICE

How many elders should there be? How is an elder chosen? What are the characteristics of an elder? What does an elder do? Again, there is much in Scripture, the New Testament especially, to teach us. It's to these examples and principles we turn next.

Plurality of Elders

The New Testament consistently demonstrates that a plurality of elders existed in the churches.[20] The church of Jerusalem had a plurality of elders (Acts 11:30; 15:2, 4, 22–23; 16:4; 21:18). Paul and Barnabas ordained elders in churches throughout Asia Minor (14:23). The church at Ephesus, founded by Paul, and later led by Timothy, had a plurality of elders (20:17; Eph. 5:17). Paul instructed Titus to ordain elders in the churches on the island of Crete (Titus 1:5). In the Epistle of James, a general epistle, James instructed that those who were seriously ill should call for the elders of that church to pray that they would be healed (James 5:17). When the word "elder" is in the singular, it refers to the office of elder in a generic sense (1 Tim. 5:19) or to a specific elder such as Peter (1 Peter 5:1) or John (2 John 1; 3 John 1).

We find evidence of the plurality of elders in early Christian documents as well:

> Several non-canonical documents reflect a situation where a plurality of presbyters was at the head of a congregation (Polycarp, *Ep.* 5–6, cf. 11; 2 *Clem.* 7.3; *Asc. Isa.* 3.23f; *Orac. Sib.* 2.264f.), even where the single bishop was clearly distinct from the presbyters, as in Ignatius (*Polyc.* 6; *Trall.* 3; *Smyrn.* 8). The church at Alexandria, according to their later reports (Jerome, *Ep.* 146; Eutychus, *Annals*, PG 111.982), was led by twelve presbyters, who chose a president as bishop out of their own number.[21]

Responsibilities of Elders

Elders had numerous duties as spiritual leaders. As noted earlier, when the office was first established in the days of Moses, elders were to share the burden of leadership (Num. 11:17). The apostle Paul urged the Ephesian elders to pay careful attention to themselves (set a godly example), to oversee, and to care for the church (Acts 20:28). The elders carefully considered, debated, and decided theological issues (Acts 15). Elders together, not a solitary bishop, ordained others to office (6:6; 14:23; 1 Tim. 4:14). Elders prayed for the sick (James 5:14) and for all of the people of God (Acts 6:4; 20:36). All elders ruled (1 Tim. 5:17), i.e., exercised ecclesiastical authority. Both in the synagogue and the church a senate of elders handled matters of spiritual discipline when members fell into sin. Teaching elders, or pastors, had responsibilities to teach and preach the Word of God (1 Tim. 3:2; 5:17) and to administer the sacraments (Matt. 28:19–20).

Certainly the Acts 15 passage just mentioned provides the prime example in the New Testament of presbyterian-representative-connectional church government. When some former Pharisees caused dissension in the church at Antioch by claiming that Paul was in error by not requiring circumcision of Gentile converts and insisting that circumcision was necessary for salvation, the church there appointed Paul, Barnabas, and other representatives to confer with the apostles and elders at Jerusalem to resolve the matter. The event illustrates several important principles:

1. A single church appealed to the larger church to resolve a theological issue (vv. 2, 22) with the expectation that the larger church had the wisdom and authority to resolve the issue.
2. Ecclesiastical authority was shared by a plurality of elders, not just the apostles (vv. 6, 22–23).
3. The decision of the representative assembly was an act of "the whole church" (v. 22).
4. The theological issue resolved constituted a binding confessional standard on all the churches (vv. 23, 30). It was not the suggestion of a convention, but the binding confessional standard of a representative assembly.
5. The statement in Acts 14:23, "presbyters were elected by show of hands," may be considered in keeping with the classical use of the term (*cheironteo*) used by the Greeks and Romans in an election, "to vote by show of hands."[22] The elders were elected representatives of the churches.

Types of Elders

Within the synagogue system there were rabbis, elders, leaders (*archesynagogos*), and almoners (those who distributed alms to the poor). It is not surprising, therefore, to find a similar arrangement in the church. The terms "bishops," "pastors," "presbyters," and "ministers" all referred to ministers of the Word. But the pastors were not the only elders. Lay leaders who had gifts for leadership (Rom. 12:8) and administrating (1 Cor. 12:28) served together with the pastors. Paul wrote, "Let the elders who rule well be considered worthy of double honor, especially those who labor in preaching and teaching" (1 Tim. 5:17). All elders rule, but some elders also have special responsibilities in preaching and teaching. This is why, in some presbyterian circles, lay elders are called "ruling elders" and ministers are referred to as "teaching elders."

The Office of Deacon

While the office of elder as a representative leader originated in the Old Testament, the office of deacon originated in the New Testament, as Luke recorded in Acts 6. With the church's rapid growth, it so happened that the Greek-speaking widows among the converts were being neglected in the distribution of food. Thus the apostles exhorted the church to choose seven men of good reputation, full of wisdom and the Holy Spirit, to oversee this ministry (v. 3). The church chose seven, all of whom had Greek names (v. 5), and the apostles ordained them (v. 6). One of the seven, Stephen, became the first Christian martyr (Acts 7). Another, Philip, was also gifted as an evangelist (8:26–40; 21:8). By the time of Paul's imprisonment and his writing to the church at Philippi, evidently the practice of ordaining deacons had spread to other churches (Phil. 1:1). As time passed, deacons took on other mercy ministries such as providing food and clothing to prisoners, providing shelter for the homeless, and job training in honorable occupations for those who had become Christians out of dishonorable occupations, among them thieves, prostitutes, and gladiators.

Spiritual Qualifications of Elders and Deacons

The spiritual qualifications of elders were first simply stated as, "men . . . whom you know to be the elders" (Num. 11:16). For deacons, the qualifications were stated simply as well: men of good reputation, full of wisdom and the Holy Spirit (Acts 6:3). Later, as the church grew and developed, these qualifications were given in greater detail in the Pastoral Epistles (1 Tim. 3:1–13; Titus 1:5–9) as Paul instructed Timothy, then pastor of the church at Ephesus, and Titus, who was planting churches on the island of Crete. These passages, taken together, paint for us a composite picture. Certain *general characteristics* are expected:

- "Known as leaders"—recognized as spiritual leaders by others
- "Filled with the Spirit"—godly, living in dependence on the Holy Spirit
- "Filled with wisdom"—able to apply biblical principles to practical situations
- "Not a recent convert"—not a relatively new Christian

Certain characteristics are expected in the elder's or deacon's *family life*:

- "Husband of one wife"—literally "a one-woman kind of man," faithfully devoted to his wife
- "Manages his own household well"—leads his family in a godly way
- "Having his children in subjection in all honor," "his children are believers, and not open to the charge of debauchery or insubordination"—an effective father to his children still in the household
- "Wives who are dignified, not slanderers but sober minded, faithful in all things"

Specific characteristics are expected in the elder's or deacon's life *within the church*:

- "Prudent"—sensible, of sound judgment
- "Of good behavior"—lives a well-ordered life
- "Hospitable"
- "Able to teach," "able to give instruction in sound doctrine and also able to rebuke those who contradict it"
- "Not addicted to wine"—does not abuse alcohol
- "Not stubborn"
- "Not quick tempered"
- "Not argumentative"
- "Uncontentious"
- "Gentle"—kind, patient
- "Not a lover of money"—not greedy
- "Loves what is good"
- "Just"
- "Devout"

Finally, certain characteristics are expected of the elder's or deacon's *community life*:

- "Above reproach"—having no glaring inconsistencies of life that would bring dishonor to Christ and the church
- "Well thought of by outsiders so that he may not fall into disgrace, into a snare of the devil"

It is obvious that the Lord, through the Holy Scriptures, places high priority on godly character for elders and deacons.

Elders and Bishops Synonymous

Obviously, a key issue in the matter of church government is whether the terms "elder" (*presbyteros*) and "bishop" (*episcopos*) are synonyms in the New Testament that describe one and the same office *or* are distinctively different terms that describe two levels of clergy, with the bishop being of higher authority.

The term "elder" or "presbyter" (*presbyteros*) denotes wisdom, maturity, and authority. As already noted, in both the Old and New Testaments elders are leaders who are spiritually mature, demonstrate wisdom, and exercise spiritual oversight. The church also borrowed the term "bishop" or "overseer" (*episcopos*) from the Greek culture, where it was used to describe an overseer of slaves, a civil servant, or the supervisor of a construction crew; a guardian, a teacher, a scout, a supervisor, an inspector.[23] It is found in the Septuagint (LXX) to describe inspectors, superintendents, taskmasters, or civil servants.[24] The Hellenistic origin of the term may explain why "bishop" is only used in the New Testament with reference to the Gentile churches of Philippi (Phil. 1:1), Ephesus (1 Tim. 3:1–2), Asia Minor (Acts 14:23), and Crete (Titus 1:5). The term "elder," then, emphasizes primarily the character of the spiritual leader, while the term "bishop" describes the role or function of the ecclesiastical officer.

One of the best arguments advanced to demonstrate that these terms are New Testament synonyms is found in J. B. Lightfoot's commentary on Philippians, in his essay "The Christian Ministry."[25] Interestingly, Dr. Lightfoot was himself Lord Bishop of Durham in the Church of England and a highly regarded New Testament and patristic scholar at Cambridge University. He offers these six proofs:

1. In the opening of this epistle St. Paul salutes the "bishops" and "deacons." Now it is incredible that he should recognize only the first and third order and pass over the second, though the second was absolutely essential to the existence of a church and formed the staple of its ministry. It seems therefore to follow of necessity that "bishops" are identical with the "presbyters." . . .
2. In Acts (xx.17) St. Paul is represented as summoning to Miletus the "elders" or "presbyters" of the

Church of Ephesus. Yet in addressing them immediately after, he appeals to them as "bishops" or
overseers of the church (xx.28).

3. Similarly, St. Peter, appealing to the "presbyters" of
the churches addressed by him, in the same breath
urges them to "fulfill the office of bishops" with dis-
interested zeal (I Pet. v. 1,2).

4. Again in the First Epistle to Timothy St. Paul, after
describing the qualifications for the office of a
"bishop" (iii.1–7), goes on at once to say what is
required of "deacons" (iii. 8–13). He makes no mention of presbyters. The term "presbyter" however is
not unknown to him; for having occasion in a later
passage to speak of Christian ministers he calls
these officers no longer "bishops" but "presbyters"
(v. 17–19).

5. The same identification appears still more plainly
from the Apostle's directions to Titus (i.5–7); "That
thou shouldest set in order the things that are wanting and ordain *elders* in every city, as I appointed
thee; if any one be blameless, the husband of one
wife, having believing children who are not charged
with riotousness or unruly; for a *bishop* must be
blameless etc."

6. Nor is it only in the apostolic writings that this identity is found. St. Clement of Rome wrote probably in
the last decade of the first century and in his language
the terms are still convertible. [*I Clement* 42, 44][26]

Presbyterian theologian Charles Hodge, who also offers
similar arguments, concludes:

With regard to the title "Bishop" there are certain points
as to which all parties may be considered as substantially
agreed. One is that in the New Testament the title is given
to those officers in the Church who are appointed to rule,
teach and ordain. Another is that the terms Presbyter and
Bishop are applied to the same officers.[27]

WHY THE RISE OF THE EPISCOPACY?

Despite the strong biblical roots of representative spiritual
leadership by elders, most church historians agree that as early

as the middle of the second century AD an episcopal system of church government had arisen. Certainly presbyterians do not deny this historical development and thus would not disagree with the claim that "episcopacy is a very ancient form of church polity." We would agree with Bishop Lightfoot's conclusion:

> The history of the name itself suggests a different account of the origin of the episcopate. If bishop was at first used as a synonyme for presbyter and afterwards came to designate the higher office under whom the presbyters served, the episcopate properly so called would seem to have been developed from the subordinate office. In other words, the episcopate was formed not out of the apostolic order by localisation but out of the presbyterial by elevation: and the title, which was common to all, came at length to be appropriated to the chief among them.[28]

Early Episcopacy

How then did the church move from a presbyterian church government to an episcopal church government so early in her history? Three basic factors were involved in effecting the transition: (1) persecution and the effort to maintain theological orthodoxy; (2) geographic and political factors; and (3) efficiency of operations.

Persecution and Maintenance of Theological Orthodoxy

Jesus had warned his disciples that they would face persecution.[29] Indeed, the church suffered persecution just as he had predicted. Christians suffered at the hands of the Jewish leaders as well as leaders of pagan religions and the Roman government. Peter and John were arrested by the Sanhedrin (Acts 4:1–22; 5:17–42), imprisoned, and beaten (5:40). Stephen the deacon was stoned to death by a Jewish mob (Acts 7). Saul of Tarsus ravaged the church (Acts 8:1–3; 9:1–2). After Saul's conversion, the former persecutor became the persecuted.[30] James, son of Zebedee and the brother of John, was beheaded by Herod Agrippa I, the first of the twelve apostles to be martyred (12:1–2).

Until Titus Vespasianus destroyed Jerusalem in AD 70 and Christian Jews fled the holy city during the siege as Jesus had warned them to do (Matt. 24–25), Christianity was regarded by the Gentile world as a part of Judaism (similar to the Pharisees, the Sadducees, the Essenes, and the Zealots). That event marked a sharper demarcation of Christians from Judaism. As more Jews were converted, Jewish opposition to Christianity and persecution of Christians intensified. With a Jewish revolt led by the false messiah Bar-cochba ("son of the star") during AD 132–35, Christian Jews were singled out for persecution by the revolutionaries. Thereafter, Christian Jews were no longer considered a sect within Judaism by either the Jews or the civil authorities. As paganism became threatened by Christianity, Christians were persecuted by religious leaders, a development evinced by the riot of the silversmiths at Ephesus (Acts 19:21–41).

The first of ten imperial Roman persecutions of the church was instituted by Nero in AD 64, by whose orders Paul and Peter were martyred. Christians endured the last of these imperial persecutions under Diocletian Galerius, AD 303–11.[31] Persecutions varied in intensity and duration; some were local, others were empire-wide. Persecution over the years made the bishop-presbyter's (senior pastor's) role more authoritative as he passed on the apostolic teachings and had custody of the Scriptures, commentaries, liturgical materials, and ecclesiastical correspondence and records.[32] Moreover, the bishop-presbyter's role became more authoritative as the church exercised pastoral discipline over its members who succumbed to moral laxity or fell into heresies. In this manner, the "monarchial bishops" arose. Ignatius of Antioch (d. AD 117) mentioned this monoepiscopacy (only one bishop as the head of a local church).[33] In reflecting upon earlier centuries of the church, fourth-century church father Jerome (c. 342–420) noted, "Ancient presbyters were the same as bishops but gradually all the responsibility was deferred to a single person, that the thickets of heresies might be rooted out."[34]

Geographical and Political Factors

The churches where the apostles had personally labored were especially respected: Jerusalem, Antioch, Smyrna, Corinth, Ephesus, Philippi, Thessalonica, and particularly Rome. These churches were regarded as "mother churches" and the wisdom of their bishop-presbyters as heirs to the apostolic teachings was especially valued.

What's more, the church took Christ's Great Commission (Acts 1:8) seriously and spread the good news throughout the Roman Empire, beginning in Jerusalem and extending to the nations. By the late second century (the time of Irenaeus and Tertullian) bishops had begun to oversee several churches within a geographical area. In the mid-third century Cyprian proposed the idea of the prominence of Peter and those who followed him as bishops of Rome,[35] though he regarded the other apostles with high honor and authority.[36] Cyprian called Rome the *matrix et radix* ("womb and root") of the church.[37]

When the imperial persecution of Christians under Diocletian ended, his successor, Constantine, declared Christianity to be a legal religion by the Edict of Milan (AD 313). Theodosius I (the Great), Roman emperor from 379 to 395, established the Christian state and persecuted pagans. The structure of the Roman government influenced not only church polity but also its theology and liturgy. The Western branch of the church, centered in Rome, was patterned after Roman courts of law. Western theology developed in a logical, rhetorical fashion. The Eastern branch of the church, centered in Constantinople, was patterned after the pomp and ceremony of the imperial court. Its liturgy developed more elaborately; its theology was more mystical than Western theology.

The church spread first within urban centers and then took root in the more rural areas. By the Council of Nicea (AD 325), urban bishops were given prominence over rural bishops. Five of the major cities of the Roman Empire had become centers for Christian expansion: (1) Jerusalem, the mother church; (2) Antioch of Syria, the first Gentile church; (3) Alexandria, the most prominent Roman city in North Africa; (4) Rome, the capital of the empire; and (5) Constantinople, the Eastern capital after the rise of Constantine. The bishops of the churches of these five "patriarchal cities" were especially influential and respected, in a manner similar to the way the senior pastor of the largest church of a particular denomination within a state is usually shown deference today. Rome was regarded as "first among equals"; Constantinople was second. Callixtus, bishop of Rome (AD 217–22), claimed to be pontifex *maximus* (highest pontiff) and *episcopus episcoporum* (bishop of bishops), though Tertullian sarcastically denounced such pretensions.[38] By the mid-fifth century, Leo I claimed to have authority over the entire church, although the Eastern branch of the church did not recognize his supremacy. Rome's prominence was further enhanced over time because heresies and heretics had been more successfully dealt with there than in Alexandria and Constantinople.

The Efficiency Factor

The episcopal system came to be seen as an efficient means of operation, especially given its modeling after Roman civil government and its effective administrative form. An authoritative bishop, with the decision-making power and the ability to delegate responsibilities to others, was more efficient than shared leadership.

Later Episcopacy

A more authoritative episcopacy developed over time in the West for a number of reasons. Rome was not only the sole patriarchal city in the West but the capital of the empire. Thus the bishop of Rome became the most prestigious of all the bishops and patriarchs. Unlike the Eastern church, the church in Rome also began to transition from Greek to Latin by the mid-second century and was thereafter able to resolve theological conflicts more readily because Latin did not have the nuances of meaning problematic to Greek. The Western church grew more rapidly than the Eastern church because it was more successful in evangelization and missions. With the barbarian invasions, the church, particularly the Western church, became a more cohesive force in the empire. Moreover, the theory of Petrine supremacy[39] and attempts by bishops of Rome to exercise universal authority led to its preeminence. Even though Rome fell to barbarian invasion in 410, many barbarians later converted to Christianity and became part of the Western church. The Eastern church was the first confronted with the rise of Islam (633–732), and within one hundred years saw the loss of the patriarchal cities of Jerusalem, Antioch, and Alexandria. Christians in the East looked to the patriarch of Constantinople as a unifying figure. Tensions between the Western and Eastern church grew, fed in part by Rome's claim to universal authority and eventuating in the Great

Schism of 1054, in which the patriarch of Constantinople and the Roman pope mutually anathematized each other.[40] During the Middle Ages the Roman papacy's power, influence, and wealth grew to its high-water mark.

THE RESTORATION OF PRESBYTERIAN CHURCH GOVERNMENT

Political and theological upheavals did not initially disrupt the episcopacy. Despite the Reformation in England, the Church of England retained an episcopal government. Nor did the Lutherans evince much concern about reforming polity. It was to John Calvin that the mantle fell to restore presbyterian-representative-connectional government to the church.

John Calvin

In the early stages of the Reformation that began in the Western church, some were concerned to reform the church more thoroughly. After the Reformation had taken root, the emperor of the Holy Roman Empire, Charles V, called for a diet (convocation) to be held in the city of Speyer in 1544 to discuss further reforms. Martin Bucer, leader of the Reformation in Strasbourg, asked John Calvin, a second-generation Reformer, to write a treatise to be presented to the emperor on why continuing reformation was necessary. Calvin concentrated on four areas in which the church needed reform: (1) worship, (2) theology (particularly the doctrine of justification), (3) sacraments, and (4) church government:

> If it be inquired, then, by what things chiefly the Christian religion has a standing existence amongst us and maintains its truth, it will be found that the following two not only occupy the principal place, but comprehend under them all the other parts, and consequently the whole substance of Christianity, viz., a knowledge first of the mode in which God is duly worshipped; and secondly of the source from which salvation is to be obtained. When these are kept out of view, though we may glory in the name of Christians, our profession is empty and vain. After these come the Sacraments and the

Government of the Church, which, as they were instituted for the preservation of these branches of doctrine,
ought not be employed for any other purpose; and,
indeed, the only means of ascertaining whether they are
administered purely and in due form.[41]

Calvin devoted almost one-third of the space in his *Institutes of the Christian Religion* to the doctrine of the church.[42] An
important aspect of the doctrine of the church is the government
of the church. Like other Reformers, he rehearsed the decline
and abuses of the church under the papacy and then advocated
a return to a presbyterian-representative-connectional form of
church government. In commenting on Ephesians 4:11 he noted
that the New Testament describes some extraordinary temporary offices, such as apostle, prophet, and evangelist, and some
ordinary permanent offices, such as pastor and teacher.[43] The
office of apostle was unique, being established by Christ as the
foundation of the church in its New Testament phase. Prophets
were those through whom revelation was given and their temporary office passed away with the closing of the Canon. Calvin
saw the evangelists as the Seventy and protégés of the apostles,
such as Luke, Timothy, and Titus. Pastor and teacher, however,
are permanent offices, with pastors being somewhat analogous
to apostles and teachers similar to prophets. Calvin argued that
the terms "bishops," "pastors," "presbyters," and "ministers"
all referred to ministers of the Word. He turned to Romans 12:7–
8 and 1 Corinthians 12:28 to justify both the office of ruling elder
(those who have the gift of government [1 Cor. 12:28] and who
rule with diligence [Rom. 12:8]) and deacon (showing mercy
[Rom. 12:8] and caring for the poor [1 Cor. 12:28]).[44]

In his commentary on 1 Timothy 5:17, Calvin posited that
the passage infers two kinds of elders, those who rule only and
those who both rule and teach. The Genevan Reformer taught
that the ancient church had three orders: (1) presbyters who
were pastors and teachers, (2) presbyters who were governors
(ruling elders), charged with censure and the correction of
morals, and (3) deacons, who collected and distributed alms for
the relief of the poor.[45] Calvin saw the office of deacon as a lay
ministry of mercy rather than as an entry-level clergy position.
In restoring the office of deacon to its original mercy ministry
function, Calvin was consistent with the actions of Reformers in

Strasbourg. In Geneva, deacons established a hospital to care for the sick, cared for widows and orphans, distributed food and funds to the destitute, and established a French refugee fund to assist Protestant refugees fleeing persecution.[46]

The people of the church were to be given a voice in choosing their ministers and governors, because, as Calvin argued on the ground of Acts 14:23, "presbyters were elected by show of hands." Calvin referred to the classical use of the term (*cheironteo*) used by the Greeks and Romans in an election, "to vote by show of hands."[47] Since the Levitical priests were brought before the people prior to consecration (Lev. 8:4–6; Num. 20:26–27), since Matthias was elected to the apostolic company (Acts 1:15ff.), and since the original seven deacons were elected by the people, so the congregation is to be given a voice in electing their pastors.[48] Calvin also referred to Cyprian's statement that the assent of the people was essential in the election of a bishop.[49] The presbyterian-representative-connectional form of church government was adopted by the Reformed Church of France, the Reformed Church of the Netherlands, the Church of Scotland, in some Swiss and German churches, and elsewhere, due in large degree to Calvin's influence. His writings were widely read, and many came to Geneva to study in the academy there.

The British Isles

The Reformation in England took a unique path. Henry VIII (r. 1509–47) wanted to be freed of papal domination, wanted to acquire much of the Roman Catholic Church's property in England, and wanted to secure a divorce from Catherine of Aragon who had borne him a daughter (Mary) but not a son. He was not interested in theological reform. In fact, Henry, who considered himself a theologian, wrote *Assertio Septem Sacramenorum* (Assertion of Seven Sacraments, 1521) against Luther, and near the end of his reign (1546) Ann Askew was burned at the stake for holding Protestant views of the Eucharist. Pope Leo X, who had excommunicated Luther, was so impressed with Henry's *Assertio* that he gave him the title "Defender of the Faith." Under Henry's son, Edward VI (r. 1547–53), Thomas Cranmer, the first Protestant Archbishop of Canterbury, led in the production of the two editions of the Book of Common Prayer, 1549 and 1552, but episcopacy was retained. Under Mary Tudor, so-called "Bloody Mary" (r. 1553–58), Roman Catholicism was restored and Protestants were persecuted. Under Elizabeth I (r. 1558–1603), Calvinist-Presbyterians had high hopes that the Church of England would be more thoroughly reformed after the example of Geneva. Even though several of their number became bishops (one, Edmund Grindal was elevated to become Archbishop of Canterbury), they were thwarted in their attempts to reform the doctrine, worship, and polity of the Church of England as they had hoped.

It was during the reign of Elizabeth that the Puritan movement developed. The Puritans, many of whom hoped for a presbyterian polity to be established, had their hopes renewed when James VI, a Stuart monarch of Scotland, ascended to the throne of England, where he became James I (r. 1603–25). Educated by Presbyterians, when the Puritans presented to him the Millenary Petition,[50] he called the Hampton Court Conference in 1604 to consider their demands. However, when one of the Puritan petitioners, John Reynolds, brought up the issue of replacing the episcopacy with presbyterianism, James replied tersely, "No bishop, no king." Charles I (r. 1625–49) was even more oppressive of the Puritans, appointing William Laud as Archbishop of Canterbury. In 1642 the English Civil War broke out, partially due to the opposition of the English Protestant gentry and the Scots to Charles' religious policies. He was eventually executed in 1649.

In the Interregnum, during the English Civil War and Oliver Cromwell's protectorate, the Church of England was disestablished and the episcopacy overthrown. Parliament unseated the bishops from the House of Lords, calling for an assembly of theologians to propose measures to create a body similar to the continental Reformed churches and the Church of Scotland. This group, which met at Westminster Abbey from 1643 to 1648, was a creature of the English parliament, *not* an ecclesiastical assembly. Charged with revising the Thirty-Nine Articles of Religion and the Book of Common Prayer, the assembly produced a Confession of Faith, Larger Catechism, and Shorter Catechism to replace the former and the Directory of Worship, which was more of a set of rubrics[51] than a prayer book, to replace the latter.

Because the assembly's commissioners were virtually to a man convinced Calvinists, they were able to arrive at a consensus on doctrinal matters more easily than on matters of church government. On that subject, views varied. Some were of Erastian convictions, believing the state to be ultimate authority over the church. Others were of *jure divino* presbyterian persuasion, believing that presbyterian church government was by divine authority *the* biblical system of ecclesiastical polity. Others wanted a return to a modified episcopal government. A vocal minority sought a congregational government.

The Westminster Assembly, as it came to be known, invited Scotland to send nonvoting delegates to participate in debate. The few Scots commissioners sought unsuccessfully to persuade the Assembly, and through it, the English Parliament, to adopt *jure divino* presbyterianism. Ultimately the assembly advocated a presbyterian but not a *jure divino* presbyterian polity for the church. The Assembly first proposed to Parliament a set of "Propositions of Church Government,"[52] which Parliament rejected in November of 1644[53] but the Church of Scotland approved in 1645. The Assembly adopted and recommended *A Practical Directory for Church Government* that consisted of a system of presbyteries and synods, but no general assembly, with the parliament (instead of the king) being the ultimate authority. Though presbyterian polity was theoretically adopted in England in 1647, it was not practically implemented.[54]

After Cromwell's death in 1658, when Charles II (r. 1658–85) gained the throne, the Church of England was reestablished, conformity to the Book of Common Prayer required, and the episcopacy restored. On his deathbed, Charles II renounced his allegiance to Protestantism and expressed his allegiance to the Roman Catholic Church. The best English Presbyterians could gain, along with Congregationalists, Baptists, and Quakers, was the status of tolerated Dissenters. Nevertheless, the work of the Westminster Assemby had and continues to be very influential not only for Presbyterians in Scotland and America, but also throughout the world.

Though presbyterian ecclesiastical polity was not at last realized in the Church of England, when the Reformation began in Scotland not only Reformed theology and worship practices but also presbyterian-representative-connectional church government were adopted. John Knox, a leading figure in the Scottish Reformation, was influenced by one of the first Reformers and Protestant martyr, George Wishart (1513–46), and shortly after 1544 adopted the principles of the Reformation. During times of persecution in England and Scotland, Knox served Reformed churches first in Frankfurt and then Geneva, where he was influenced by Calvin's teaching. After his return to Scotland in 1559 he was instrumental in forming the General Assembly of the Church of Scotland a year later. He was the major writer of the Scots Confession, which stated the church's theology, and one of the five ministers who wrote the *First Book of Discipline*, which stated the church's presbyterian polity. The church's polity was further detailed in the adoption of the *Second Book of Discipline* (1578), which clearly defined the gradation system of church courts.[55]

Presbyterianism in America

American Presbyterianism differed from its Scottish predecessor. Whereas in Scotland the general assembly was established before the presbyteries, in colonial America the Presbyterian Church began first with congregations, then with the organization of the Presbytery of Philadelphia in 1706, the Synod of Philadelphia in 1717, the Synod of New York in 1741, and the General Assembly in 1788 (also formed in Philadelphia). When the General Assembly was formed, eight preliminary principles[56] of representative church government were adopted that reflected America's more democratic, free-church perspective rather than duplicating the Church of Scotland's polity, which most American commissioners regarded as an aristocratic, top-down perspective that gave the General Assembly too much authority.[57]

STRENGTHS OF THE PRESBYTERIAN SYSTEM

Biblically Based Polity

Presbyterians do not hold to "apostolic succession" in the sense that the Roman Catholic Church, Eastern Orthodox churches, or some high church Anglicans do. That is, that there is an unbroken chain of ordained bishops who can trace their ordinations all the way back to the apostles and that only such bishops have the power to ordain.[58] Neither do Presbyterians hold a "Landmark" Baptist view, that from the present to the first century, there is an unbroken chain of local churches practicing believer's baptism and congregational government.[59] Presbyterians, along with Lutherans and low church Anglicans, believe that true apostolic succession is maintaining and propagating the faith delivered to the church by the apostles who were also authors of the New Testament, and following the apostolic practice of obedience to the revealed will of God given in Holy Scriptures. The Reformed and Lutheran view of church history is neither that the church is infallible, as claimed by the Roman Catholic and Eastern Orthodox churches, nor that the church was immediately overwhelmed with pagan syncretism after the death of the apostles, as was the view of some sixteenth-century radical Reformers or nineteenth-century "Restorationists." Rather, Reformed Christians hold that the church is simultaneously and always holy yet imperfect, wise but not infallible. In so doing, Reformed churches identify with the long lineage of the church throughout her entire history, recognizing other branches of the church as valid expressions of the church universal, recognizing the ordinations and sacraments of other Christian communions, receiving members from other denominations, and allowing Christians from other denominations to receive communion in our churches. This perspective, when applied to church polity, means that Presbyterians, from the Reformation forward, have not regarded presbyterian polity as necessary to the existence of the church, but as essential to the perfection of the church.[60] Yet, as we have sought to demonstrate above, the Scriptures are not silent on the issue of church government. The chief advantage of presbyterian polity is its being the system most closely in general conformity to the principles of biblical polity.

Doctrinal Fidelity

No system of church polity can absolutely guarantee theological integrity among its ministers and office-bearers. Apostasy and heresy have cropped up in branches of the church with all types of church government. Nevertheless, presbyterian church polity has built-in safeguards that work *if* the system is faithfully followed. First, a Reformed-Presbyterian church has a binding confessional doctrinal standard that is not just an advisory consensus statement.[61] Second, the doctrinal standards of a Reformed-Presbyterian church are derived from Scripture, relying upon the Holy Spirit, benefiting from the wisdom of the theological consensus of the church throughout the ages. Finally, ministers and office-bearers are required to adhere to the biblical system of doctrine for ordination and continued ministry.

Mutual Accountability

In a church with a presbyterian-representative-connectional system, there is mutual accountability not only in doctrinal integrity, but also for one's manner of life.[62] Historically, the Reformed-Presbyterian churches have regarded the "marks of the church" to be (1) the faithful preaching of the Word, (2) the proper administration of the sacraments, and (3) the practice of discipline.[63] In a presbyterian system, the members of the local church are accountable to the elders of that church, ministers and churches are accountable to the presbytery, and presbyteries are accountable to the general assembly. Carefully detailed procedures are to be followed once a judicial process of discipline has been instituted. Moreover, there is the possibility of appeal to the larger church, the presbytery, or even the general assembly.[64]

Cooperative Ministry

To be a presbyterian church involves not only a mutual commitment to a confessional doctrinal standard and mutual accountability, but also a commitment to cooperative ministry. That is based on an ecclesiology which posits that the church is more than the local church, that local churches ministering together as a regional church or national church can accomplish more than local churches ministering separately. Because the church is a covenant community of the people of God, local churches are not independent, but interdependent, not only in doctrinal confessions and accountability, but also in cooperative ministry. This is not to say that churches with other forms of church government cannot have effective cooperative ministries,[65] but that for presbyterians cooperative ministry is a matter of theological principle, not merely practical strategy.

Checks and Balances

The abuse of power is one of the recurring sins throughout the long history of the church. Most Reformed Christians believe that sin taints the entirety of human personality.[66] Those who believe in human depravity recognize the practical truth of the statement, "Power corrupts and absolute power corrupts absolutely," not only in the political sphere but in the church as well. A hierarchal episcopacy, or a monoepiscopacy, offers greater opportunity for the abuse of power by individual leaders. A purely congregational system offers an opportunity for the "tyranny of the majority." The presbyterian system of representative-connectional government by a plurality of elders in a gradation of church courts poses an effective check on the abuse of power by an individual leader. Moreover, the presbyterian system features not only majority rule, but also preserves the rights of a minority within the local church and the larger church.

CONCLUSION

In this chapter we have argued that church polity is not a matter of indifference in the Bible and that the presbyterian form of church government is biblical, historical, and practical. Presbyterian-representative government was instituted by God in the Old Testament, developed in the synagogue, continued in the New Testament phase of the church until the mid-second century, and restored to the church in the sixteenth-century Reformation. Because Presbyterian polity conforms most closely to the general principles of biblical polity, it should be employed in the church today. Presbyterian polity is essential not to the existence of the church, but to its perfection.

AN EPISCOPALIAN'S RESPONSE

Peter Toon

Dr. Taylor provides a very clear presentation of the claimed origins and basis of presbyterian polity. I congratulate him on his clarity and the width of his coverage. I note that he argues that church polity is not a matter of indifference in the Bible and that the presbyterian form of church government is biblical, historical, and practical. He claims that presbyterian-representative government was instituted by God in the Old Testament, developed in the synagogue, continued in the New Testament phase of the church until the mid-second century, and restored to the church in the sixteenth-century Reformation. Further, because he holds that presbyterian polity conforms most closely to the general principles of biblical polity, he believes that it should be employed in the church today. Finally he claims that presbyterian polity is essential not to the existence of the church, but to its perfection.

My judgment is that while he provides a most readable essay he is wrong in most of his major conclusions, claims, and beliefs. (However, I think that he is right in claiming that presbyterianism is practical, for it has worked from the sixteenth century to the present.) This is because he chooses to ignore the history of the church of God, and the divine providence watching over her, from circa AD 100 to 1500. Theologically, it appears that the Bible for him exists in its own space and time, without beginning or context, and that it does not belong in real terms to the church in her space and time. If he were to take most seriously the way that the canon of Scripture, and particularly that of the New Testament, came into existence, in the context of the full display of episcopal polity, he would have to adjust the way that he reads the evidence. We all need to remember that the Bible of the early Christians was the Old Testament—the Septuagint—and that the full canon of the New Testament was not universally agreed upon or fully available for all until perhaps as late as the third century. And also we cannot separate the acceptance and approval of the Canon from the presence of bishops in the church as those who made (under God) the final decisions as to that Canon.

So naturally, I am interested that in his presentation Taylor has something to say about the episcopal polity. In fact, he readily concedes that the system of episcopacy and the Threefold Ministry were in place from the middle of the second century and that they became and then remained the sole form of polity until the sixteenth century, from which time they had competition from presbyterian polity in parts of old Europe. It seems to me that this concession alone, because of its implications, undermines his case and means that his whole biblical edifice is built upon supposition rather than fact.

WHAT IF THERE HAD BEEN EARLY PRESBYTERIAN POLITY?

I do not think that in the period of the apostles, and in the period immediately after their deaths, there was in place any one standard and uniform system of church polity everywhere without exception. There were so many differences between regions and cities in the multiracial and multiethnic Roman Empire, and communication was so slow, that we should expect that different apostles and evangelists made local arrangements that were practical and realistic, but based upon standards they held in common and in mind. Suggestions of this variety are there for all to see if we read the Acts of the Apostles and the epistles of Paul, Peter, James, and John.

But, for the sake of argument, let us agree that at least in some regions or some individual churches there was in place a system (from the little that we know about it) that can be called presbyterian, in that presbyters ruled in one way or another and that there was no church officer above them (except an apostle when they were still alive).

Yet whatever form of presbyterianism might have existed here or there, Taylor readily concedes that it did not last long at all! This is very odd indeed. Why should what is supposedly right and good disappear so quickly, smoothly, and uniformly everywhere, without apparent protest from those who were deeply involved in it? However, to account for its disappearance he seeks to explain why his preferred system lasted for so little time in the years after the apostles and why an episcopal polity developed quickly and smoothly from it.

He supplies three reasons: persecution and maintenance of theological orthodoxy; geographical and political factors; and efficiency. To these I would add the church's study and meditation upon the Scriptures (i.e., the Septuagint) in the light of the Christian message (not yet fully settled into the canon of the New Testament).

Now I am ready to accept that the consideration of historical factors causing or allowing a change or development in space and time in God's church can be an interesting and perhaps important study. And we can speculate on the basis of the meager records we possess why episcopal polity rather quickly became the only and prized polity. However, in supplying historical data, Taylor does not consider the theological question that I see arising here—a rather critical matter. By this I mean the possibility that the change from his supposed presbyterianism (or my picture of a variety of local arrangements) into the single episcopal system was guided by no less a personal power than the Lord of the church and the providence of the Holy Trinity.

If the church (as he accepts) was going through difficult and rough times in a hostile environment in the second century, is it not more reasonable to suppose that God was protecting and guiding his church in all general matters, rather than leaving her to flounder in the waves of tribulation and uncertainty? Is it not more reasonable to suppose that the emergence of episcopal polity was by the design of the Lord Christ himself and executed in space and time through the presence and guidance of the Holy Ghost, the Paraclete, according to the will of the Almighty Father? Is it not reasonable to suppose that God the Holy Trinity intended a hierarchy of ministers so that holy order could be reflected and kept more efficiently in the church?

The proposal that there was initially a pure or right polity that quickly changed into a less than pure or right polity, or even into an impure or erroneous polity, suggests that the church was going down the broad way that leads to perdition rather than seeking to walk in the narrow way that leads to life. And in historical records there appears to be no internal evidence to suggest that any members of the early church believed that she was going in the wrong direction in her general acceptance of episcopacy. In fact, what we know suggests the opposite—that the development of the Threefold Ministry was natural and was God's will, confirmed by the study of the Bible (i.e., the Septuagint).

THE REAL REASON FOR THE DEVELOPMENT
OF THE EPISCOPACY

Believing that the order they knew in the second and third century of the church was God's will, Christian writers actually used an Old Testament analogy that Taylor does not use and would probably resist using—the hierarchy of the divinely ordained priesthood. Even as there were the high priest, the priest, and the Levite in the old economy, so in the new economy there are the bishop, the presbyter, and the deacon.

We recall that from the earliest times the Eucharist was seen as an unbloody sacrifice replacing the bloody sacrifice no longer offered in the destroyed temple of Jerusalem. So, from around AD 100, in the *Didache*, we read: "Assemble on the Lord's Day, breaking bread and celebrating the Eucharist; but first confess your sins that your sacrifice (*thysia*) may be a pure one. . . . For it was of this that the Lord spoke, 'Everywhere and always offer me a pure sacrifice' [Malachi 1:10–11]" (ch. 14). This text from Malachi was very significant for the early church and is often cited by its writers. Further in chapter 13 of the *Didache*, we read that the charismatic prophets are the Christian "high priests."

At much the same time, Clement of Rome claims that Christian liturgical offerings and services should be constructed on the analogy of the Old Testament basis of high priest, priest, and Levites (*1 Clement* 90). And not too long afterward, Tertullian speaks of the bishop as the *summus sacerdos* (in *Baptismo* 17), and

Hippolytus of Rome refers to the "high priestly spirit" of the bishop (*Apostolic Tradition*, III, 5).

The church fathers were not claiming that the Threefold Ministry of the new covenant is a continuation of the Threefold Ministry of the temple of the old covenant, but the analogy is being used both to set forth the holy order of the Christian ministry instituted by God and also to insist that the Eucharist is an offering to the Father, through his Son, and in the Spirit. Of course, this teaching is not to be equated with the medieval doctrine of the Mass as a propitiatory sacrifice!

Thus, the Christian theology of the ministry did not simply base itself on the eldership of the old covenant, as Taylor claims. But let us move on into the sixteenth century.

AN INCONSISTENT APPEAL TO
THE CHURCH FATHERS

Strangely enough, Protestant Christians whom we now call Presbyterians do accept the authority of the teaching of the Fathers (bishops) in the absolutely basic teachings of the Christian faith. If we go to any of the confessions of faith produced by Presbyterians in the sixteenth and seventeenth centuries, we shall see that they are wholeheartedly committed to the patristic dogmas of the Trinity and the person of Christ (taken from the first four, perhaps first six, ecumenical councils of the early church). By whom were these dogmas produced? By bishops, of course, assembled in councils in the first five centuries!

These same Presbyterian confessions of faith commit to the canon of Holy Scripture. By whom was this canon fixed and who was responsible for what was included in the New Testament canon? Bishops in synods and councils, of course, in the third and fourth centuries.

Now you cannot have it both ways. If the foundational dogmas of your confessions of faith, and if the very canon of Scripture from which you make your case, are both the products (in terms of human agency) of synods, wherein bishops were the primary members and decision makers, then you surely have to concede that the episcopal polity (at least at this stage) had not revealed itself to be outside the guidance and providence of Almighty God. If it were, how could it get right the very basic truths of the Bible and the Christian faith?

THE UNCERTAINTY OF EARLY PRESBYTERIAN POLITY

Though there is no scholarly consensus as to the precise way that churches were governed in the first and early second centuries, that is, in the apostolic and subapostolic age, no one doubts that episcopal polity was in place from AD 200 until the sixteenth century in the whole of the known Christian church and has been in place for the majority of Christians ever since.

The only period when all historians and theologians agree that presbyterian polity has been in place is from the Protestant Reformation in Europe to the present. Apparently only Presbyterians think it was in place in the first century and perhaps part of the second. Thus, to claim that presbyterian polity is the sole polity to which the New Testament witnesses is, first of all, to make a disputed claim. Second, it is to claim a polity that, it appears, was totally unknown to the Christian leaders who approved what we now call the canon of the New Testament (from which source documents the claim of presbyterian polity is made!).

CONCLUSION

Let me end by noting Taylor's claim that presbyterian polity is necessary not to the essence of the church but to its perfection. That it is not necessary to its essence is demonstrated by the fact that there was no presbyterian government of the church anywhere for many centuries! For on Taylor's best estimate, from circa 150 to circa 1530 there was no such polity to be seen. Further, in the critically important period of the early church's expansion into and through the Roman Empire, and then in facing the invading tribes from the north of the empire, the church did not have the slightest appreciation of, or even memory of, presbyterian polity.

Finally, since all are agreed that there was no presbyterian polity in God's church for over thirteen centuries, how can anyone claim that this polity is necessary to its perfection? The logic of this requires us to believe that God abandoned his full care of the church from sometime soon after the apostolic period until the Swiss Protestant Reformation got on its way in the sixteenth century. Could the God of mercy be so unkind to his elect people? Presbyterian polity belongs neither to the *esse* of the church nor to its *plene esse*. I will accept, however, that an argument can be made that from 1530 it may belong to its *bene esse*!

A SINGLE-ELDER CONGREGATIONALIST'S RESPONSE

Paige Patterson

Anyone searching for a succinct and cogently argued defense of the presbyterian perspective on church government needs look no further than this chapter by Roy Taylor. Standing in a long and venerable line of Presbyterian divines, Taylor represents their cause well.

AREAS OF AGREEMENT

Among the many perspectives with which I find broad agreement, I will choose to list only a few which seem to be especially important in light of other chapters in this book. First, Taylor's discussion of the historic rise of the episcopacy as a form of church government chronicles at least one of the sociopolitical realities that resulted in a change from the way the earliest assemblies operated. In so doing, he calls attention to the fact (to which even Peter Toon must admit), namely, that episcopacy is a development across time, not the practice of churches in the New Testament period or even the second century. This change must be explained. What exactly was the deficiency in the earliest churches which had to be altered in passing centuries? And was the development really an improvement?

A second major contribution of Taylor's essay is the marshaling of evidence that the terms "bishop," "elder," and "pastor" were synonymous in the New Testament period. Citations from Jerome, Calvin, and Hodge all testify to this. Meanwhile, Taylor even cites both Cyprian and Calvin to the effect that the elders were chosen or elected by the churches. Cyprian's observation that the election of elders requires the "assent of the people" sounds remarkably like the kind of congregationalism I would advocate.

In addition, I am grateful for Taylor's avowal that no form of church government guarantees "theological integrity." Further, he is certainly on target when he points out what a good many Baptists need to hear, that the chant "no creed but Christ" is simplistic. Ecclesiastical life abounds with examples of churchmen and theologians who chant that mantra but so remake Christ in their own image as to deny the Jesus of the Bible. Others seize one aspect of the teaching of the Lord while they effectively jettison those aspects of his teachings that they determine are unpalatable to contemporary tastes.

Also, I would be remiss not to express gratitude for the observation in note 65 concerning the missionary efforts of Southern Baptists. The fact that British Baptists of William Carey's era as well as independent Baptists and nondenominational Bible churches (all of which are fiercely independent of hierarchical connectionalism and often congregational in government) are among the other more successful practitioners of missions might suggest that denominational bureaucracies of the type Taylor advocates are seldom an asset to world mission endeavors.

A POINT OF CLARIFICATION

On the subject of "apostolic succession," I would have to give a mixed review. On the one hand, I wholly endorse the definition that Taylor proposes:

> True apostolic succession is maintaining and propagating the faith delivered to the church by the apostles who were also authors of the New Testament, and following the apostolic practice of obedience to the revealed will of God given in Holy Scriptures.

On the other hand, he mentions the Landmark Baptist view almost as if it were the predominant view among Baptists. While I know that the author knows better, I fear that some readers might come away thinking that most Baptists are Landmarkers. Most Baptists are confident that what remains of the mission of the apostles is the apostolic testimony found in the New Testament. Following that testimony is what links a church directly to the apostles.

By the same token, I know of very few of the radical Reformers of the sixteenth century who believed that God had ever left himself without a witness. They, as I, believed that the church was, by the time of Constantine and certainly in the aftermath of his declaration that Christianity was no longer illegal, "overwhelmed with pagan syncretism." I have never seen a really convincing argument to the contrary, although Rome and, I think, Peter Toon, make ongoing attempts. This conclusion does not suppose that there were no genuinely regenerate believers after AD 313. Neither does it advance the thesis that there were no local assemblies that rejected the Constantinian synthesis and longed for and sought for the purity of the New Testament way. Nevertheless, contemporary Baptists, for the most part, would endorse Taylor's definition of apostolic succession. Most would not endorse Landmarkism.[67]

AREAS OF DISAGREEMENT

My differences with Taylor begin with his misunderstanding of the nature of congregationalism, as stated in the initial part of his chapter. Those who advocate congregational government would almost wholly reject this idea of the congregation voting on "minute details of church ministry operations." In my own chapter, I have identified as aberrant that abuse of the congregational paradigm. However, the alternative is not a "*de facto* presbyterian government," since congregations always have the prerogative of taking anything they wish under advisement, including the continuing service of the elder(s) (1 Tim. 5:17–20).

Although congregationalism is no guarantee that a church will get things right, this paradigm still seems preferable to me for three reasons. First, any sort of hierarchical system is in the nature of the case a bureaucracy, and bureaucracies are seldom efficient and often self-serving. Second, the long history of abuse in hierarchical forms of church government provides its own warning. Finally, the burden of proof for the necessity of abandoning the congregationalism that seems often present in the

New Testament still rests upon the advocates of elder rule and presbyterianism.

The two major differences between these positions focus on the final nature of scriptural authority and the question of the relationship of the church to the Old Testament people of God. First, regarding the authority of Scripture, I was surprised to read the advocacy of "church courts" consisting of sessions, presbyteries, synods, and general assemblies. Where is the precedent or mandate for these "courts" in the Bible? Some argument might be marshaled for presbyteries in the New Testament sense, but the others are without mention in the early church. Surely this system of "courts" belongs to a post-New Testament era. If so, then how does Taylor's scheme differ from that of Toon? Both essentially find the New Testament pattern inadequate or, at the very least, in need of future development.

While I find this position untenable, I understand it better in light of Taylor's confession that "most Christians would turn first to the Bible. But there are other factors to consider as well, such as common sense, culture, Christian wisdom, local circumstances, biblical precedents, and general biblical principles, not just biblical commands and prohibitions." While I join him in affirming that all of those factors are important, and I would even add "the history of interpretation," I remain uncomfortable with placing any factors such as common sense, culture, local circumstances, or Christian wisdom in a sentence parallel with the Bible and biblical principles. In my own view, the Bible is the final authority not only for faith but also for *practice*.

Unlike Toon, I do not think that Taylor wants brazenly to bring tradition in the front door of the church, but I fear that imprecision in the matter of biblical authority has caused him to allow tradition to be smuggled in the side door and honored, at least in ecclesiology, alongside the Scriptures. Lacking scriptural support, these various "church courts" can only be endorsed on the basis of tradition. For me, tradition is too prone to error. Give us a sure word from God or else either abandon the concept of these courts, or at least acknowledge the practice as "optional."

Apparently, Taylor rejects Toon's proposal of the consensus of the first five centuries with the various councils. But instead of replacing that paradigm with Scripture alone, he wants to substitute the Diet of Speyer to establish a "presbyterian-representative-connectional" form of church government. Acknowledging that there were some elders who especially "labored in the Word" (1 Tim. 5:17), where is the evidence in the New Testament actually differentiating two classes of elders, teachers and governors, or clergy and laity? Where in the New Testament is the distinction between clergy and laity at all? The New Testament knows only the saints of God with elders and deacons chosen by the churches to equip the whole congregation to do the work of the ministry (Eph. 4:12).

The identification of the church with Israel in the Old Testament is the basis of another difficulty. Baptists, both dispensational and nondispensational, have generally noted that while Israel in the Old Testament and the church in the New Testament are both the people of God, the family of the faith—the church—nevertheless, is a separate entity that marks a new dispensation in God's plan and purpose. Taylor correctly identifies commonalities between the Old Testament people of God and the church. These include sharing the same Savior, the same destiny, and the same basis and instrumentality of salvation. He fails, however, to mention the profound differences between Israel and the church, which are no less striking than the similarities.

First, the post-Pentecostal era boasts a permanent indwelling of the Holy Spirit in each believer, a condition apparently unknown in Israel (John 14:17). This fact, in turn, abrogated the necessity of a separate priesthood, since each believer became the "temple" for the Holy Spirit, enjoying direct access to God through the great High Priest Jesus (Heb. 10:19–21). Further, believers make up the body of Christ, an idea unknown and unforeseen in the Old Testament (1 Cor. 6:19). The church is the bride of Christ, and it seems doubtful to me that this distinction will be entirely lost even in the eternal kingdom (Rev. 21:9). The church belongs to "the fullness of the Gentiles" as opposed to the Old Testament work of God primarily focused on Israel as separate from all other nations (Rom. 11:25).

The sometimes devastating results of improperly distinguishing between Israel and the church can be observed in the tendency to equate New Testament baptism with circumcision and, therefore, with the determination to baptize infants. Aside from being without precedent or mandate in the New Testament, such a practice has the tendency to encourage people as they reach an age of understanding simply to consider themselves "children of the covenant" without having received the new birth. Jesus said, "Unless one is born again he cannot see the kingdom of God" (John 3:3). Clearly this regeneration experience is not synonymous with baptism.

A connection of grace certainly exists between the operation of God in the Old Testament and the revelation of the church in the New Testament era. But by the same token the church is a mystery of God anticipated in the Old Testament only by references to a coming new covenant, promises of a Messiah, and the vision of an era of Gentile responsiveness to God (Jer. 31:27–40, Isa. 9:1–3). According to Paul, this *mystery* of the church was not made known to the sons of men in other ages but was revealed by the Spirit only to his holy apostles and prophets, namely, that the Gentiles should be included in the plan of God (Eph. 3:1–7). This *mystery*, Paul continues, was hidden by God, only to be made known by the church (vv. 9–10). Even Taylor recognizes that the office of deacon is unique to the New Testament. Consequently, the church should not be viewed as a mere continuum of Israel.

In conclusion, contemporary churches should seek to restore the New Testament patterns of church government and function without the complications of paradigms drawn either from the Old Testament or from the later developments of Christian traditions whether Roman, Orthodox, or Reformed. The simplicity of believer-priests functioning in Spirit-filled cooperation with one another, exercising the gifts of the Spirit under the headship of Christ, is the approach that takes into account not only the evidence of how the New Testament church operated, but also the theology of salvation which makes each believer a priest with access to God through Christ.

When the church at Corinth had a problem member with whom to deal, even Paul, armed with apostolic authority, could not demand the obedience of the church (1 Cor. 5). Still less can one find any record of a hierarchy of ecclesiastical "courts" to which adjudication of an issue was remanded. The entire local church carried all of the privileges and all of the responsibilities of the body of Christ. Only in the sovereign distribution of gifts did individual believers differ from one another.

Following the ascension of the risen Lord, authority in the church was bequeathed to the apostles. These operated with less authority than Christ himself as may be seen in the incident of Peter's error, which required the rebuke of Paul (Gal. 2:11–21). Nevertheless, the authority vouchsafed to the apostles as provided by the inspired Scriptures is that which informs believer-priests in each local expression of the body of Christ. Accordingly, the church is not free to deviate from the apostolic patterns observable in Holy Scripture.

A PLURAL-ELDER CONGREGATIONALIST'S RESPONSE

Samuel E. Waldron

COMMENDATIONS

I want to begin my response to Taylor's chapter by commending him for the very clear and in many respects correct treatment of church government he has provided. To begin with, Taylor does not leave us guessing as to how he defines presbyterianism. In his opening paragraph he states expressly that it "is a representative form of church government by elders elected by the people of God." Later he provides another helpful description of his view: "The presbyterian system of church government is representative and connectional." He makes a helpful distinction between the word "Reformed," which designates a system of theology, and "presbyterian," which denotes a form of church government. This enables me to say—as I want to—that I am Reformed, but not presbyterian or paedobaptist in my view of the church and its government. I am glad that Taylor allows me to make this distinction.

Other aspects of Taylor's chapter deserve commendation. Taylor's notice that an unqualified kind of democratic congregationalism becomes unworkable as congregations become larger and that they develop either *de facto* presbyterian or episcopal systems is interesting. His observation that the "senior pastor" view "is actually a replication of the older monoepiscopacy of the second century" is shrewd. I also, of course, agree emphatically with his insistence that all elders are bishops and that a plurality of elders in each church is normative. Finally, I certainly agree with Taylor's insistence that the system of church government that most closely conforms to "the principles of biblical polity" ought to claim the allegiance of every Christian.

QUESTIONS

Before coming to my major objections of Taylor's view, I want to pose a number of critical questions about Taylor's defense of presbyterianism.

Is Church Government Biblical and Not Merely New Testament?

Taylor insists that presbyterians (because they hold a strong view of the continuity of the church and Israel) prefer to speak of the 'biblical church,' not just the 'New Testament church.'" I heartily concur with Taylor's insistence on the idea that

> The catholic or universal church, which (with respect to the internal work of the Spirit and truth of grace) may be called invisible, consists of the whole number of the elect, that have been, are, or shall be gathered into one, under Christ, the head thereof; and is the spouse, the body, the fulness of him that filleth all in all.[68]

I also concur with Taylor's insistence that every saint in both Old and New Testaments has the same Savior, the same destiny, and the same salvation—by grace alone, Christ alone, and faith alone. What is missing in Taylor is an appreciation of the fact that one point at which there is emphatic discontinuity between the *Old Israel* and the *New Israel* is their external polity. The Old Testament church was a physical nation. The New Testament church is a spiritual nation. This contrast is written large on the face of the Bible.

The central (and only explicit) reference to the inauguration of the new covenant speaks clearly to the issue of this emphatic discontinuity with regard to the nature and polity of the people of God in the New Testament.

"Behold, days are coming," declares the LORD, "when I will make a new covenant with the house of Israel and with the house of Judah, not like the covenant which I made with their fathers in the day I took them by the hand to bring them out of the land of Egypt, My covenant which they broke, although I was a husband to them," declares the LORD. "But this is the covenant which I will make with the house of Israel after those days," declares the LORD, "I will put My law within them and on their heart I will write it; and I will be their God, and they shall be My people. They will not teach again, each man his neighbor and each man his brother, saying, 'Know the LORD,' for they will all know Me, from the least of them to the greatest of them," declares the LORD, "for I will forgive their iniquity, and their sin I will remember no more" (Jer. 31:31–34).

This contrast may be seen throughout the New Testament:

"Therefore I say to you, the kingdom of God will be taken away from you, and given to a people, producing the fruit of it" (Matt. 21:43).

But as many as received Him, to them He gave the right to become children of God, even to those who believe in His name, who were born, not of blood nor of the will of the flesh nor of the will of man, but of God (John 1:12–13).

Beware of the dogs, beware of the evil workers, beware of the false circumcision; for we are the true circumcision, who worship in the Spirit of God and glory in Christ Jesus and put no confidence in the flesh (Phil. 3:2–3).

This drastic discontinuity between the nature and polity of the old church and the new church is behind Jesus' use of the future tense in his first recorded mention of the church: "I also say to you that you are Peter, and upon this rock I will build My church; and the gates of Hades will not overpower it" (Matt. 16:18).

Thus, when Paul builds on this saying of Jesus he makes clear that the church is built on the foundation of the apostles and prophets (Eph. 2:20). The prophets mentioned here are not the Old Testament prophets. The order is wrong for this meaning and more importantly the parallel uses of this phrase, "apostles and prophets," clearly refer to New Testament prophets (3:5; 4:11; 1 Cor. 12:28–29). The language of Jesus and Paul constrains us to speak of a new beginning with regard to the nature and polity of the visible church of God on earth—a new beginning inaugurated by the redemptive-historical events associated with the first advent of Christ.

The fact that such discontinuity is so emphasized in the Bible with regard to the nature and polity of the New Testament church requires that we allow the New Testament to have a normative significance for the issue of church government. To be specific, information about elders in the Old Testament may be helpful in understanding what the New Testament teaches. (I have used it that way myself in my chapter.) There are undoubtedly lines of continuity. It cannot, however, be decisive for the details of church government. The emphatic discontinuity asserted by the Bible with regard to the nature and polity of the New Testament church does not allow this.

Are There Two Types Of Elders? Are There *Lay* Elders? Are All Elders Not Pastors?

Taylor affirms that there are two types of elders, that there are *lay* elders, and that all elders are not pastors. These three assertions are closely related and may conveniently be addressed together.

The problem with the assertion that there are two types of elders is partly that it does not go far enough. As we have seen, the key text upon which presbyterians ground this assertion indicates a wonderful diversity possible in a biblical eldership. First Timothy 5:17 says: "The elders who rule well are to be considered worthy of double honor, especially those who work hard at preaching and teaching." This text makes two distinctions and, thus, distinguishes three concentric circles of elders in Ephesus. Here there is, first, a distinction between all the qualified elders of the church at Ephesus and those who rule well. Remember that all the qualified elders must both rule and teach. First Timothy 3:2 asserts that all elders must be able to teach (cf. Titus 1:9). First Timothy 3:4–5 affirms that all elders must rule the church. Within this larger circle of qualified elders, there are those who rule well, who excel beyond their peers. Apparently, their gifts and godliness enable them to be more useful than the elders in general. The text implies that these elders who rule well may be worthy of double honor—financial support—even though they may not "work hard at preaching and teaching." Thus a second distinction becomes clear in the text, not just one as presbyterians claim. Within this circle of elders who rule well are those "who work hard at preaching and teaching." The financial support of the church is to be focused on this innermost circle of elders but may expand to include the elders who rule well.

Another problem with Taylor's view is this: the teaching elder–ruling elder distinction is in constant danger of accentuating a difference beyond what the Bible supports. If presbyterians are to speak of teaching and ruling elders, they must make clear that all elders must both rule and teach. They must also make clear that their distinction between only two types of elders oversimplifies the diversity of the eldership taught in the New Testament.

The improper accentuation of the difference between ruling elders and teaching elders becomes clear in Taylor's willingness to speak of "lay elders." Taylor's use of this terminology raises all sorts of questions that he does not bother to answer. For instance, it immediately implies a distinction between clergy and laity. Taylor has not justified this distinction. The Bible speaks of the elders and the brethren. Where does it ever speak of the clergy and the laity? Do not all elders have hands laid on them (1 Tim. 5:22)? Are they not all in that sense ordained? It is common in presbyterian churches that teaching elders are not members of the local churches they shepherd, but only of their local presbytery. Ruling elders in contrast must be members of those local churches. It is stretching 1 Timothy 5:17 way beyond what it fairly implies to make it support this or Taylor's distinction between clergy and *lay* elders.

The improper accentuation of two types of elders also becomes clear in Taylor's assertion that not all elders are pastors. He says, "But the pastors were not the only elders. Lay leaders who had gifts for leadership (Rom. 12:8) and administrating (1 Cor. 12:28) served together with the pastors." Though Taylor holds that all elders are bishops (overseers), he clearly does not think that all elder-overseers are pastors (shepherds).

Now Taylor is commendably committed, as we have seen, to the idea that we must have a biblical polity. He is obliged, therefore, to justify this distinction between elders and pastors.

Where is his evidence for this? In his paragraph affirming this distinction he cites only three texts: 1 Corinthians 12:28, Romans 12:8, and 1 Timothy 5:17. There is no distinction between elders and pastors visible in any of these texts. Indeed, the Greek word for "pastors" or "shepherds" is absent from them. There is a mention of gifts of leadership and administration in the first two. There is a distinction between different kinds of elders in the last. But that is all. Surely Taylor must provide us with better evidence than this to justify a distinction between elders and pastors, especially when he has affirmed so fervently that we must make no such distinction between elders and bishops!

But bad as this is for Taylor's thesis, the situation is actually worse. For there is clear evidence against this distinction between elders and pastors. As I show in my chapter, both Acts 20:28 and 1 Peter 5:1–2 require elder-overseers to pastor (shepherd) the flock of God. This is a strange task for them, indeed, if they are neither pastors nor shepherds. Pastors are mentioned in Ephesians 4:11 where they are also described as teachers in the phrase, "and some as pastors and teachers." Does this provide evidence that pastors are to be equated with teaching elders, but distinguished from ruling elders? No! First Timothy 3:2 and Titus 1:9 make clear that all elders must be able to teach. The evidence overwhelmingly suggests that the pastor-teachers of Ephesians 4:11 are simply elder-overseers.

There is certainly a diversity of gifts within the New Testament vision of eldership. There are certainly degrees of teaching ability. There is, however, no evidence to suggest a methodological distinction between two types of elders, *lay* elders, or a distinction between elders and pastors.

OBJECTIONS

"The presbyterian system of church government is representative and connectional." This helpful description of presbyterian polity provides the framework for my two major objections against it. I want to suggest that New Testament church polity is neither strictly and legally representative nor strictly and legally connectional.

New Testament Church Polity Is Not Strictly and
Legally Representative

I have carefully qualified this objection to a presbyterian system of church government by saying that it is not *strictly and legally* representative. Let me first explain my qualification. I certainly do not deny that in a loose and general sense the elders of a church may represent that church. They certainly may be sent as representatives to associational meetings. It is probably most appropriate that elders act in such a capacity. They may represent their church in other ways as well. Writing letters or extending greetings on behalf of their congregation are examples of this.

Presbyterians, however, mean something more than this when they speak of church government being representative. They mean that the board of elders of a church legally and representatively *is* that church. Their decisions, therefore, constitute the decisions of the church. The consent of the church is not necessary to confirm or consent to such decisions, because the church has already given its consent in the decision of their representatives, the elders.

The greatest and clearest illustration of this strict and legal representative character of the elders may be found in the matter of church discipline. Taylor writes, "Both in the synagogue and the church a senate of elders handled matters of spiritual discipline when members fell into sin." In a presbyterian system of church government, matters of church membership and church discipline may be decided by the elders alone. They are the church representatively in this matter. No vote of the assembled church membership is necessary. The church membership may be informed. Their support may be sought. The decision of the elders is, however, decisive.

It is noteworthy that Taylor cites no scriptural support for this view. No doubt, he believes that it follows from the general authority of the elders and passages like Acts 15 (which will be discussed below). The problem for him is that the two major New Testament passages on church discipline teach otherwise. Matthew 18:15–20 is the first of these:

> If your brother sins, go and show him his fault in private;
> if he listens to you, you have won your brother. But if he
> does not listen to you, take one or two more with you, so

that by the mouth of two or three witnesses every fact may be confirmed. If he refuses to listen to them, tell it to the church; and if he refuses to listen even to the church, let him be to you as a Gentile and a tax collector. Truly I say to you, whatever you shall bind on earth shall have been bound in heaven; and whatever you loose on earth shall have been loosed in heaven. Again I say to you, that if two of you agree on earth about anything that they may ask, it shall be done for them by My Father who is in heaven. For where two or three have gathered together in My name, there I am in their midst.

The passage seems clear, does it not? Yet presbyterians assume that "church" here means the church represented in her elders, not the whole church assembled. Of course, this makes perfect sense on their premises, *but we are now asking exactly about those premises*. Upon what basis do they have the right to assume this? The problem with their theory is there is no basis in the entire New Testament to support it. Rather, in numerous places, the church is clearly distinguished from its elders, or it is clear in some other way that the entire church assembled is in view. (Consider, for example: Acts 5:11; 8:1, 3; 9:31;11:26; 13:1; 14:23, 27.)

Another proof of the arbitrary character of the notion of the church represented in its elders is found in the only other reference to the church in Matthew. Matthew 16:18 clearly does not have this in mind when it says that Christ will build his church and the gates of hell will not prevail against it. The substance of Matthew 18:15–20 itself is against this interpretation. Surely, it is the whole church that is to hold the offender to be a Gentile. This strongly suggests that it is the whole church, not just the elders representing the church, that was told of the offense and admonished the offender.

It is likely that presbyterians will appeal to the Old Testament for their idea of the church representative being composed of its elders. We have already seen, however, that just at the point of the nature and polity of the church there is discontinuity between the old church and the new. Even if such a notion could be proven from the Old Testament, it would not, therefore, be conclusive for such an idea in the New Testament.

The word *ekklesia* is used seventy-seven times in the LXX translation of the Hebrew Old Testament. There are a few cases in which it may refer to a representative assembly (2 Chron. 1:3 is a possibility). There is one where it must, but this seems to be an exceptional situation (Ezra 10:14). There are many where it clearly does not refer to a representative assembly of elders (Deut. 4:10; 9:10; 18:16; Judg. 20:2; Ezra 2:64; 10:1).

There is little or no reason, therefore, to think that Matthew 18:15–20 refers to the elders of the church. There are many reasons to think that it does not. When we come, however, to 1 Corinthians 5:1–13—the other major passage on church discipline in the New Testament—even this shadow of a doubt disappears.

This passage is plainly given to the whole church at Corinth, the same church addressed in 1 Corinthians 1:2 ("the church of God which is at Corinth, to those who have been sanctified in Christ Jesus, saints by calling, with all who in every place call on the name of our Lord Jesus Christ, their Lord and ours"). The elders of the church in Corinth are never mentioned in this letter. Indeed, from the contents of the epistle itself it remains uncertain whether this church even as yet had elders (the term "church," however, is used twenty-three times and each time clearly refers to the entire membership of the church called together). In this particular passage there is every indication that the offender is removed by action of the assembled church.

> It is actually reported that there is immorality among *you* (v. 1).
>
> *You* have become arrogant (v. 2).
>
> In the name of our Lord Jesus, when *you* are assembled, and I with *you* in spirit (v. 4).
>
> Clean out the old leaven so that *you* may be a new lump, just as *you* are in fact unleavened (v. 7).
>
> I wrote *you* in my letter not to associate with immoral people (v. 9).
>
> But actually, I wrote to *you* not to associate with any so-called brother (v. 11).
>
> [emphases mine]

Thus, when Paul finally issues the command in verse 13 ("Remove the wicked man from among yourselves"), it is clear that the entire church assembled is in view and not just the elders. Thus, the entire church is obligated to take that action which "removes" the wicked man.

Yet more, in 2 Corinthians 2:5–8, there is a likely reference to this very situation:

> But if any has caused sorrow, he has caused sorrow not to me, but in some degree—in order not to say too much—to all of you. Sufficient for such a one is this punishment which was inflicted by the majority, so that on the contrary you should rather forgive and comfort him, otherwise such a one might be overwhelmed by excessive sorrow. Wherefore I urge you to reaffirm your love for him.

Here Paul is again addressing the entire church. As earlier, there is no mention of the elders of the church. He tells them all to forgive, comfort, and reaffirm their love to the disciplined man. Even more pointedly he tells them that this man was punished with church discipline by "the majority."[69] In this context this can mean nothing else than the majority of the membership of the church at Corinth and certainly assumes some sort of vote by which the discipline was enacted.

Thus, in the two major passages where we would on presbyterian terms expect to find the elders acting as the representatives of the church, we find nothing of the sort and no mention of elders at all. It is the entire church assembled together and acting corporately that enacts church discipline. Though presbyterians must find in these passages their representative form of church government, it is startlingly absent.[70]

New Testament Church Polity Is Not Strictly and Legally Connectional

In my chapter I anticipated the key position that Acts 15 and the council at Jerusalem would play in Taylor's argument for connectionalism. Taylor agrees: Acts 15 "provides the prime example in the New Testament of presbyterian-representative-connectional church government." So as not to repeat my comments, I simply want to respond to the four conclusions that Taylor draws from Acts 15.

Taylor's first conclusion is: "A single church appealed to the larger church to resolve a theological issue." By "larger church"

Taylor means a higher representative court of elders from many different churches. He says earlier in his chapter, "By 'connectional' we mean that local churches see themselves as part of the larger church, that local churches are not independent but are accountable to the larger church, and that local churches do not minister alone but in cooperation with the larger church." In proof of this appeal to the larger church, Taylor cites Acts 15:2 and 22. These verses do say that Paul and Barnabas went up "to Jerusalem to the apostles and elders." They do not, however, assert that in so doing Paul and Barnabas went to a representative assembly of elders from many churches. It is clear from Acts 15:2 and 16:4 that the apostles and elders in question were only those in the church at Jerusalem. Not even Paul and Barnabas were numbered among these apostles and elders (Acts 15:2, 4; 16:4).

Taylor's second conclusion is this: "Ecclesiastical authority was shared by a plurality of elders, not just the apostles." This is true, but not in the sense that Taylor means. The elders mentioned surely did share ecclesiastical authority with the apostles *over the church at Jerusalem*. They may also have had a unique authority as the elders of the mother church of Christianity. It is also possible that their involvement in the decision may simply have been because the circumcision troublemakers had claimed some authority from the church at Jerusalem. Thus, their involvement was necessary to show the solidarity of the church at Jerusalem with the apostles in this decision, and because they were responsible for those who went out ministering from Jerusalem.

Taylor's third conclusion is that the "decision of the representative assembly was an act of 'the whole church.'" By this statement Taylor means us to understand that there were elders in Jerusalem that acted as (the representatives of) the whole church universal. The problem with this understanding is that it completely misreads the meaning of the phrase "the whole church." The church in view here is not a representative assembly. No such assembly is found in Acts 15 or in the entire New Testament. It is rather and clearly a reference to the "church" that with the apostles and elders received Paul in Jerusalem and heard his report (v. 4), the local church at Jerusalem. The wording of Acts 15:22 distinguishes the apostles and elders from the whole church. It is "the apostles and the elders, with the whole church." This wording plainly suggests that the whole church is not the representative assembly (the elders), but some group in addition to the elders (the membership of the local church in Jerusalem). The following clauses further support this reading of the text by referring to the selection of Judas and Silas ("leading men among the brethren") to send with Paul and Barnabas as representatives of the church in Jerusalem.

Taylor's fourth conclusion is that "the theological issue resolved constituted a binding confessional standard on all the churches." Taylor is certainly correct in this. The question is, however, *why* it was authoritative and binding. We have seen that it is primarily because of the authority of the apostles in Jerusalem and perhaps secondarily because of the unique status of the elders of the church in Jerusalem. There is no reason to think, as we have proven, that this council was a representative assembly or that its decrees were binding for that reason.

The council in Jerusalem, composed of the apostles and the elders of Christianity's mother church and attended and blessed by the apostle of Christ to the Gentiles, was a unique, redemptive-historical event and not a precedent for a presbyterian system of church government today.

Chapter 2: Presbyterianism Notes

L. Roy Taylor

[1]The sixteenth-century French-Swiss Protestant Reformer, John Calvin, is the most well-known and influential theologian of the Reformed tradition. Reformed theologians are often called "Calvinists." Actually Calvin was a second-generation Reformer. Ulrich Zwingli is more accurately regarded as the first Protestant Reformer in the Reformed tradition. Reformed theology shares with most orthodox Christians an affirmation of the ecumenical creeds of the historic church (Apostles' Creed, Nicene Creed, etc.) and additionally emphasizes the sovereignty of God, the covenantal grace of God, the human enigma of our being created in the image of God, our suffering from the pervasive character of sin adversely affecting the total human personality, the supremacy of Scripture over ecclesiastical tradition but at the same time the value of church wisdom developed over the centuries. Continental Reformed churches (Switzerland, France, Hungary, the Netherlands, etc.) called themselves Reformed to emphasize their theological distinctives. Most of them also have a presbyterian form of church government. Some Reformed churches, such as the Hungarian Reformed Church, retained an episcopal church government with the church being governed by bishops. Most Presbyterian churches are Reformed in theology. Some Presbyterian denominations, such as the Cumberland Presbyterian Church, hold to presbyterian church government, but reject some of the distinctive doctrines of Reformed theology. Reformed churches in Scotland used the term "presbyterian" to indicate their opposition to an episcopal form of church government imposed upon them by the Church of England, particularly in the period between 1560 (the First General Assembly of the Church of Scotland) and 1662 (the restoration of the monarchy and the Great Ejection of Puritan ministers from the Church of England under Charles II). There are other Christians among Anglican, Congregational, Baptist, and other branches of the church that adhere to Reformed theology in varying degrees but do not hold to presbyterian church government. So as a general rule we could say that most Presbyterians are Reformed but not all Reformed churches hold to presbyterian church government.

[2]In most churches elders and deacons are ordained officers of the church.

[3]Ignatius, *Epistle to the Magnesians*, 6.1.

[4]An older term is the church "senate," but that is not commonly used today.

[5]The *Book of Church Order of the Presbyterian Church in America* (pp. 11–14) says, "For the orderly and efficient dispatch of ecclesiastical business, it is necessary that the sphere of action of each court should be distinctly defined. The Session exercises jurisdiction over a single church, the Presbytery over what is common to the ministers, Sessions, and churches within a prescribed district, and the General Assembly over such matters as concern the whole Church. The jurisdiction of these courts is limited by the express provisions of the Constitution." (Used by permission of the Office of the Stated Clerk of the General Assembly.)

[6]Edvard Schweizer, *Church Order in the New Testament* (London: SCM Press, 1961), 1.

[7]See the preface to the Ordinal of the Book of Common Prayer, 1662 (Church of England), and preface to the Ordinal of the Book of Common Prayer, 1789 (Protestant Episcopal Church USA).

[8]Declaration of Principles of the Reformed Episcopal Church, adopted December 2, 1873, Principle II, www.recus.org/doctrinalstmts/declaration.htm.

[9]As per the Westminster Confession of Faith (I, 6): "The whole counsel of God concerning all things necessary for His own glory, man's salvation, faith and life, is either expressly set down in Scripture, or by good and necessary consequence may be deduced from Scripture: unto which nothing at any time is to be added, whether by new revelations of the Spirit or traditions of men. Nevertheless, we acknowledge the inward illumination of the Spirit of God to be necessary for the saving understanding of such things as are revealed in the Word: and that there are some circumstances concerning the worship of God, and government of the Church, common to human actions and societies, which are to be ordered by the light of nature, and Christian prudence, according to the general rules of the Word, which are always to be observed."

[10]This understanding of a continuity and unity of the people of God spanning both the Old and New Testaments is the basis for the uniquely Reformed perspectives on baptism and communion. That is why Presbyterians practice "covenant baptism" of infants, yet do *not* hold to baptismal regeneration, nor do they regard such baptisms as mere dedications. That is also why many Calvinists believe that in the Lord's Supper believers truly commune with Christ spiritually and benefit from proper preparation for communion, participation in communion, and proper reflection after communion. Many Calvinists believe that Christ is genuinely present in the sacrament event, but reject both the doctrine that Christ's presence is localized in the sacramental elements (bread and wine) and the idea that the Lord's Supper is just a memorial. Our concern in this book is only church government, however.

[11]For a discussion of the similarities and differences from a Reformed perspective, see John Calvin *The Institutes of the Christian Religion* (Book II, Chs. X–XI), where he specifies three basic similarities and five differences between the testaments.

[12]Key biblical texts on this issue are Romans 4 and Galatians 3. For other discussion see Charles Hodge, *Systematic Theology*, vol. 2 (Grand Rapids: Eerdmans, 1965), 354–77; William Sanford Lasor, "The People of God," in *The Truth about Armageddon* (Grand Rapids: Baker, 1982); Geerhardus Vos, *The Kingdom of God and the Church* (Nutley, N.J.: Presbyterian and Reformed, 1972); Jakob Jocz, *The Jewish People and Jesus Christ* (Grand Rapids: Eerdmans, 1979).

[13]Elders as *civil* government leaders had been instituted shortly after the Exodus (see Ex. 18). Numbers 11 records an incident a couple of years later and deals with the institution of others as *spiritual* leaders.

[14]This is the origin of the tradition in post-exilic Judaism for the Sanhedrin's having seventy members plus the high priest.

[15]The Lord's promise through Ezekiel was a basis for the formation of synagogues after the destruction of the temple: "Thus says the Lord GOD: Though I removed them far off among the nations, and though I scattered them among the countries, yet I have been a sanctuary to them for a while in the countries where they have gone" (Ezek. 11:16).

[16]"God-fearers" were Gentiles who accepted monotheism (the Lord of Israel as the one true and living God) and the Hebrew Scriptures as the Word of God, and who lived by the moral law but had not been circumcised and did not follow the Jewish ceremonial law.

[17]Acts 9:20–22, 28–30; 13:5–14:7; 16:13; 17:1–10; 18:4–11, 18–21; 19:8–20.

[18]For an interesting perspective on the success of the gospel among the Jews, see R. C. H. Lenski's introductory remarks in his commentary on the Epistle to the Hebrews supporting his theory that Apollos was the author of Hebrews. Lenski argued that the majority of the synagogues in Rome had become Messianic or Christian synagogues and that the epistle was written primarily to encourage the Christian Jews of Rome.

[19]In a similar manner the persecution that resulted in the death of the first martyr, the deacon Stephen (Acts 7), was a significant transition. We will discuss the institution of the office of deacon below. For an extended discussion of the significance of these two persecutions' effects upon the church see J. B. Lightfoot's essay, "Paul and the Three" in his *Epistle of St. Paul to the Galatians* (Grand Rapids: Zondervan, 1962), 292–374.

[20]By "plurality of elders" we mean that the minister or pastor is not the only elder in a local church; that there are several elders in a local church, chosen by the congregation.

[21]Everett Ferguson, ed., *Encyclopedia of Early Christianity* (New York: Garland, 1988), 752.

[22]Calvin, *Institutes*, Book IV, Ch. III.15. See also Liddell-Scott, *Lexicon*, for numerous such examples. See also Arndt and Gingrich, *A Greek-English Lexicon of the New Testament* on the same term.

[23]See Henry George Liddell and Robert Scott, *A Greek-English Lexicon* (Oxford: Oxford University Press, 1968), 657.

[24]2 Kings 11:19; 2 Chron. 24:12, 17; Neh. 11:9, 14, 22; Isa. 60:17.

[25]J. B. Lightfoot, *St. Paul's Epistle to the Philippians* (Grand Rapids: Zondervan, 1953), 181–269.

[26]Lightfoot, *Philippians*, 96–98.

[27]Charles Hodge, *Discussions in Church Polity* (Philadelphia: Grant, Faires, and Rodgers, 1878), 242.

[28]Lightfoot, *Philippians*, 196.

[29]Matt. 5:10; 10:16–26: Mark 4:17; 13:9; Luke 10:3; 21:12–19; John 15:18–25; 16:1–4.

[30]Acts 9:23–25, 29; 13:50; 14:5, 19; 16:19–24; 17:13; 18:12–17; 19:21–41; 20:3; 21:27–28:31.

[31]Some regard these ten persecutions as a fulfillment of Christ's word to the church of Smyrna that the church would be tested for "ten days" (Rev. 2:10). These persecutions instigated by emperors were by Nero (AD 64), Domitian

(90–96), Trajan (98–117), Hadrian (117–38), Marcus Aurelius (161–80), Septimus Severus (202–11), Maximus the Thracian (235–36), Decius (249–61), Valerian (257–60), and Diocletian Galerius (303–11).

[32]After Constantine came to power, he issued the Edict of Milan in AD 313, thus ending the imperial persecutions. A controversy then ensued over whether pastors who had surrendered the Scriptures and other Christian materials to the Roman government during persecution should be readmitted to the ministry and whether the baptisms they had administered were valid.

[33]Ignatius, *Epistle to the Magnesians*, 6.1.

[34]G. P. Fisher, *The History of the Church* (London: Hodder and Stoughton, 1913), 52.

[35]See Cyprian, *On the Unity of the Church*, 1.4, in which he argues that Peter was the first among the apostles and the origin of church unity. While this section also asserts Peter's primacy, not merely his prominence, it is regarded by patristic scholars as a later emendation.

[36]Cyprian, *On the Unity of the Church*, 1.4; *Epistles of Cyprian*, 48.3.

[37]Cyprian, *Epistles of Cyprian*, 48.3.

[38]Tertullian, *On Modesty*, ch. 1.

[39]Petrine supremacy is the view that Peter was chosen by Christ to be the primary apostle and visible head of the entire church on earth in Christ's absence, that Peter became bishop of Rome, and that his successors are head of the entire church. As noted earlier, this view was advocated by Cyprian (d. AD 258), bishop of Carthage.

[40]As a result of Vatican II, the Eastern Orthodox Church and the Roman Catholic Church lifted these mutual anathemas in 1963.

[41]John Calvin, *The Necessity of Reforming the Church* (Audubon, N.J.: Old Paths Publications, 1994), 4–5.

[42]See John Calvin, *Institutes*, Book IV, Chs. I–XX.

[43]Calvin, *Institutes*, Book IV, Ch. III.5.

[44]Calvin saw two types of "deacons" in the New Testament: (1) men who hold an official office, collecting and distributing alms and administering the affairs of the poor (as the original seven in Acts 6), and (2) women (often widows as in 1 Tim. 5:9–10) who devote themselves to the care of the poor and are personally involved in such a ministry. See *Institutes*, Book IV, Ch. III.9.

[45]Calvin, *Institutes*, Book IV, Ch. IV.1.

[46]See Hughes Oliphant Old, *Worship That Is Reformed According to the Scriptures* (Atlanta: John Knox Press, 1984), 153–54. The French refugee fund encompassed a number of ministries, among them providing: housing, furniture, tools for craftsmen to begin their businesses, apprenticeship fees for young men's job training, and dowries for women who wanted to marry. The fund also sent missionaries back into France and printed Protestant literature for missionaries to distribute.

[47]Calvin, *Institutes*, Book IV, Ch. III.15. See also Liddell-Scott, *Lexicon,* for numerous such examples. See also Arndt and Gingrich, *A Greek-English Lexicon of the New Testament* on the same term.

[48]Calvin, *Institutes*, Book IV, Ch. III.15.

[49]Cyprian, *Letters*, lxvii.4.

[50]So called because one thousand ministers supported it.

[51]I.e., principles and instructions on conducting worship rather than a prescribed liturgy to be followed in detail.

[52]The propositions as proposed by Cornelius Burgess were: (1) "that the Scriptures holdeth out a Presbytery in a Church, and (2) That a Presbytery consisteth of ministers of the Word, and other such public officers as have been already voted to have a share in the government of the Church." William M. Hetherington, *History of the Westminster Assembly of Divines* (Edmonton: Still Waters Revival Books, 1993), 180.

[53]Hetherington, *History*, 180–82.

[54]Hetherington, *History*, 280.

[55]The lowest being the local church session, the next highest being the presbytery, and the highest being the general assembly.

[56]The Presbyterian Church in America, in setting forth the form of government founded upon and agreeable to the Word of God, reiterates the following great principles which have governed the formation of the plan:

1. God alone is Lord of the conscience and has left it free from any doctrines or commandments of men (a) which are in any respect contrary to the Word of God, or (b) which, in regard to matters of faith and worship, are not governed by the Word of God. Therefore, the rights of private judgment in all matters that respect religion are universal and inalienable. No religious constitution should be supported by the civil power further than may be necessary for protection and security equal and common to all others.

2. In perfect consistency with the above principle, every Christian Church, or union or association of particular churches, is entitled to declare the terms of admission into its communion and the qualifications of its ministers and members, as well as the whole system of its internal government which Christ has appointed. In the exercise of this right it may, notwithstanding, err in making the terms of communion either too lax or too narrow; yet even in this case, it does not infringe upon the liberty or the rights of others, but only makes an improper use of its own.

3. Our blessed Saviour, for the edification of the visible Church, which is His body, has appointed officers not only to preach the Gospel and administer the Sacraments, but also to exercise discipline for the preservation both of truth and duty. It is incumbent upon these officers and upon the whole Church in whose name they act, to censure or cast out the erroneous and scandalous, observing in all cases the rules contained in the Word of God.

4. Godliness is founded on truth. A test of truth is its power to promote holiness according to our Saviour's rule, "By their fruits ye shall know them" (Matthew 7:20). No opinion can be more pernicious or more absurd than that which brings truth and falsehood upon the same level. On the contrary, there is an inseparable connection between faith and practice, truth and duty. Otherwise it would be of no consequence either to discover truth or to embrace it.

5. While, under the conviction of the above principle, it is necessary to make effective provision that all who are admitted as teachers be sound in the

faith, there are truths and forms with respect to which men of good character and principles may differ. In all these it is the duty both of private Christians and societies to exercise mutual forbearance toward each other.

6. Though the character, qualifications and authority of church officers are laid down in the Holy Scriptures, as well as the proper method of officer investiture, the power to elect persons to the exercise of authority in any particular society resides in that society.

7. All church power, whether exercised by the body in general, or by representation, is only ministerial and declarative since the Holy Scriptures are the only rule of faith and practice. No church judicatory may make laws to bind the conscience. All church courts may err through human frailty, yet it rests upon them to uphold the laws of Scripture though this obligation be lodged with fallible men.

8. Since ecclesiastical discipline must be purely moral or spiritual in its object, and not attended with any civil effects, it can derive no force whatever, but from its own justice, the approbation of an impartial public, and the countenance and blessing of the great Head of the Church.

If the preceding scriptural principles be steadfastly adhered to, the vigor and strictness of government and discipline, applied with pastoral prudence and Christian love, will contribute to the glory and well-being of the Church.

[57]For a fuller discussion see Paul R. Gilchrist, *Distinctives of Biblical Presbyterianism* (Atlanta: World Reformed Fellowship, 2002), in which he discusses the differences between a "democratic presbyterianism" espoused by continental Reformed churches, the sixteenth-century Church of Scotland, some of the Scots commissioners to the Westminster Assembly, such as George Gillespie and Alexander Henderson, and an "aristocratic presbyterianism" advocated by Samuel Rutherford and Robert Baillie. In the former, ecclesiastical authority flows from the lower courts to the higher with the consent of the governed. In the latter ecclesiastical authority flows from the higher courts to the lower. See also Louis Berkhof, *Systematic Theology* (Grand Rapids: Eerdmans, 1939), 583–84; William Cunningham, *Historical Theology* (Edinburgh: Banner of Truth, 1969), I, 57, II, 536; James Bannerman, *The Church of Christ* (Edinburgh: Banner of Truth, 1974), 266.

[58]See Bannerman, *The Church of Christ,* II, 436–51.

[59]The Landmark Baptist movement was led by J. R. Graves in the nineteenth century, primarily in the South.

[60]I.e., not *esse* (the being, or existence) of the church, but *bene esse* (the well-being or perfection) of the church.

[61]The statement, "No creed but Christ" is simplistic. A brief assertion such as "Jesus saves" is a theological statement that must be explained from the teachings of Scripture by answering such questions as "Who is Jesus?" "What is unique about Jesus?" "What does it mean to be saved?" "Why do we need to be saved?" "From what are we saved?" "To what are we saved?" "How are we saved?" Discovering these answers is theology.

[62]*Disciplina,* for the early fathers of the church, meant a Christian manner of life, maintaining a Christian lifestyle. It included pastoral instruction, discipleship,

and oversight, not just corrective discipline that involved church censures. See Jean Danielou, *The Origins of Latin Christianity* (Philadelphia: Westminster Press, 1977), III, 464.

[63]Though Calvin did not specify discipline as one of the marks of the church in the *Institutes*, he certainly discussed it at length. Discipline was practiced in Geneva. Reformation-era Reformed confessions such as the first Scots Confession and the Belgic Confession include discipline as one of the marks of the church.

[64]Most Presbyterian books of church order are divided into three sections: (1) form of government, (2) rules for discipline, and (3) directory of worship.

[65]The Southern Baptist Convention, for example, is composed of churches that are congregationally governed, but as a denomination has fielded the largest Protestant missionary force in history, primarily through its "cooperative program."

[66]Total depravity is the first of the so-called "five points of Calvinism." This does not mean that people are as actively wicked as they could be, nor does it deny human dignity. Rather, it means that sin has adversely affected how people think, feel, decide, and act.

Paige Patterson

[67]Landmarkism was the term associated with the teachings of J. R. Graves, J. M. Pendleton, and Amos C. Dayton, which in the 1850s attempted to insist on a succession of Baptist churches, though not always by that name, from the time of Christ to the present. Most Baptists saw neither the necessity nor the historical evidences for such a view and hence rejected the idea.

Samuel E. Waldron

[68]*The 1689 Baptist Confession of Faith*, chapter 26, paragraph 1.

[69]The Greek phrase is *hupo ton pleionon* which literally means "by the more."

[70]This is why, by the way, Taylor is at such pains to find the election of elders by the church in Acts 14:23. In my chapter I deduced the election of elders mainly from the general power of the assembled church supported by the two passages just discussed. There I found the major reason to argue that elders should be elected by the church. To a lesser degree some indication of this is also found in the selection of deacons by the entire church mentioned in Acts 6:1–7. I argued that Acts 14:23 is at best a doubtful reference to the election of officers by the church. The "stretching out of the hand" suggested by the Greek word is more probably a reference to the laying on of the hands of the apostles in setting apart these men to office. The text says that *they*—not the churches—stretched out their hands. Taylor, however, makes this passage his basis for asserting that elders were elected. He must do this because on his view both Matthew 18 and 1 Corinthians 5 refer to the action of the elders as the representative church and not to the entire church. This leaves him with only the most doubtful basis for this crucial part of his system.

Chapter Three

SINGLE-ELDER CONGREGATIONALISM

SINGLE-ELDER CONGREGATIONALISM

Paige Patterson

Mythological trappings of the chronicle aside, when on February 23, AD 155, Polycarp, the near centenarian pastor of the church in Smyrna, walked to the stake and was burned, the church there had not just suffered the loss of one of its elders; it had lost its pastor. When Chrysostom addressed his parishioners in Saint Sophia's for a final sermon in Constantinople in AD 404, then slipped across the Bosporus under cover of night into exile, the Constantinopolitan church had lost its pastor. The people of London's Metropolitan Tabernacle knew that with the passing of the incomparable Charles Haddon Spurgeon in 1892, they had lost their pastor. On January 10, 2002, when W. A. Criswell loosed from earthly moorings and entered heaven's rest, the saints at First Baptist Church of Dallas, Texas, lost their pastor even though he had formally retired some years earlier.

From apostolic times the hand of God has rested upon certain men, most often associated with a local parish or congregation. Whether Knox in Edinburgh, Hus at Bethlehem Chapel in Prague, Edwards at Northampton, Zwingli in Zurich, Hubmaier in Nikolsburg, Boice in Philadelphia, or Truett in Dallas, these stellar figures of church history have been by virtue of calling, gifts, dedication, and what my father termed "moral ascendancy"the acknowledged under-shepherds of their flocks even while exercising monumental influence beyond those geographical and congregational constraints.

Discussion of ecclesiastical government is doomed from the outset unless it begins with Christ, the head of the church. Edmund Clowney was on target when he observed:

> Our understanding of the government of Christ's church must begin with the Lord himself and his *kingdom authority*. He is the Head of the church; his rule is unique and incomparable. A second principle derives from the first. The church shows the *organic life* of Christ's body: it lives as an organism, not just an organization. The third principle is no less essential. The church is not like the kingdoms of this world, for it is organized for service, not dominion. All government in the church is *stewardship*: *i.e.* its leaders are servant-managers, who use their authority only to advance the interests of those they represent and serve.[1]

The lordship of Christ assumed, the thesis of this chapter is not that it is unscriptural to have multiple elders in a local church. To the contrary, such practice has clear precedent and mandate in the Scriptures and is augmented by the pragmatics of caring for the spiritual needs of large flocks of spiritual sheep. However, the churches of the New Testament recognized only two offices—those of pastor and deacon.[2] Pastors, also identified as elders and as bishops, were the spiritual leaders of the congregation, while deacons assisted in caring for the physical needs of the congregation. Each assembly needed a single pastor, and this would be augmented as growth dictated. Even when multiple elders were necessary, one of the elders remained the decisive spiritual leader of the flock.

This chapter will further contend that initially the churches were essentially autonomous and congregational in polity. This congregational polity functioned by means of prayerful inquiry into the mind and direction of the Holy Spirit, giving full recognition to the permanent indwelling of the Holy Spirit in each regenerate believer. The pastors were expected to be decisive spiritual leaders and interpreters, with accountability first to God and then to the autonomous congregation.[3] Furthermore, congregations related to each other through a loose confederation based on common commitment to Christ and to the doctrine of the apostles. The doctrine of the apostles eventually became codified in the New Testament documents. In turn, these documents became the authority under which the congregations of the late first- and early second-century congregations exercised their gifts and ministries.

THE HISTORICAL BACKGROUND OF CONGREGATIONALISM

The *Oxford Dictionary of the Christian Church* defines "congregationalism" as "that form of Church polity which rests on the independence and autonomy of each local church."[4]According to this source, the principles of democracy in church government rest on the belief that Christ is the sole head of his church, the members are all priests unto God, and these units are regarded each as an outcrop and representative of the church universal.[5]

Leon Morris traces the beginnings of congregationalism to Robert Browne's treatise *Reformation Without Tarrying for Any*, published in 1582 by English separatists living in Holland.[6] Browne argues convincingly for autonomous congregations functioning without constricting connection either to the magistrates of civil government or to the prelates of ecclesiastical structure. When the Westminster divines approved the Westminster Confession in 1643, dissenting brethren issued the Savoy Declaration of 1658, insisting on congregationalism. Excerpts from that declaration follow:

> V. These particular Churches thus appointed by the Authority of Christ, and intrusted with power from him for the ends before expressed, are each of them as unto those ends the seat of that Power which he is pleased to communicate to his Saints or Subjects in this World, so that as such they receive it immediately from himself.

> VI. Besides these particular Churches, there is not instituted by Christ any Church more extensive or Catholic intrusted with power for the administration of his Ordinances or the execution of any authority in his Name.

> IX. The Officers appointed by Christ to be chosen and set apart by the Church so called, and gathered for the particular administration of Ordinances and execution of Power or Duty which he intrusts them with, or calls them to, to be continued to the end of the World, are Pastors, Teachers, Elders, and Deacons.[7]

Confessions of faith among various "free church" congregationalists demonstrate a fair amount of diversity regarding ecclesiastical government and officers. Baptist and Anabaptist confessions frequently exhibit a form of the approach advocated above. For example, the earliest Anabaptist confession, the Schleitheim Confession of 1527, says:

> We are agreed as follows on pastors in the church of God. The pastor in the church of God shall, as Paul has prescribed, be one who out-and-out has a good report of those who are outside the faith. This office shall be to read, to admonish and teach, to warn, to discipline, to ban in the church, to lead out in prayer for the advancement of all the brethren and sisters, to lift up the bread when it is to be broken, and in all things to see to the care of the body of Christ, in order that it may be built up and developed, and the mouth of the slanderer be stopped.
>
> This one moreover shall be supported of the church which has chosen him, wherein he may be in need, so that he who serves the Gospel may live of the Gospel as the Lord has ordained. But if a pastor should do something requiring discipline, he shall not be dealt with except [on the testimony of] two or three witnesses. And when they sin they shall be disciplined before all in order that the others may fear.
>
> But should it happen that through the cross this pastor should be banished or led to the Lord [through martyrdom] another shall be ordained in his place in the same hour so that God's little flock and people may not be destroyed.[8]

Here it is made evident that among the Swiss Brethren and the South German Anabaptists (as generally among all Anabaptists) the congregation as a whole chose the pastor, so identified as "this one." No other official is mentioned in the document. Most of these diminutive, harassed Anabaptist assemblies could boast just this one pastor, but even in larger congregations there was one clear leader. Most Anabaptists, who were thorough biblicists, however, also would have endorsed the office of deacon. In northern Europe, the Waterlander Mennonites adopted a confession in 1580 or 1581. That confession reiterates the hand of the congregation in the selection of its ministers and seems to suggest a division of ministers into "teachers, bishops, and deacons."[9]

These same themes of election to office by the gathered church and the offices of elders and deacons, the latter of whom could be either male or female, are repeated explicitly in *A Declaration of Faith of English People* remaining in Amsterdam, Holland in 1611.[10] The influential London Confession of 1644 was a confession of Particular Baptists in England, which continues the insistence on congregational church government and selection of officers, but mentions four ministers—pastors, teachers, elders, and deacons.[11] In 1656, Thomas Collier and others sought to draft a confession that would bring Particular Baptists and General Baptists into a union or at least to the discussion table. The Somerset Confession was the result, which mentions only "ministers" as officers but characteristically urges that these be selected by the congregations themselves.[12]

Perhaps the most influential of all the early Baptist confessions was that which eventually became known as the Second London Confession of 1677. Deliberately an attempt of Particular Baptists to incorporate major insights from the Westminster Confession of 1646, in order to show solidarity with Presbyterians in the wake of the restored ascendancy of Anglicanism and even Catholicism, once again the "suffrage" of the church is the terminology employed making clear both the congregational selection of officers and the two offices of elder and deacon.

> A particular Church gathered, and compleatly [*sic*] Organized, according to the mind of Christ, consists of Officers, and Members; And the Officers appointed by *Christ* to be chosen and set apart by the Church (so called and gathered) for the peculiar Administration of Ordinances, and Execution of Power, or Duty, which he instructs [*sic*] them with, or calls them to, to be continued to the end of the World, are Bishops or Elders and Deacons.[13]

The New Hampshire Confession of 1833 serves as the basis for the *Baptist Faith and Message* adopted by the Southern Baptist Convention first in 1925 and then revised in 1963 and in 2000. New Hampshire Baptists did not speak to the polity issue, although congregationalism was almost universally the practice among New England Baptists. They did, however, specify that the offices were to be "bishops or pastors and deacons."[14] Expanding this statement, the *Baptist Faith and Message* (2000) of the Southern Baptist Convention overwhelmingly adopted by the convention June 14, 2000, reads:

> VI. The Church
> A New Testament church of the Lord Jesus Christ is an autonomous local congregation of baptized believers, associated by covenant in the faith and fellowship of the gospel; observing the two ordinances of Christ, governed by His laws, exercising the gifts, rights, and privileges invested in them by His Word, and seeking to extend the gospel to the ends of the earth. Each congregation operates under the Lordship of Christ through democratic processes. In such a congregation each member is responsible and accountable to Christ as Lord. Its scriptural offices are pastors and deacons. While both men and women are gifted for service in the church, the office of pastor is limited to men as qualified by Scripture.
> The New Testament speaks also of the church as the Body of Christ which includes all of the redeemed of all the ages, believers from every tribe, and tongue, and people, and nation.[15]

Several important features are discernible in this confessional statement. First, local congregations are said to be "autonomous"—that is, a law unto themselves. However, it turns out this autonomy is limited since it "operates under the Lordship of Christ through democratic processes." How this can actually function and why it should happen in this way will be developed in what follows. Pastors and deacons constitute the only officers mentioned and the confession specifies that the office of pastor is limited to men.

This brief survey of the confessional statements of Baptist and Anabaptist groups is sufficient to demonstrate two important facts. First, from the time of the Reformation until the present era, a not inconsiderable number of churches in the free church movement have viewed themselves as autonomous entities.[16] They function without answerability beyond their local assembly except to Christ. Second, the vast majority of these churches recognize two officers identified by the New Testament documents—pastors and deacons. Each congregation seems to have chosen a pastor, who even in the eventuality of added elders, was clearly "the pastor."

Such is clearly the state of affairs. However, most of these congregations also operated under the aegis of the absolute authority of the Bible. Consequently, the ultimate question must be to decide whether or not such a perspective represents the teachings of Jesus and the apostles as found in the pages of the New Testament.

THE WITNESS OF THE NEW TESTAMENT

The case in the New Testament for congregationalism and for single, primary elder leadership can be constructed along several lines. The initial consideration involves the recognition of the nature of salvation and its relationship to the church. Second, the language of the New Testament regarding the officers of the church and the qualifications set forth in the Bible must be analyzed. Finally, examples of the activity of the earliest church must be assessed.

The Nature of Salvation

Paramount in congregationalism is the conviction that the church itself is composed only of men and women who have passed from death to life by means of the new birth or regeneration. This process includes the remarkable event of the permanent indwelling of the Holy Spirit, as anticipated and promised by Jesus, effected initially at Pentecost, and confirmed by the witness of the New Testament epistolary literature. Because every believer was thus indwelt by the Holy Spirit, he or she now had direct access to God and was invited to come boldly before him (Heb. 4:16). Consequently, a levitical-type priesthood was unnecessary because every believer was a priest. This understanding of the priesthood of all believers was recognized though not consistently applied by Martin Luther.[17]

Five times the New Testament mentions this priesthood. Three of these references occur in the Apocalypse (Rev. 1:6; 5:10; 20:6) in references to a kingdom of priests. Only in 1 Peter 2:5 and 9 is there an explanation of the nature of this assignment. In those verses the followers of Christ are said to constitute a "spiritual house" made up of "living stones" for the purpose of exercising a "holy priesthood." This priesthood is further defined regarding its activity: "offer[ing] up spiritual sacrifices accept-able to God through Jesus Christ." In verse 9, the assignment is expanded to include proclaiming "the praises of Him who called you out of darkness into His marvelous light."

Old Testament priests were "bridges" between God and the people, representing God to the congregation and the congregation to God. But these priests were limited to a few of the members of only one tribe, Levi. Furthermore, only priests could enter the Holy Place, and only the high priest could enter the Holy of Holies. What changes dramatically in the New Testament is that individual believers are invited to appear "boldly" before the throne of grace on the merits of the blood of Jesus, the great High Priest who entered once for all into the Holiest.

Believer-priests with regenerate hearts have access directly to God. The Holy Spirit indwells each believer-priest. Although these believer-priests have different callings and enjoy almost infinite combinations of spiritual gifts, each has instant and complete access to God. Leon Morris describes this position:

> Nor is it any less fundamental that the way into the very holiest of all presences is open to the humblest believer (Heb. 10:19–20).... The apostles, it is true, exercise a certain authority, but it is the authority of founders of churches and the Lord's own apostles. After their death there was no divinely instituted apostolate to take their place.[18]

Consequently, congregationalists generally have recognized an ontological equality of all the saints even while recognizing that some are called by God and appointed by the church to positions of leadership. Therefore, the ministries of the church should derive from the action of the corporate body seeking the face of God and the leadership of the Holy Spirit and expressing that through some process, which for lack of a better term may be called a vote. Better still is the idea that the congregation arrives by whatever means at a *spiritual consensus*. Mark Dever states the case well:

> Baptists and Presbyterians have had two basic differences in their understandings of elders. First and most fundamentally, Baptists are congregationalists, that is, they understand that the final discernment on matters rests

not with the elders in a congregation (or beyond, as in the Presbyterian model), but with the congregation as a whole. Baptists, therefore, stress the consensual nature of church action. Therefore, in a Baptist church, elders and all other boards and committees act in what is finally an advisory capacity to the whole congregation.[19]

Wolfhart Pannenberg, concerned about the progress of ecumenical studies, recognizes that the doctrine of the priesthood of believers is a major barrier between Protestants and Catholics. He observes that the Second Vatican Council noted that "the office of priest differs from the universal priesthood of all believers not only in degree but also in its very essence (Lumen Gentium II.10)."[20] Nevertheless, Pannenberg is hopeful that some strategy can be found to bridge this gap. But the gap is in fact a vast chasm. In simplest of terms, if every believer is a priest, the necessity of an official priesthood is negated.

A pragmatic objection to this approach is sometimes raised. Even regenerate congregants are still not infallible in discerning the direction of the Holy Spirit. Worse still, some churches such as Corinth in the New Testament era exhibit more than a little carnality among infantile saints. Even more debilitating, everyone knows that unregenerate people hold membership in churches, and this paradigm gives less than mature Christians and even unbelievers a voice in the affairs of the church.

This objection is not problematic to congregationalists. First, other systems of church government are susceptible to the same foibles, as ecclesiastical history has consistently and embarrassingly demonstrated. Second, authority invested in the "many" of the congregation is less likely to be abused and much easier to be corrected than authority vested in the "few" of other ecclesiastical systems. Third, congregational churches operating with a careful, redemptive approach to church discipline based on the New Testament have in place a significant corrective to the aforementioned problems.

To summarize, a congregational form of church government, in which the assembly as a whole recognizes and selects its pastors and deacons in response to the prompting of the Holy Spirit, is in keeping with the New Testament instruction regarding the regeneration of all believers, the permanent indwelling of the Spirit in each believer, and the elevation of each believer to the assignment of believer-priest. This system is misconstrued and abused when it creates the "rugged individualist" who introduces upheaval and divisiveness into the church of God.[21] The point cannot be pressed too forcefully that there is no authorization in the congregationalism of the New Testament for divisive conduct, long or regular "business meetings," or even the right of someone to speak his mind. In fact, Christianity is far more about servanthood than it is about personal rights. The paradigm functions in a New Testament pattern when critical decisions within the fellowship of the church begin with the saints of God on their faces seeking God's will and ultimately arriving at spiritual consensus.[22]

The Language of the New Testament

Most congregationalists recognize only two offices in the local church—pastor and deacon. How can this be correct, given the New Testament also clearly speaks of elders and bishops? The answer proceeds along two fronts: first, the language of the New Testament and, second, the listed qualifications for church office.

The terms "pastor" (Gk. *poimen*), "elder" (Gk. *presbyteros*), and "bishop" (Gk. *episcopos*) are used interchangeably in the New Testament.[23] The emphasis of each word is different, calling attention to the various roles of a pastor, but all describe one and the same church office. This is nowhere made more lucid than in 1 Peter 5:1–3.

> The elders who are among you I exhort, I who am a fellow elder and a witness of the sufferings of Christ, and also a partaker of the glory that will be revealed: Shepherd the flock of God which is among you, serving as overseers, not by compulsion but willingly, not for dishonest gain but eagerly; nor as being lords over those entrusted to you, but being examples of the flock.

Here, all three words "elder," "bishop" (overseer),[24] and "pastor" (shepherd) occur in the same text, all referring to the same office. Peter addresses himself to the elders (Gk. *presbyterous*), identifying himself as a "fellow elder" (Gk. *sumpresbyteros*). He requests that these elders "shepherd" (Gk. *poimanate*) the flock of God among them, "taking oversight" (Gk. *episkopountes*) of those flocks. Two of the three terms are verbs, but, as such, point to the function of the corresponding nouns. Therefore, at least functionally, all three ideas, two of which describe the work of the elder, are present.

The word "elder" is certainly the most prominent of the three.[25] It carries with it the rich history of the elders of Israel. Furthermore, the wisdom of long experience recognized in the senior population of almost all societies nuances the word. The elder was a recognized community leader worthy of the respect and honor accorded to the senior population of a community. As a church official, an elder did not have to accumulate many years to be so designated (note Timothy and Titus), but by virtue of the office the same sort of deference was owed by the assembled church.

A pastor is a shepherd. A good shepherd leads his sheep to sustenance—food and water, protects them from predators and other harm, comforts them and medicates their wounds, and presides over the growth of his flock. So the pastor is responsible for feeding his flock through the teaching and preaching of the Word of God. He leads them by example to the rivers of living water to slake their spiritual thirst. The pastor protects his sheep from heretical predators who would harm them. He comforts and spiritually medicates those who have suffered. Finally, he leads in the task of growing the flock—through evangelism and missions.

As overseer or bishop, an elder must assume administrative oversight of the congregation. This word probably focuses more on the leadership role of an elder or pastor. As we shall see later, the word vests in him considerable authority to lead and direct, but never without accountability to the congregation.

One of God's gifts to the church is the gift of "pastor" (Eph. 4:11). Elders are to be appointed "in every city" (Titus 1:5), and these are to "rule well" (1 Tim. 5:17), not be subject to frivolous accusations (v. 19), and be well cared for (v. 17). Qualifications for a bishop are explicit and demanding (1 Tim. 3:1–7; Titus 1:5–9). The burden of proof rests on those who would distinguish among these words as used in the New Testament. A cursory reading uninformed by later developments in Christian history would understand all three words to apply to the spiritual leader(s) of local congregations.

Another line of evidence concerns the qualifications for service in these offices listed in the New Testament documents. The simple point to be made here is that there is no list of requirements for anything other than bishops (elders) and deacons. In 1 Timothy 3:1–7 and Titus 1:5–9, the qualifications for bishops (Timothy) and elders (Titus) are so similar that a case can surely be made that both refer to the pastors or spiritual leaders of the churches. In 1 Timothy 3:8–13 the qualifications of deacon are provided. Although the seven set aside by the Jerusalem church are not statedly "deacons," the attributes of the men called for in Acts 6:1–6 as well as the nature of their assignment have generally been acknowledged by the church as the orders for deacons. Because such lists exist apparently for only two offices and because, furthermore, the activities ascribed to pastors, elders, and bishops in the pages of the New Testament seem to be essentially the same, there is little reason to believe that the earliest church boasted a system any more complicated than that of a congregation of believers under the lordship of Christ led by Spirit-filled pastors and deacons.

Examples of Congregationalism in the New Testament

Pictures of life of the first-century church abound in Acts and the epistles. The majority of these snapshots concern themselves with the expansion of the gospel and the growth of the church. Infrequently and almost incidentally we are introduced to a vignette of governance. However, even from this relative scarcity of insight, it seems possible to observe churches apparently functioning under congregational determination.

First, there is the poignant story of the incestuous relationship of a congregant of the church at Corinth. Paul addresses the issue of Corinthian laxity in 1 Corinthians 5 and apparently again discusses the issue in 2 Corinthians 2:6–8. In 1 Corinthians 5, Paul scolds the church at Corinth for toleration of known, heinous sin in one of its members and insists that it take action to exclude the offender when assembled in the name of the Lord Jesus Christ (v. 4).[26] Finally, the church is told that God judges those outside of its authority, while those inside the church are to adjudicate issues in the membership and "put away" from themselves those who imperil the purity of the church (vv. 12–13).

Several factors need to be noted here. First, if anyone had the authority from the outside to exclude the offender, surely it was the apostle Paul. Yet he appeals to the church to take this action. A careful study of the Corinthian correspondence warrants the conclusion that Paul was unable to control the situation in which evidently rival partisan parties battled for control in the church (see 1:10–17). Rather, Paul appeals to the church on many issues. And his appeal is not to the elders, bishops, pastors, or deacons, but to the church. In fact, J. M. Pendleton noted, "It deserves notice too, that the members of the Corinthian church could not, in their *individual capacity*, exclude the incestuous man. It was necessary that they should be 'gathered together.'"[27]

When Paul revisits the incident in 2 Corinthians 2:5–11, he is convinced that the exclusion of the offender has worked its redemptive purpose and pleads that "this punishment ... by the majority is sufficient" (v. 6). Now the brother ought to be restored to fellowship so that his sorrow would not be too great. The very mention of the action of the *majority* in punishment suggests spiritual consensus in the church. Furthermore, Paul could no more restore the man by command than he could banish him by mandate.

The primacy of the congregation in such serious action as the exercise of what Anabaptists termed "the ban," accords with congregational responsibility for capital punishment in the Old Testament (Deut. 13:9; 17:7; et al.). The idea both places seems to relieve one individual or a small group of the burden of assessing the penalty but to instead involve the congregation. In this way, the larger entity must bear the responsibility for the decision to punish, making a correct decision more likely and reducing the possibility of accusations and bitterness toward individuals later.

This congregational approach to church government seems to be in keeping with the counsel of Jesus in Matthew 18:15–17. A series of approaches to an offending brother culminates in "tell it to the church" (v. 17). Clearly the final action anticipated by Jesus was not to be the verdict of a group of presbyters, still less of bishops or a council external to the local church. "Tell it to the church" strongly implies that the adjudication of such an issue lay with the gathered congregation.

Additional cases of apparent congregational polity include Acts 11:22 where the church in Jerusalem sent Barnabas to Antioch to minister to the rapidly growing congregation there. In Acts 13:1–3 it appears to be the entire church at Antioch that commissions Barnabas and Saul. Meanwhile, in Acts 6, clearly the Jerusalem church receives instruction from the apostles to choose seven men to attend to the ministry to widows. The church responds positively, chooses seven, and places them before the apostles (vv. 5–6). Even in the case of the selection of Matthias to replace Judas, the entire group of 120 were involved in the nomination of two and may very well have participated in the casting of lots (1:12–26).

In Acts 15:22–23, the solution of the Jerusalem council was approved by the apostles and the elders, but this was done in connection "with the whole church" (v. 22). In 2 Corinthians 8:19, Paul explains that Titus was appointed "by the churches" to travel with Paul to collect an offering for the saints in Jerusalem. While all of this evidence may come short of establishing a hands-down case for congregational polity, it does, at least, demonstrate two things. First, the early church clearly had nothing resembling an episcopal form of government. Second, congregations as a whole exercised considerable influence, perhaps even final determination in major considerations for local churches.

EVIDENCE TO THE CONTRARY

But what of the New Testament passages that seem to promote either the episcopal or the presbyterian form of church polity? Certainly such texts exist. As a sampling, one may mention the conclusion of the discussion between Jesus and Simon Peter at Caesarea Philippi recorded in Matthew 16. Jesus bestows the keys of the kingdom, which have to do with binding or loosing in heaven and on earth. Whether these keys represent the preaching of the gospel having been bestowed on Peter alone, on all of the disciples, or on the whole church, or determining precisely what actually constitutes binding and loosing are the subjects of endless debates. But the verses could be read to establish something approaching episcopal authority.

Paul instructs Titus to appoint elders in every city on the island of Crete (Titus 1:5). This passage does not appear to grant the congregations in Crete any authority in the matter, though this hinges somewhat on how the word "appoint" is understood. Therefore, this verse could suggest a form of episcopacy.

Advocates of presbyterian polity will focus on 1 Timothy 5 where elders are to be rewarded if they "rule well." Here the word employed is *proistemi*, which has a wide range of meanings including *govern, rule, lead, prefer*, and so on.[28] While it is admittedly a strong word, there is no necessity bound up in the concept that in the context of the churches would limit the exercise of congregational polity.

Another text to which advocates of presbyterianism might appeal is Hebrews 13:7, 17.

> Remember those who rule over you, who have spoken the word of God to you, whose faith follow, considering the outcome of their conduct. . . . Obey those who rule over you, and be submissive, for they watch out for your souls, as those who must give account. Let them do so with joy and not with grief, for that would be unprofitable for you.

The word translated "rule" in these two verses is, if anything, even a stronger word than the one used in 1 Timothy 5. Here *hegeomai*, like the previous word *proistemi*, boasts a variety of nuances in Greek including *lead, rule*, or *command* with reference to war. Otherwise it can mean *rule, political supremacy*, or *authority*. But the chief sense of the word seems to encompass the concept of *lead*.[29]

And these two verses hint that "lead" may be the central emphasis. The Hebrew Christians are told to "remember" those who lead them and to follow the example of the faith of such leaders (v. 7). Further, they are to "obey" them and "be submissive" because these are the ones who watch for their souls (v. 17). Thus, apparently the author of Hebrews is writing a hortatory passage to those who neither he nor the ones who have "rule" can absolutely enforce.

THE CASE SUMMARIZED

Having said all of this, one must acknowledge that any reading of the New Testament reveals examples of all three forms of church government, or at least provides passages which could be so interpreted. This admonition places evangelical Christians—who want to behave biblically and "do church" right—in a bit of a dilemma. What are sincere Christians to conclude about ecclesiology? Do they admit that the New Testament documents are contradictory on this issue? Should they conclude that the form of church polity is really not that crucial and that each church or group of churches may simply do as they please?

Personally, I believe that the answer to this enigma is bound up in the temporal circumstances represented in the New Testament. The first century was an age of transition. Jesus had bought his church with his own blood. The church was launched, if not born, on the Day of Pentecost and developed rapidly under apostolic and subapostolic direction (Titus, Timothy, etc.). By the concluding years of the century all of the apostles were gone and the witness of the apostles permanently deposited in Holy Scripture. As I have indicated elsewhere:

> A general answer to that question [of authority] is possible based on data previously mentioned. To review, the pattern of authority in the primitive church is as follows: All authority in heaven and in earth the Father has vested in Jesus (Matthew 28:18). That authority has been passed along to the apostles and to the church (Luke 10:19), though with some limitations. The apostolic witness to Christ, as found in the New Testament, is conceived to be the voice of God through the apostles (1 Corinthians 14:37; 2 Peter 1:21; 3:16) and thus carries full authority for the church. Elders governing and leading at the will of the churches, therefore, have general authority to adjudicate matters that have not already been settled either by Jesus or in the Scriptures. They do not, under any circumstances, have the authority to reverse the Scriptures or make exceptions to the teachings of Scripture due to circumstance or culture.[30]

Leon Morris is aware of the dilemma posed by the documents. He says:

> A consideration of all the evidence leaves us with the conclusion that it is impossible to read back any of our modern systems into the apostolic age. If we are determined to shut our eyes to all that conflicts with our own system we may find it there, but scarcely otherwise. It is better to recognize that in the NT church there were elements that were capable of being developed into the episcopal, presbyterian, and congregational systems and which in point of fact have so developed.[31]

But Morris may be too cynical here if in fact the picture of the church in the New Testament is that of transition.[32] Apostolic authority would in the nature of the case carry significance for the early church second only to that of Christ. The apostles were the interpreters and evangels of Jesus. However, with the exception of those occasions when they were writing under inspiration (1 Cor. 14:37; 2 Tim. 3:16; 2 Peter 1:16–21), the apostles were themselves fallible men. Consequently, even their profound authority had its limits. As these leaders began to fade from the scene, they left the legacy of sacred Scripture, inspired by the same Holy Spirit who now permanently indwells the individual believer. Increasingly, each church became autonomous, free to strive for spiritual consensus. This included the choice of the ministers: the deacons and elders (the latter of whom are also denominated pastors and bishops).

Hans Küng recognizes this developmental process in the earliest churches:

> At the end of the Pauline period the two fundamental conceptions of Church organization (which may briefly be termed the Pauline-Gentile and the Palestinian) begin to influence one another to a certain degree, or at least to interlock, so that the different titles become somewhat confused. The identification of the titles "bishop" and "presbyter" was inevitable in view of the similarity of the functions they fulfilled. There may also have been certain connections, although indirect, linguistic or factual ones, between the Greek *episkopoi*, the word *episkopos*, that is, an overseer in the secular sense, as used in the Septuagint (cf. Num. 31:14; Neh. 11:9–22; 1 Macc. 1:51) and the Jewish synagogue overseer, although he was never described as an *episkopos*, as well as the "overseer" (*paquid* or *mebaqqer*) in the Dead Sea sects (1 QS 6:12–20; cf. Dam. 9:17–22; with reference to the elders 1 QS 6:8). In Acts the same men are described as presbyters and *episkopoi*: for instance, the elders of Ephesus are referred to as *episkopoi* (Acts 20:17 and 28). Luke must have introduced this word (which he otherwise never uses, but which was increasingly current in the Pauline communities, cf. Phil. 1:1), on purpose, in order to equate the *episkopoi* of the Gentile communities with the presbyters in the Judaeo-Christian communities, and thus in the interests of Church unity and warding off heresy to unite two different traditions. The same kind of reason

probably leads him to say that Paul and Barnabas appointed presbyters in all communities (14:23).[33]

Even if one wishes to view this transition from the apostolic community in a different way, Küng certainly is correct in observing that change was taking place in the first-century church. Congregations were beginning to take seriously the implications of the priestly status of each believer.

These autonomous congregations seem to have had at least one elder, adding additional elders as the necessities of the ministry required. However, even if these were strong leaders, they were just that and did not constitute a governing oligarchy for the church. And as the examples with which this chapter began illustrate, even with plurality of elders, one chosen man of God seems always to have been "the pastor." Although the major consideration is the witness of Scripture, it is worth noting that the contemporary landscape provides the same view even in congregations practicing "elder rule" or even just "plurality of elders." There are few cases of prospering congregations not led ultimately by a primary pastor figure.

ON BEHALF OF THE SINGLE ELDER

Throughout this assessment there have been references to a single elder in local churches. An attempt has also been made to acknowledge that there is nothing in the Bible to inhibit a congregation from appointing as many elders as needed. Furthermore, a case for a single elder or the case for mandatory multiple elders, in my estimation, cannot be established on the basis of Scripture. What seems evident is that each congregation needs to have elder leadership. Some churches have more than one as the need arises. Why then argue for a single elder who is at least the decided leader of the congregation?

First, the general pattern that emerges in the Bible is that God calls a leader from among the people. Moses was clearly *the leader* assisted by Aaron and others. In the book of Judges God would raise up one judge at a time to deliver Israel from oppression. Individual prophets come and go, but aside from the mysterious "schools of the prophets," these appear to labor under individual calling and mandate. There are twelve apostles, but soon Peter seems to emerge as the *de facto* leader. The testimony of Acts 15 seems to suggest that however many elders there were, James the half brother of the Lord seems to be recognized as *the pastor* in Jerusalem.

Second, this pattern is also true to the development of church history and to the psychology of leadership. John Chrysostom was the obvious pastor at Antioch and later at Saint Sophia's in Constantinople. Augustine was the clear leader at Hippo. Jonathan Edwards was the pastor at Northampton, etc. Even in congregations where more than one elder functions, the contemporary milieu often finds one designated as *senior pastor*, almost always a reference to his priority in leadership rather than to his age.

Third, most scholars acknowledge the synagogue's influence on the life and worship of the early church. And most synagogues apparently had a stated leader, a *archisunagogos*, the president of the synagogue. W. White says:

> The chief executive of the synagogue was called in Heb. *rosh hakeneset*, Gr. *archisunagogos*, "president of the synagogue." This official was known also among pagan associations, but by the 1st Christian cent. was more commonly applied to the Jewish officials and by the 5th cent. exclusively so. The name has also been found upon epigraphic inscrs. He was responsible not merely for the upkeep and operation of the house but also for the order and sanctity of the service (Luke 13:14). Three individuals in the NT are so designated: Jairus (Mark 5:22; Luke 8:41); Crispus (Acts 18:8); and Sosthenes (18:17).[34]

This is perfectly understandable given that the psychology of human leadership demonstrates that a leader emerges by way of election, coup, selection by some group, or by other natural means in almost every social endeavor of life. This ordering of authority seems to be a part of the psyche of humans and is called for in the home (1 Cor. 11:1–3; Eph. 5:22–6:4) as well as in the civic arena (Rom. 13:1–7).

Finally, note that the letters sent to seven historical congregations in Asia Minor appearing in the Apocalypse are addressed to "the angel of the church" at Ephesus, at Smyrna, etc. Various proposals can be found for the identification of these "messengers" thus addressed and a final conclusion is doubtless not possible. However, the majority of the commentators seem to favor the position that this is John's reference to the pastor of the congregation.

How the commendations, warnings, and promises of these letters could have been communicated to the constituents of those assemblies if "angels" is meant to be taken in its usual sense has little rationale. By the same token, the letters would most logically have been addressed to the pastors of those churches to be read by them to the congregation.

If this reading of these "messengers" as pastors is correct, then the evidence that each of these churches had a single elder with highest authority and leadership responsibilities becomes clear. As already noted, this is what we would expect from the New Testament, from church history, from contemporary congregations, and from the human social order.

In conclusion, I reiterate my conviction that a hands-down case cannot be made for "single elder" primacy or "multiple elder" oligarchy. There simply are no "commandments" on this issue. The case then must be made on the basis of what can be determined from observing leadership practice throughout the Scriptures.

THE CONCLUSION

Since it is difficult to find any place where God called a committee, I believe that the pattern in both Testaments is for God to call individual leaders for his people. A congregational polity encourages maximum freedom, participation, and responsibility for every believer-priest. A church should choose its elders and deacons based on the qualifications set forth in the New Testament and under the leadership of the indwelling Holy Spirit. One of these should be the primary leader and preacher-teacher for the flock. This pattern has an enviable track record of evangelism and missionary expansion from the time of the Reformation until now and represents a restoration of the pattern of New Testament churches at the close of the first century.

AN EPISCOPALIAN'S RESPONSE

Peter Toon

As far as I can tell from the evidence of this chapter, Dr. Patterson is wholly enthusiastic about congregational church government, but he has virtually no interest in the history of the one, holy, catholic, and apostolic church from the end of the first century until the early decades of the sixteenth century. True enough, he can cite examples of great preachers/leaders from the early centuries (e.g., Chrysostom), but such bishops were very particularly in their writings, convictions, and work, committed episcopalians.

In this lack of regard for thirteen centuries of church life, he is typical, I fear, of so many American evangelicals and of Baptists in particular. He appears to believe that God's providential guiding of the early church in terms of polity (not to mention dogma, worship, piety, and discipline) ceased to exist, or the church herself ceased to reflect the knowledge of the will of God, until Luther came on the scene in the sixteenth century. And then it was only a small part of the universal church that got it right! He ignores or passes by the decrees of church councils and synods held in the early centuries, when the church was finding her way through persecution and the onslaught of powerful heresies (like Gnosticism) to serve the Lord and to preserve his church with sound doctrine and polity, in purity and holiness.

THE CONSEQUENCES OF IGNORING PRE-REFORMATION CHURCH HISTORY

In cutting off some 1,400 years of church history Patterson effectively reduces his participation in the communion of the saints. He cuts himself off from the grace of God revealed in the saints of those years, from their perseverance, and from their examples to us. Thus he is poor when he could be rich and he is left with a half-empty basket when it could be full. True enough, he misses the errors and heresies, the corruption and the decay, evident at times in these fourteen centuries, but this is only a slight gain in comparison with the acceptance of these centuries and the riches of grace to be found in reading the works of the Fathers and the saints of the medieval period, East and West. To a woman and man they all believed that episcopacy was what God had ordained for his church.

Further, it is the case that all the baptized of these centuries, whether they were holy or less than holy, whether they had mistaken views concerning images and the sacrifice of the Mass or not, are in a vital sense our brothers and sisters in Christ; and, if we are all saved by grace, then we shall meet them on equal terms in the life of the age to come. And, let us recall, many of the bishops of these centuries were faithful pastors who often suffered for the faith of Christ.

Patterson seems not to realize or take into account that the canon of the New Testament from which he seeks to extrapolate his democratic congregationalism was recognized, fixed, and made effective by a church whose polity was decidedly, clearly, and overtly episcopal—a church existing on earth as dioceses in fellowship with each other and having one bishop over each diocese, assisted by presbyters and deacons. I suggest that what he ought to have argued for—as in harmony with the sacred Scriptures and with the providential rule of God over the church—was a simple form of monoepiscopacy; that is, the rule of one bishop with his presbyters over one diocese with the people of God therein approving and receiving this ministry. We know that as the church expanded, she developed a territorial and hierarchical form of episcopacy that (1) enlarged the pastoral care of the local bishop through the geographical enlargement of his diocese, and (2) advanced the status of bishoprics of big cities above those of smaller ones.

It is possible to argue for a model of episcopacy based on that known in the second century when the local bishop was the celebrant at the Sunday Eucharist and was assisted in his pastoral care and discipline by a group of presbyters and deacons.

And the advantage of such an argument is that it is deeply in harmony with both the New Testament and the polity of the church of God as it emerged everywhere in the Roman Empire. I myself would join him in such an argument and for such a renewal of historical episcopacy!

SOLA SCRIPTURA?

Patterson's position seems to me to belong to a *sola scriptura* approach which hangs in free space, with no real context except a selected history from the sixteenth century to the present, and, most pertinently, the context of the modern American supermarket of religions wherein denominations compete one with another, and in which the long, historical existence of the church of God in space and time is not even a minor selling point for most of them. It appears to this writer that utilitarian and pragmatic principles (of the supermarket) are used—perhaps unwittingly and unconsciously—to make the Bible speak a modern doctrine of local democracy with one leader in charge and up front. I cannot point to any one sentence or paragraph to demonstrate this. Rather it is the general tone and mind-set that sets forth this position.

The modern extreme Protestant (in contrast to the classic reformed Catholic) approach to church authority/polity seems to know what it is looking for as it reads the Bible for evidence, and thus what is discovered therein is usually what is being looked for. Since so much of modern American philosophy, politics, education, and (church) life is dominated by utilitarian and pragmatic considerations, it is not surprising that they become part of the mind-set of American Christians as they search for a model of church government and authority. One can only begin to shed them by recognizing that the church of God is one and has existed through space and time continuously from the apostolic period to the present day, and that hierarchy (holy order) and unity across space and time have always been part of her nature as a divine society on earth.

From my perspective as an English episcopalian, it is difficult to argue with someone like Patterson who enters the debate ruling out the major evidence concerning the case. True enough, there is a period when there seems to be diversity of organization and polity (and for which we have very little information outside the New Testament documents); but, by the middle of the second century, and certainly by the beginning of the third century, it is clear to all with eyes to see that episcopal polity was universally accepted and that it remained so.

There is no trace of any clear evidence for what in modern times has been called congregationalism until well into the sixteenth century (or perhaps more accurately, the seventeenth century). However, and this is important from where I stand, basic elements in the modern claims for the Congregational Way are actually incorporated into the episcopal system—e.g., the ministers (bishops, presbyters, and deacons) are elected by the baptized members of the congregation and then later can only be ordained by the officiating bishop(s) when the people present in the service give their approbation and permission.

And, we may ask, if the teaching of the New Testament is so clearly for congregationalism, as Patterson thinks, then why is it that during the period of intense scrutiny of the New Testament document and Canon acceptance, there is not the slightest sign that the existing episcopal polity was being questioned as contrary to the mind of Christ?

It is my judgment that nothing would be achieved by my offering alternative readings of the New Testament evidence (verses and the like) for episcopal polity—that is, offering a differing exegesis and interpretation.[35] What weighs heavily with me is that the church of God, which had the awesome duty of collecting and approving the canon of the New Testament in the third and fourth centuries, saw no problem whatsoever in accepting the developing episcopal polity/ministry as being the natural, God-ordained continuance of the apostolic ministry of the first fifty or so years of the church's history.

Of course, one can argue with hindsight that in some particulars the church made mistakes in its development of episcopal polity, which opened the door to later serious errors. For example, likening the bishop, presbyter, and deacon to the high priest, priest, and Levite of the Old Testament had some practical benefits, but it did allow, especially in the medieval period, the development of a false doctrine of the bishop and presbyter as sacrificing priests who offer the Eucharist/Mass in union with Christ at Calvary. Further, recognizing the importance of churches in several great cities (Alexandria, Jerusalem, Antioch,

Constantinople, and Rome) and calling their bishops by the Old Testament name of "patriarch" opened the door for excessive development of this approach in Rome, so that eventually the bishop there was said to be not only the patriarch of the West (correct!) but the actual successor of the apostle Peter and the vicar of Christ on earth (incorrect!).

To argue that episcopal polity is the one approved by and set in place by the Lord of the church is not at all to concede that false developments of this polity which began in the late patristic period are guided and accepted by the Lord of the church. After all, the church is called to minister in an evil age and sinful world, and it has often chosen to adopt the mind-set and ways of the world it is called to save! It did so in the fourth century and it does so in the twenty-first century. Yes, the church is holy in union with Christ Jesus, but in practice she often fails in her high calling.

THE ORIGINS OF CONGREGATIONALISM

Turning now to the origins of congregationalism, one must remember that it was a period when many social and political changes were occurring in old Europe and thus democracy for the church became an option. Furthermore, the sixteenth and seventeenth centuries saw a massive reaction to much of what the medieval church had stood for and taught. In such reaction the danger was (and the reality became) that the baby was thrown out with the bathwater. The Bible was read without reference to the way it had been understood by the church which authorized the Canon, making it possible to set aside God's providential guidance and rule of his church over the preceding fifteen centuries. Nothing really mattered between AD 100 and 1520! And this approach is still exceedingly common in American evangelicalism.

One response to the obvious corruption of the church in the late medieval period—and that adopted by the major divines of the Church of England—is to say that just because episcopal polity had been seriously warped, it did not make episcopacy as such to be wrong. Rather, it made it a candidate for possible reform and renewal (as occurred in northern Europe in Scandinavia and England in the sixteenth century). The authority of the pope could be discarded and the episcopate renewed without the loss of the basic episcopal system.

THE NATURE OF CHURCH UNITY

Another important area where the advocate of the congregational system actually has a different approach to that of the church of the second century concerns the nature of church unity and the doctrine of the church as visible and invisible. Unity in the early church is, practically speaking, the unity of the episcopate. The bishop of the local church/diocese is ordained and consecrated by three bishops from other churches so as to affirm and demonstrate the unity of the church on earth across space and through time. Unless he is so consecrated, neither he nor his diocese can be said to be in the one catholic church. Thus a bishop in this or that city is the successor of the bishop who went before him and is in communion with the bishops of the cities around him and through them with all the dioceses in the world. So, if a presbyter moves from one city church to another he takes along a letter of introduction from his bishop and is accepted as a presbyter in the church to which he goes. Further, the invisibility is related to the visibility of the church as is one side of a coin to another, for in the ministry and sacraments of the visible church the invisible grace of God and communion of saints is known.

CONCLUSION

Anticipating arguments against what I have written, I reiterate the following in conclusion: The fact that modern congregationalism (wherein the congregation hires and fires a senior pastor) can and does work well in modern America and in other places does not constitute an argument for such a polity being required or approved by the Lord Jesus and as being set forth as a blueprint in the New Testament canon. No doubt there have been many faithful pastors/preachers, and an even greater number of saintly souls who have listened to them, within congregational assemblies! For these we heartily thank God. But despite the learned arguments of Dr. John Owen (of whom I am the biographer and who is perhaps the greatest congregationalist divine), congregational polity is only functional, not apostolic! It is one way of reading the New Testament evidence *if* one ignores the history of the early church and *if* one comes out of a society wherein democratic notions are being discussed or are already in place.

Patterson's arguments are only convincing to those who blot from their minds, memories, and evaluation the real evidence: that episcopal polity was the polity of the church of God from earliest times to the sixteenth century and has been since then, right until the present day, the polity of the greatest part numerically and geographically of the fractured church of God.

A PRESBYTERIAN'S RESPONSE

L. Roy Taylor

Dr. Patterson presents a case for a form of congregationalism in which the local church is autonomous, governed by a spiritual democracy (congregational vote), its lay officers are deacons and the pastor is usually its only elder. This is a form of ecclesiastical government with which I am familiar not only from study but also from experience.[36] First, I will address the single-elder issue (i.e., whether the pastor should be the only elder in a local congregation), and then I will address the issue of congregationalism.

SINGLE-ELDER LEADERSHIP

Patterson agrees with the proposition that the New Testament uses the terms "elder," "bishop" (overseer), and "pastor" to refer to the same office ("pastors, also identified as elders and as bishops"). While using the term "single-elder congregationalism" to describe his position, he acknowledges that in larger churches, there could be several elders (ministers) who are spiritual leaders in the church, though the senior pastor would be the most prominent. After conceding this, he focuses most of his chapter on the congregational (autonomous) church government of independent churches.

He emphasizes that "the churches of the New Testament recognized only two offices—those of pastor and deacon," with the pastors being the spiritual leaders of the local church and the deacons assisting in caring for the physical needs of the congregation. He does not seem to be advocating a "pastor-led church" which functions more like a monoepiscopacy than a congregationally governed church.

Two questions must be asked about single-elder leadership. One, does the term "elder" as used in the Bible refer only to ministers (pastors, teaching elders) or does the term encompass lay leaders as well? Two, in a congregationally governed local church, is the role of deacons only that of "caring for the physical needs of the congregation" or is it not more accurate to say that in many Baptist churches deacons have a role of spiritual leadership, not just mercy ministry?

THE TERM "ELDER"

Few would dispute the reality that whoever is the pastor[37] has the primary role of spiritual leadership in the congregation, no matter a local church's form of government. Patterson cites as examples several well-known pastors—Polycarp, Chrysostom, Spurgeon, and Criswell. And though certainly there are instances of conflicts between the pastor and the congregation, the pastor is considered the beloved spiritual leader of the flock, as it should be.

The question remains, however, about the breadth of the term "elder." From my view the New Testament does not limit the use of the term "elder" to what we now refer to as "pastor" or "minister." In 1 Timothy 5:17, Paul subdivides elders into two categories. All elders rule; some elders rule and, additionally, labor in preaching and teaching. This is the basis for the presbyterian distinction between ruling elders (laymen) and teaching elders (ministers), as I noted in chapter 2.[38] When the original seventy elders were chosen to assist Moses (Num. 11), they were ordinary men, not long-term prophets like Moses. They prophesied only once after their selection (Num. 11:25), as a demonstration that the Spirit of the Lord was upon them. The synagogue system, which influenced the church order of the first century, had lay elders as well.[39] There is no reason to believe that there was a change from the inclusion of lay elders in the Old Testament to an exclusion of lay elders in the New Testament. The church at Jerusalem was a megachurch with several thousand members (Acts 2:41; 4:4; 5:14). The apostles served as pastors of the Jerusalem church (Acts 6:2, 4, 6 [the apostles were also elders, 1 Peter 5:1]). Not all of the churches of the New Testament were megachurches requiring numerous pastors, yet each church had a plurality of elders.[40] It is reasonable to conclude, in light of the Old Testament and synagogue precedent, that there were lay elders among them. Moreover, there are early-church references to churches with a plurality of elders, not all of whom were ministers.[41]

The concept of ruling elders sharing spiritual leadership with pastors (teaching elders) does not remove from the pastor his prominent role of leadership nor does it diminish the affection and esteem in which he is held by the flock. Not all churches that are congregationally governed are credo-baptist;[42] some are paedo-baptist.[43] In fact, the Congregational churches, whose Savoy Confession Patterson quoted, practice infant baptism and have a plurality of elders, some of whom are ministers (pastors) and others of whom are lay leaders. Though single-elder congregationalism is the practice among many Baptist churches in America, Baptist and Anabaptist congregationally governed churches have had more than pastors and deacons as officers (as Patterson points out in his quotation of several Anabaptist and Baptist confessions). There is no uniform practice among Baptists and Anabaptists of having only two offices, pastor and deacon. Some included elders as well. Patterson concludes, "[A] hands-down case cannot be made for 'single elder' primacy or 'multiple elder' oligarchy. There simply are no 'commandments' on this issue." Yet I would refer the reader to chapter 4 of this book for Samuel Waldron's defense of "plural-elder congregationalism."

THE ROLE OF DEACONS

Just as there were almoners in the synagogues, the early church found it necessary to appoint officers to take care of the distribution of food among its widows (Acts 6). Though the term "deacon" is not used, most regard Acts 6 as the institution of the office of deacon mentioned in Paul's letters to the churches at Philippi and Ephesus.[44] In the late first and early second centuries, the deaconate was a lay ministry of mercy. As the episcopal system began to develop in the second century, the office of deacon became an entry-level clergy position.[45] In the Reformation era, Reformed churches restored the office of deacon to its original function as is continued in Presbyterian, continental Reformed, and Congregationalist churches. John Owen, the most prolific writer of the seventeenth century on congregational government, in his work, *The True Nature of a Gospel Church*, advocated a plural-elder congregationalism with elders having spiritual leadership and authority. His view of deacons was similar to that of Calvin, i.e., not an office of spiritual leadership, but a ministry of mercy, an office of sympathy and service. British Congregationalist John Huxtable, in his 1947 abridgement of Owen's far lengthier treatise, noted, "In present-day congregationalism, these officers [Teaching elders, Ruling Elders, and Deacons] are differently named. Deacon nowadays is the equivalent of Owen's elder; and the deacon duties, as Owen understood them, are often performed by a finance committee."[46]

It appears that a similar phenomenon has occurred in Baptist churches in America, judging by published materials for deacon training. The "Deacon Family Plan," widely used among Southern Baptists, is a program of spiritual care for families of the church very similar to under-shepherd ministries led by Presbyterian elders.[47] Henry Webb regards deacons as spiritual leaders, not simply almoners: "They [deacons] also share with the pastor the responsibility of leading the church in the accomplishment of its mission."[48] One cannot help but ask—if deacons are functioning as elders, why not call them "elders"?

CONGREGATIONALISM

Now we turn our attention to whether the Bible teaches congregational church government. Dr. Patterson offers several arguments: (1) the kingship of Christ as the only king and head of the church, (2) the nature of salvation and its relationship to the church, which is essentially an argument concerning regenerate church membership and the priesthood of the believer, (3) the language of the New Testament regarding church officers and their qualifications, and (4) examples and activities of the early church.

The Kingship of Christ

Patterson quotes with approbation Edmund Clowney's statement regarding Christ being the only king and head of the church. Clowney, a Presbyterian, reiterates the traditional Reformed position that was formulated to counter the Roman Catholic claim that the bishop of Rome is the vicar of Christ, the head of the church on earth, and to repudiate the Act of Supremacy of 1534 which made Henry Tudor (Henry VIII) "the supreme head of the Church of England" instead of the pope.[49] The belief that Christ is the only king and head of the church is a view that Baptists share with Presbyterians and other Dissenters. This is not the issue. The issue is whether Christ's authority is vested in the congregation only. Presbyterians hold that, "The power which Christ has committed to His Church vests in the whole body, the rulers and those ruled, constituting it a spiritual commonwealth. This power, as exercised by the people, extends to the choice of those officers whom He has appointed in His Church."[50]

The Nature of Salvation

Patterson argues that the nature of salvation (regeneration and the priesthood of believers) implies the necessity (or at least the preferability) of congregational church government. Baptists and Anabaptists distinguish themselves from other branches of the church in that they do not baptize infants, and hold that only people who have been baptized subsequent to a profession of faith are members of the church. It is assumed that this is the best procedure to insure a regenerate church membership. Presbyterians, Anglicans, Lutherans, Methodists, and others baptize infants and regard baptized children as noncommunicant members of the church until they make a profession of faith and are thus admitted to the Lord's Table and assume the full privileges of membership.[51] In churches with noncommunicant and communicant members, only communicant members vote at congregational meetings.

As Patterson notes, no system guarantees that 100 percent of the members of a local church are regenerate. In response, he argues that all systems of church government have the same problem with human nature, a statement with which I agree. He then asserts that the "many" of congregationalism is less susceptible to the abuse of power than the "few" of representative leadership of presbyterianism or episcopalianism. However, in my estimation, it is easier for a few knowledgeable and determined people to manipulate a convention (congregationalism) than it is to manipulate a deliberative representative body.

Patterson also argues that congregationalism can best practice church discipline. While I agree that the practice of discipline is one of the marks of the church, I respectfully disagree that congregationalism is the best venue for discipline, particularly in larger churches and in cases dealing with sensitive and controversial matters.

The priesthood of believers is the Protestant antidote to the sacerdotalism that had developed in the Roman Catholic Church in which priests were regarded as necessary intermediaries between people and God through the administration of its seven sacraments. Luther and other Reformers rightly asserted that the Bible teaches that *all* Christians have direct access to God and that the mediation of priests is not necessary. Indeed, all Protestants hold to the priesthood of believers; it is not a doctrine unique to Baptists. One could argue that believers voting on the election of an elder in a Presbyterian congregational meeting or a deputy voting on the election of a bishop at an episcopal convention are following the leading of the Holy Spirit as regenerate believer-priests, just as much as a Baptist in a congregational meeting voting on electing a deacon.

The Authority of Church Officers

We have already considered to a degree the nature and qualifications of church officers. Patterson argues for there being only two offices (pastor and deacon), but allows there are biblical arguments and historical precedents (even within Baptist and Anabaptist circles) for plurality of elders (teaching elders and ruling elders) as well as deacons. The point at issue is whether teaching elders and ruling elders lead the church only through example in an advisory capacity or if they have any spiritual authority.

Elders have numerous duties according to the Scriptures, as I pointed out in detail in my chapter. "Overseeing" the church is, by nature, an exercise of authority, not in a sacerdotal sense but in a pastoral one. Deciding theological issues binding on the whole church is not just offering pious advice. Both in the synagogue and the church, a senate of elders handled matters of spiritual discipline when members fell into sin, also an exercise of authority. Preaching the Word is an authoritative exercise, not simply giving opinions on the meaning of a biblical text.

The Example of New Testament Churches

Patterson's final argument is an inference drawn from the example of New Testament churches in (1) practicing discipline (Matt. 18:15–17; 1 Cor. 5:4, 12–13; 2 Cor. 2:5–11); (2) electing deacons (Acts 6); (3) commissioning missionaries (Acts 11:22; 13:1–3); (4) settling theological issues (Acts 15:22); and (5) collecting funds for various needs (2 Cor. 8:19).

Congregationalist John Owen set forth a good case for church discipline being carried out by elders elected by the church rather than through a congregational meeting. He first argued that the office of apostle was a temporary office (during a transitional time of the church, as Patterson argued). The apostles had extraordinary powers, one of which was to "deliver someone over to Satan for destruction in order that one's soul be saved."[52] But Christ now exercises his authority in the church through ordained offices (Eph. 4:11–15). When the elders of the church exercise discipline, they are exercising the power of the keys of the kingdom of heaven, which Christ has given to the church (Matt. 18:17–18). Owen argued:

> This excommunication, as we have proved before, is an act of church authority exerted in the name of our Lord Jesus Christ: and if so, then it is the act of the officers of the church … for there is no authority in the church, properly so called, but what resides in the officers of it.[53]

Patterson notes that though 1 Timothy 5:17 speaks of elders who "rule"(*proistemi*), it does not rule out congregational polity. A consideration of other passages in which the term *proistemi* is used has to do with leadership (Rom. 12:8) and a father's ruling his children (1 Tim. 3:4–5, 12). It is, by the nature of the case, a strong word, connoting authority, not just advice. Hebrews 13:7, 17, and 24 are even stronger—*hegeomai*, to lead, conduct, command, rule over, guide, or govern. These terms, *proistemi* and *hegeomai*, indicate that those who are chosen as elders lead not only by inspiring example, but also have a type of spiritual authority, though not a sacerdotal power. Having said that, I agree with Patterson's statement on the limitations of elders' authority:

> Elders governing and leading at the will of the churches, therefore, have general authority to adjudicate matters that

have not already been settled either by Jesus or in the Scriptures. They do not, under any circumstances, have the authority to reverse the Scriptures or make exceptions to the teachings of Scripture due to circumstance or culture.[54]

To argue that Acts 6 proves the necessity of congregationalism and excludes a presbyterian government does not follow. Deacons are officers of a local church, in both a presbyterian and congregational system. Moreover, the Antioch church's commissioning of Barnabas and Saul of Tarsus as missionaries does demonstrate that "congregations as a whole exercised considerable influence, perhaps even final determination in major considerations for local churches," but it does not prove that they were totally independent. Finally, the council of Jerusalem (Acts 15) does not present a strong argument for congregationalism, a convention of independent churches. Elders sat with the apostles in that council (Acts 15:2, 4, 6, 22–23; 16:4). The "whole church" included not just the church of Jerusalem but elders from other churches as well. The council issued decrees (*dogmata*)—authoritative theological rulings—not consensus statements or mere pious advice (Acts 16:4).

CONCLUSION

Single-elder congregational government has been extant in the church since the sixteenth century, and in these days when many mainline denominations are deviating from foundational doctrine and morality, ecclesiastical independency is an appealing option. Nonetheless, we must determine whether the Bible teaches that churches are to be *independent of* each other or *interdependent upon* each other in fulfilling the Great Commission.

A PLURAL-ELDER CONGREGATIONALIST'S RESPONSE

Samuel E. Waldron

COMMENDATIONS

I cannot begin my response to Paige Patterson without expressing personal appreciation for his part in the conservative resurgence among Southern Baptists. The fact that we are both Baptists and congregationalists also provides me with much to commend in his chapter. His chapter contains a fine defense of congregationalism. It also manifests sensitivity to some of the contemporary abuses of congregationalism as when he remarks that it ought not to create a forum for "the rugged individualist" and does not give anyone "the right ... to speak his mind." I also appreciate the way that he defended a biblically mandated church government. He sums up the key point well when he says, "The first century was an age of transition." Finally, I certainly appreciate his clear statements that it is not "unscriptural to have multiple elders in a local church" and that the "terms 'pastor' ... 'elder' ... and 'bishop' ... are used interchangeably in the New Testament." Of course, as will become clear in this response, I believe that Patterson does not see clearly or work through consistently the implications of these admissions. Nevertheless, there is much to appreciate in his chapter.

CRITICISMS

I want to isolate three areas of disagreement in my response to Patterson's article. In so doing I hope to make clear the biblical elements of ecclesiology that contrast with Patterson's position.

The Purely Pragmatic Necessity of Multiple Elders

It is, I think, fair to say that when Patterson allows for multiple elders to be scriptural, he does so on what may be called purely pragmatic grounds. Patterson clearly envisions that local churches will have one elder and that this first and primary elder will be supplemented with further elders merely as need for ministry arises. He says, for instance, that "the thesis of this chapter is not that it is unscriptural to have multiple elders in a local church. To the contrary, such practice has clear precedent and mandate in the Scriptures and is augmented by the pragmatics of caring for the spiritual needs of large flocks of spiritual sheep." A little later he adds, "Each assembly needed a single pastor, and this would be augmented as growth dictated." Later still he remarks, "These autonomous congregations seem to have had at least one elder, adding additional elders as the necessities of the ministry required." Again, Patterson observes, "What seems evident is that each congregation needs to have elder leadership. Some churches have more than one as the need arises."

These statements by Patterson give the clear impression that local churches normatively and originally have a single elder and only add more (under the leadership of the original elder) as increased ministry makes necessary. Now the fact is that this picture of the local church and its eldership distorts the original, biblical portrait of the eldership. The New Testament gives not a single example of any local church with only one elder. Instead it gives numerous examples of churches where a plurality of elders existed and continued from the inception of organized leadership: Jerusalem (Acts 11:30), Antioch in Syria (13:1), Lystra, Iconium, Pisidian Antioch (14:23), Ephesus (20:17), the churches of Crete (Titus 1:5), the churches of the Jewish dispersion to whom James wrote (James 5:14), probably the churches to whom Peter wrote in Pontus, Galatia, Cappadocia, Asia, and Bythinia (1 Peter 5:1–2), Philippi (Phil. 1:1), probably the churches to whom Hebrews was written (Heb. 13:7, 17, 24), and finally the unidentified church whose presbytery laid hands on Timothy (1 Tim. 4:14).

A further problem with the picture Patterson provides is that it is insensitive to the fact that elders are part of a presbytery or council of elders. Biblically speaking, it is necessary to speak of the abnormality of a lone elder. *The Friberg Greek Lexicon*, for instance, gives the following as one of its definitions of elder: "as designating honorable officials in local councils."[55] We have seen the evidence for this in the local church. In the Bible we also read, however, of the elders of Israel (Ex. 3:16 and many other times), the elders of a city (Ruth 4:2 and many other times), and the twenty-four elders in heaven (Rev. 4:10 and several other times in the book of Revelation). The Sanhedrin is also called the presbytery of the Jews (Luke 22:6; Acts 22:5). The incongruity of Patterson's position in this regard can be pointedly epitomized. He sees nothing abnormal in one-man presbyteries. Nor does he see anything deficient in elderships composed of one elder.

In my chapter I acknowledge that it is not necessarily sinful to have only one elder. We know of churches without any elders at all (Acts 14:23). The reason, however, that these churches lacked elders is that they had just been planted and were not fully organized. When—soon—they were organized, a plurality of elders was immediately appointed in each church by the apostles: "they ... appointed elders for them in every church."

Thus, though we cannot say that lacking a plurality of elders is sinful, we still must say that it is abnormal. The deficiency of the churches in view in Acts 14:23 (and Titus 1:5) was supplied not by the appointment of a single elder, but by the appointment of a plurality. If it was abnormal and deficient for a church to have no elders, it was also clearly abnormal and deficient for that church to have only one. The New Testament teaches that it is abnormal and deficient for the church to have one elder, but Patterson teaches that it is normal and frequently sufficient.

The Normative Character of a Single, Primary Elder

Patterson repeatedly insists that it is normative for one of the elders—if a church has more than one—to be the decisive spiritual leader of the other elders. Indeed, it is not too much to say that this is one of the major emphases of his chapter. He says, "Even when multiple elders were necessary, one of the elders remained the decisive spiritual leader of the flock." As he prosecutes his argument, he affirms: "The case in the New Testament for congregationalism and for single, primary elder leadership can be constructed along several lines." Later he asks, "Why then argue for a single elder who is at least the decided leader of the congregation?" In his concluding paragraph he affirms that of the elders a church should choose "one [to] be the primary leader and preacher/teacher for the flock."

Before discussing the biblical evidence related to Patterson's assertions, two preliminary observations may helpfully clarify the issue here brought forward. As noted previously, it is gratifying to see that Patterson has given up any attempt to defend *single-elder congregationalism*. He has chosen rather to defend *primary-elder congregationalism*. In so far as this reflects movement toward *plural-elder congregationalism*, this is, from my perspective, encouraging.

At the same time, it is important to note a measure of ambivalence on Patterson's part with regard even to the *primary-elder congregationalism* that he has chosen to defend. At the end of his defense of the primary-elder idea he admits: "In conclusion, I reiterate my conviction that a hands-down case cannot be made for 'single elder' primacy or 'multiple elder' oligarchy. There simply are no 'commandments' on this issue. The case then must be made on the basis of what can be determined from observing leadership practice throughout the Scriptures."

It is difficult to avoid the suspicion that something strange is going on here. First, why is this issue so important to Patterson, if there are "simply no commandments" about it? Second, it is interesting to see Patterson implying that the primary biblical evidence is not clear on this issue, so that we must have recourse to "observing leadership practice throughout the Scriptures." This sounds suspiciously like Toon's attempt to appeal to early tradition, because in his opinion there is no one form of church government found in the books of the New Testament. Perhaps it is not that the New Testament is unclear, but rather that Patterson is not inclined to look too closely at what it actually says.

As a matter of fact, when we examine the New Testament teaching on eldership and church government, a number of principles relevant to the primary-elder theory do clearly emerge. We have already had occasion to emphasize the first. As we have shown, the New Testament teaches that a plurality of elders is normative. Far from a single eldership being the normal or original state of New Testament churches, the opposite, so far as we can tell, was the case everywhere. As soon as there were elders, there were pluralities of elders. Since in none of these passages is a primary elder mentioned, this—to say the least—is not encouraging for the primary-elder theory.

The second observation as well does not need to be made the subject of extended comment. Patterson himself admits, as we noted at the outset, that bishops, pastors, and elders are simply different ways of describing the same church officers holding one and the same church office.[56] There is, therefore, no terminological or official distinction made between the pastor or the bishop and the rest of the elders. Indeed, there is no terminological or official distinction of any kind to be found in the New Testament in which one of the elders is given a title or said to possess an office that the others do not.[57] The straightforward, and one would think obvious, implication of this patent, biblical fact is that all hold the same office and have equal authority. This does not at all encourage the theory that one of the elders should exercise "decisive leadership" over the others. One rather thinks that it would encourage mutual accountability of all the elders to one another!

What about that general evidence from leadership practice in the Scriptures to which Patterson appeals? I have two things to say about it.

First, it does not prove that there ought to be a primary elder with an office or authority that the rest of the elders do not possess. Patterson appeals to the example of Moses, but he was the mediator of the old covenant occupying a position that made him the representative of God, the type of Christ, and the rough equivalent of the later kings of Israel. His example is simply irrelevant for the present purpose. Patterson appeals to Peter. Peter, however, held precisely the same office—apostle of Christ—as the rest of the Twelve. Patterson surely does not want to teach in Rome-like fashion that Peter possessed some sort of official primacy in relation to the other apostles. Patterson appeals to James the half brother of the Lord. Again, there is simply no evidence that James possessed any office or authority not possessed by others in the church in Jerusalem. James is never explicitly called an elder, but, if he were, there were clearly other elders in the church (Acts 15:2). James is never called a pastor, but, if he were, there were clearly other pastors in the church. (On Patterson's own admission, all the elders were pastors.) James is called an apostle of Christ (1 Cor. 15:7; Gal. 1:19), but there were certainly other apostles in Jerusalem. James is ranked with them, but not above them. (In Galatians 2:9 James, Cephas/Peter, and John are all called pillars.) And, by the way, what happened to the primacy of Peter, when James came to have the primacy? Both were at the council in Jerusalem. Was there a church split? Did both possess the primacy? But then what happens to Patterson's theory of leadership? We also wonder what happened to Jesus' teaching about leadership in all this talk about who will be first (Luke 22:24–27).

Patterson also appeals to the "angels" of the churches addressed in Revelation. Patterson is astute enough to admit that a final conclusion about the identity of these "angels" is not possible. A wide variety of opinions and a lack of any consensus may be found in the commentators. Nevertheless, he attempts to leave the impression that it is quite likely that these "angels" were "the pastors of those churches." Again Patterson slips into the pastor-elder distinction that he himself admits is not biblical. This is, in fact, the chief problem with this interpretation. It finds in the highly symbolic language of Revelation a distinction that is nowhere present in the rest of the New Testament. As we have seen, there is no terminological or official distinction to be found in the plain teaching of the rest of the New Testament in which one of the elders is given a position, title, or authority not possessed by the rest of the elders. Are we now to use the highly symbolic language of Revelation to impose such a distinction on that teaching? Are we on the basis of Revelation 1–3 to distinguish between the "angel" and the rest of the elders? This appears to violate some very fundamental rules of biblical interpretation.

The fact is that there are alternative interpretations (each held by respected commentators) that do not violate the plain teaching of the rest of the New Testament. The angels of the churches are also interpreted as (1) literal, guardian angels of the churches, (2) the human messengers (or angels) through whom the letters were sent to the churches, (3) the spirit or personification of each of the churches, (4) a general reference to the ruling-teaching function or government of each church.

Patterson makes a number of appeals that may be described as a general appeal to "the development of church history and to the psychology of leadership." Here he appeals to various illustrations of primary leaders in church history (Chrysostom, Jonathan Edwards), the synagogue (the *archisunagogos* mentioned several times in the New Testament), the family, and civil government. Patterson sums up this argument by saying: "Since it is difficult to find any place where God called a committee, I believe that the pattern in both Testaments is for God to call individual leaders for his people."

Patterson's use of the term "committee" in the preceding quotation is pejorative and prejudicial. The fact is, however, that we have at least two very pertinent illustrations of the Son of God calling a plurality of leadership for his church. He appointed, not one, but twelve apostles to lead the church universal. He called, not one, but a plurality of elders to lead the local churches of the New Testament. The reason for this procedure is not difficult to discover. The church universal and the church local already had a primary bishop and pastor: Jesus Christ himself (1 Peter 2:25)!

Second, some of the general evidence from the practice of leadership that Patterson cites points to an element of truth in his position that is consistent with plural-elder congregationalism. I note in my chapter, plural-elder congregationalism in no way requires that an artificial uniformity (in which absolute uniformity is jealously guarded) be imposed on the eldership of any local church. In line with this I want to point out that Patterson fails to make an important distinction. This failure introduces an unfortunate ambiguity into his argument. Simply put, if we are ever to understand the biblical teaching on this issue, *official authority and mere influence or power must be carefully distinguished*. For instance, Patterson and I agree that in the home the husband or father is the authority or head. He is officially responsible for his home to God. I think, however, we would both agree that it is no violation of the husband's headship for a godly wife to exercise a great deal of influence over the decisions he makes as head. I think Patterson would agree that (as long as the final decision remains the husband's) such influence is perfectly consistent with the wife's submission to the husband's headship. This is the distinction on which I want to insist with regard to the eldership. An elder may exercise great influence on his fellow elders without undermining their authority.

Another illustration may further clarify this distinction. When Absalom drove his father David, the rightful king of Israel, from Jerusalem, he certainly exercised great power over his father. His power over the king did not mean, however, that he had authority over the king or a right to rule Israel. Notwithstanding his temporary power, that right and authority still belonged to David. *Again, the lesson is that authority, right, and office are not the same as sheer power or mere influence.* It is this distinction that Patterson has failed to apply to eldership. The fact that one of the elders exercises greater influence does not give him a right to an office the other elders do not possess. To claim such an office is to usurp their authority. He may and must exercise his God-given influence without the usurpation of claiming to be king when he is not.

Now I am perfectly happy to admit that in many elderships one of the elders may have a great deal more influence than the others. I am perfectly happy to concede that there is no violation of biblical teaching in this. I am perfectly happy to acknowledge that it will not be uncommon for one of a church's elders—because of his level of teaching or preaching gift, his personality, his age and experience, or his godliness—to have more influence than the others. I am perfectly happy to allow that the evidence Patterson compiles may prove something like this. I am even perfectly happy to say that the greater influence God may give to one of the elders should not be resented or minimized by the others.

I am perfectly happy to grant all this *with only two qualifications.* First, the official authority must remain with the eldership as a whole. To put this another way, no elder should claim an office or authority not possessed by all. Second, the situation where one elder has such influence must not be seen as necessary or normative. In other words, I do not believe that it can be proven that a church must have an elder with such unusual influence. According to Galatians 2:9, for instance, the church at Jerusalem had at least three pillars: James, Cephas, and John. Jesus sent his disciples out *two by two.* For a long time, with wonderful results, and until a sad and unnecessary division, the missionary team of Paul and Barnabas had dual leadership. Calvin exercised wide and wonderful influence *as one of the* ministers of Geneva. The wisdom of God affirms: "Two are better than one because they have a good return for their labor. For if either of them falls, the one will lift up his companion. But woe to the one who falls when there is not another to lift him up. Furthermore, if two lie down together they keep warm, but how can one be warm alone? And if one can overpower him who is alone, two can resist him. A cord of three strands is not quickly torn apart" (Eccl. 4:9–12).

Why is this a matter of practical importance? A whole book, perhaps, could be written in response to this question. I can only point out several practical advantages of the viewpoint I am here advocating. I simply want to preface these comments by affirming that no system of church government is a panacea or solution for all the problems that sin may cause.

The same history that Patterson cites also shows that a talented leader has his own weaknesses. A sense of accountability to equals—the other elders—will tend to deliver him from the spiritually fatal notion that he is above the law. Working with an eldership will tend to deliver him from the accusation of one-man rule. Working with other godly leaders may tend to minimize exposing to the church the sometimes-large blind spots of such talented leaders. It also may tend to deliver the church from becoming marked by the foibles and idiosyncrasies of one talented leader. The plural-elder system with the flexibility I am advocating allows the development of younger leaders within the church by eliminating the sense that there is room for only one leader and one ministry in the church. Above all, a church led by a plurality of elders will have in its very system of leadership a constant reminder that the head of the church is *not* the pastor or the bishop, but *the Lord Jesus Christ.*

Let me emphasize that a plural-elder system makes all this possible without requiring that the gifts of a talented elder be suppressed. Let such an elder exercise all the influence he can for good. This is no violation of plural-elder congregationalism.

The Advisory Nature of Pastoral Authority

My third area of disagreement with Patterson is his view of the advisory nature of pastoral authority. Patterson advocates the idea of *spiritual consensus* as the way to reach decisions. By itself I have nothing to quarrel with in this idea. In fact, I advocate something like it in my own chapter. What concerns me is the Mark Dever quotation Patterson uses at this point. Dever is due much credit for his work to reform the church in our day and to advocate the importance of a plurality of elders. Yet I am uncomfortable with the view of pastoral authority revealed when Patterson cites Dever saying, "Therefore, in a Baptist church, elders and all other boards and committees act in what is finally an advisory capacity to the whole congregation."

The view that the eldership's authority in the church is *finally advisory* does not do justice to the biblical evidence, in my opinion. Now I certainly admit the difficulty of combining pastoral authority and congregational rights in a coherent theory of church government. I also admit that the Bible clearly teaches the necessity of congregational suffrage both in the selection of officers and in the enactment of church discipline. I simply cannot see, however, how one can really take seriously the various titles and descriptions of the pastoral office in the New Testament and conclude that pastoral authority is advisory. As I point out in my chapter, there are seven descriptions of the ruling officers of the church and the majority of these designations (elder, overseer, shepherd, governor, and steward) emphasize the real authority they possess.

The view that pastoral authority is finally advisory also fails to recognize how far the radical democracy practiced in most congregational churches today has moved not only from biblical norms but from the congregationalism of our Puritan predecessors. The congregational government that the Puritans advocated involved elements *monarchical*, *aristocratical*, and *democratical*, but today it has become a simple democracy in many churches. Reducing the authority of the eldership to an advisory capacity jettisons the biblical evidence that might correct this imbalance.

CONCLUSIONS

Patterson's chapter—good as it is—at last becomes a clever defense of the status quo. I suggest that the reader ask himself whether Patterson has critiqued contemporary practice in light of the New Testament or interpreted the New Testament in light of contemporary practice.

The problem quickly becomes visible in Patterson's chapter. In his opening sentence he affirms that with the death of Polycarp the church at Smyrna "had not just suffered the loss of one of its elders; it had lost its pastor." We have seen the element of truth in such a statement. Some pastors do exercise preeminent influence for good. Polycarp was one such pastor. Yet we have seen the inconsistency in Patterson's statement. He himself denies that the New Testament teaches any such pastor-elder distinction as he here makes.

But I want to point out here how bound this assertion is by contemporary practice. It would have been no less unbiblical for Patterson to say that they did not simply lose one of their elders. They lost their bishop! It would have been more historical. Bishop was the name beginning to be given to such pastors at this time in church history. Why, then, does Patterson speak so unbiblically and unhistorically? Patterson's thinking is bound by contemporary practice.

To say that the church at Smyrna had lost their bishop would reveal too clearly the real nature and tendency of the primary-elder theory. The same theory with a different name led to episcopacy and then to Rome in the early church. Patterson is a congregationalist. I am certain that he does not really want to take even one step on the road that leads in that direction!

Chapter 3: Single-Elder Congregationalism Notes

Paige Patterson

[1]Edmund P. Clowney, *The Church* (Downers Grove, Ill.: InterVarsity, 1995), 202.

[2]W. A. Criswell says, "Although many see different offices in these titles, there are at least three compelling reasons for believing that *poimen* (pastor), *episkopos* (bishop), and *presbuteros* (elder) are descriptive names for the same office. Although the words translated *bishop* and *elder* are used more often in the New Testament, the following discussion will use the term *pastor* because it is most familiar to Baptists. First, other than the names themselves, there is no suggestion in the New Testament that more than one pastoral office ever existed. Paul told Titus, for example, to ordain elders, but he did not mention bishops or pastors. He gave Timothy qualifications for bishops, but not for elders or pastors. In Ephesians 4:11, though other preaching offices are mentioned, we find only one pastoral office, the pastor. If more than one such office existed, the New Testament does not make it clear. Second, the three terms often are used synonymously and are never distinguished from one another.... Third, whenever the officers of the church are listed formally, invariably there are only two, pastors and deacons." *The Doctrine of Church* (Nashville: Convention, 1980), 69–70.

[3]The contributors to one anthology on the doctrine of the church offer an opposing perspective. They say, "Though discussions were carried on as to who would be elders, no one can honestly and fairly prove these men were voted on in a popular congregational, electoral fashion. The best indication we have from Scripture is that they were appointed for their positions by other elders/leaders. Shepherds should be able to spot shepherds. They are given the responsibility to make important spiritual decisions. This is the role of leadership. More than likely they had been Jewish elders before they received Jesus as their Messiah and Savior. They had perpetuated elder leadership roles by appointment of other elders." Mal Couch, gen. ed., *A Biblical Theology of the Church* (Grand Rapids: Kregel, 1999), 194. It should be noted, however, that just as it cannot be proven that congregations chose their elders, neither can it be proven that they were selected (at least universally) by other elders. That being the case, logic seems more on the side of congregationalism as a result of the priesthood of the believers.

[4]F. L. Cross and E. A. Livingstone, eds., *The Oxford Dictionary of the Christian Church* (New York: Oxford University Press, 1997), 399.

[5]*The Oxford Dictionary of the Christian Church*, 399.

[6]Walter A. Elwell, ed., *Evangelical Dictionary of Theology* (Grand Rapids: Baker, 1984), 240.

[7]Philip Schaff, *The Creeds of Christendom*, vol. III (Grand Rapids: Baker, 1977), 724–25.

[8]William L. Lumpkin, *Baptist Confessions of Faith*, rev. ed. (Valley Forge, Pa.: Judson, 1969), 27.

[9]*Baptist Confessions of Faith*, 58–59.

[10]*Baptist Confessions of Faith*, 121–22.

[11]*Baptist Confessions of Faith*, 166.

[12]*Baptist Confessions of Faith*, 212.

[13]*Baptist Confessions of Faith*, 287.

[14]*Baptist Confessions of Faith*, 365–66.

[15]*Baptist Faith and Message* (Nashville: LifeWay, 2000), 13.

[16]The author has focused on Baptists and Baptistic groups since the Reformation only because of the large and well-known status of these. There were, of course, pre-Reformation groups, which exhibited some of these same characteristics, and there are numerous other Christians who practice congregational polity today. In addition to Baptists and Congregationalists, many independent assemblies that function autonomously have arisen.

[17]Werner Jeanrond suggests that this failure on the part of Luther was not unusual for the Reformation period. "Structurally, the medieval Church consisted of two ('ontologically') different sections, the clergy and the laity. The clergy had become the ruling class while the laity was the group to be looked after (not always only spiritually) by the clergy. This ecclesiastical organisation was questioned in the Protestant Reformation which retrieved the biblical image of the priesthood of all people. But this retrieval was at first more of a programmatic nature, while the actual situation in the local church remained unchanged. The Protestant 'pastor' continued to take care of his flock, the Protestant potentate took over the role of the civil patron of the Reformed Church from his Roman Catholic predecessor. However, the ecclesial reorganisation in many (though not in all) Protestant movements led eventually to a much more substantial participation of the 'laity' in Church governments, whereas in the Roman Catholic Church the principle of clerical authority was refined even further. Here the clerical absolutism has on the whole remained unchanged until today." Colin E. Gunton and Daniel W. Hardy, *On Being the Church* (Edinburgh: T. & T. Clark, 1989), 91.

[18]Elwell, *Evangelical Dictionary of Theology*, 240.

[19]Mark Dever, *Nine Marks of a Healthy Church* (Washington, D.C.: Center for Church Reform, 1998), 22.

[20]Wolfhart Pannenberg, *The Church* (Philadelphia: Westminster, 1983), 103–4.

[21]Protestant Reformers understood the necessity for leadership as Brachlow notes, "Despite the challenge of Continental protestant reformers to the authority of the hierarchy at Rome, they never doubted that the church required the guidance of a separate, ordained ministry. 'Fanatical men' might think a formal ministerial order superfluous, Calvin said, but it was his settled opinion that the prophets and godly teachers of the visible church were 'necessary and highly approved' by the Word." Stephen Brachlow, *The Communion of the Saints* (New York: Oxford University Press, 1988), 157–58.

[22]There are other ways to look at the officers of the early church. In his well-known book on ecclesiology Dana notes, "Here we are not on as definite and secure ground as one might wish to assume. It surprises the student who anticipates a rigid scriptural pattern for official functions in the church to discover that there was no unvarying uniformity in the official staff of the New

Testament churches. But we can discern with sufficient assurance what officers ministered in the churches in the Apostolic Age taken as a whole. There were certain officers who served in a general missionary capacity, going from church to church, with no permanent relationship to any particular church. These we may call general officers. Then there were officers related distinctively and permanently to a local church, whom we will describe as local officers." H. E. Dana, *A Manual of Ecclesiology*, rev. 2nd ed. with L. M. Sipes (Kansas City, Kans.: Central Seminary Press, 1944), 246.

[23]See Acts 20:17, 28 where Paul does the same thing.

[24]Saucy mentions this use of more than one word to describe the bishop. "After listing those for a 'bishop' (vv. 1–7), he proceeds immediately to those for the office of a deacon. No mention is made of the elder, but later, in reference to the elder, he ascribes to him the functions performed by the bishop (cf. 1 Ti 5:17 with 3:4). Thus the two terms are apparently used for the same officers." Robert L. Saucy, *The Church in God's Program* (Chicago: Moody Press, 1972), 141.

[25]R. Alastair Campbell notes the particular impact of the Jewish heritage of Christianity when he says, "Although the earliest churches developed rapidly within a Graeco-Roman environment, their primary cultural heritage was, of course, Jewish. Accordingly, we began our survey of the New Testament background by looking at the elders in Ancient Israel. We saw that they constituted a form of leadership that was collective and representative, with an authority derived from their seniority relative to those they represented, whether household, clan, tribe or nation. 'The elders' was shown to be a term of honour for those whose power was based on relationships that already existed, rather than a precise office, entered through appointment, election or ordination." *The Elders* (Edinburgh: T. & T. Clark, 1994), 238.

[26]Many Anabaptists took this in connection with the phrases, "let us keep the feast" (5:8), and "not even to eat with such a person" (5:11) as an indication that the exclusion enjoined is that of forbidding access to the Lord's Table, the fellowship meal of the church.

[27]J. M. Pendleton, *Church Manual* (Philadelphia: Judson, n.d.), 105.

[28]Henry George Liddell and Robert Scott, *A Greek-English Lexicon* (Oxford: Clarendon, 1966), 1482–83.

[29]*A Greek-English Lexicon*, 762–63.

[30]Paige Patterson, "The Meaning of Authority in the Local Church," in *Recovering Biblical Manhood and Womanhood*, eds. John Piper and Wayne Grudem (Wheaton, Ill.: Crossway, 1991), 258.

[31]Elwell, *Evangelical Dictionary of Theology*, 241.

[32]The somewhat confusing picture of church governance in the New Testament is highlighted by F. J. A. Hort's contrast between information about the churches at Jerusalem and Antioch. "One other supplementary observation should be made before we leave this fifteenth chapter. In all that we read there and previously about the young Ecclesia of Antioch we learn absolutely nothing about its government or administration. The prophets and teachers have, as such, nothing to do with functions of this kind. Doubtless a man like Barnabas, coming as an envoy of the Ecclesia of Jerusalem (so, not simply of the Apostles, xx. 22) and

shewing such sympathy with the local conditions of things, would acquire by the mere force of circumstances a considerable moral authority, and this would presently be shared with St Paul, when he too had come out of his Cilician retirement. Of course by its very nature this position was temporary as well as informal. Strange to say, we hear nothing about Elders. Since we know that the Ecclesia of Jerusalem had long had Elders, and St Paul on returning from his journey in Asia Minor had appointed Elders for each local Ecclesia, it is hardly credible that they were wanting at Antioch, to say nothing of the influence of the precedent of the great Jewish population. But in the Acts we hear only of 'the brethren' (xv. 1, 32, 33) or 'the disciples' (xi. 26, 29; xiv. 28) or 'the multitude' (xv. 30) or 'the ecclesia' (xi. 26; xiii. 1; xiv. 27). Evidently at this time the general body of disciples at Antioch must have taken at least a large share in the acts of the Christian community." *The Christian Ecclesia* (London: Macmillan and Co., 1914), 90–91.

[33]Hans Küng, *The Church* (New York: Sheed and Ward, 1967), 407–8.

[34]Merrrill C. Tenney, gen. ed., *The Zondervan Pictorial Encyclopedia of the Bible*, vol. 5 (Grand Rapids: Zondervan , 1977), 563.

Peter Toon

[35]There is of course a very large literature from episcopalians across the centuries in which it is argued that the New Testament does actually provide the embryonic basis for the Threefold Ministry by the way in which the apostolic churches were founded and organized. Much of this was produced to counteract claims from presbyterians and congregationalists that the New Testament contains blueprints for either presbyterianism or congregationalism. Today, it is generally argued by episcopalians that the New Testament evidence, read alone and without the context of the early church, wherein the books of the New Testament were read and collected, contains *no* blueprint for later, specific form of polity. This is because the apostolic age is one of expansion and development and the results of this work of the Lord are only seen in a settled form in say AD 150 or 200. I commend the essays by my former teacher, Professor Henry Chadwick, "Episcopacy in the New Testament and Early Church" and "Ministry and Tradition," in *Tradition and Exploration* (Norwich: Canterbury, 1994). Further, I commend the study of Part X, "The Christian Ministry," in *Anglicanism*, eds. P. E. More and F. L. Cross (London: S.P.C.K., 1951), along with Part V, "Church and Ministry," in *The Study of Anglicanism*, eds. S. Sykes, John Booty, and Jonathan Knight (Minneapolis: Fortress, 1988).

L. Roy Taylor

[36]I grew up in a Southern Baptist church and began my preaching ministry in a Southern Baptist church. Later I became a Presbyterian (through my own study) while a student at a Southern Baptist seminary.

[37]Solo pastor in a church that has only one minister, or senior pastor in a church that has several ministers.

[38]See pages 81.

[39]James, most likely the first written of all New Testament books, refers to the local church as a synagogue (James 2:2).

[40]See pages 79–80.

[41]Everett Ferguson notes: "Several non-canonical documents reflect a situation where a plurality of presbyters was at the head of a congregation (Polycarp, *Ep.* 5–6, cf. 11; 2 *Clem.* 7.3; *Asc. Isa.* 3.23f; *Orac. Sib.* 2.264f.), even where the single bishop was clearly distinct from the presbyters, as in Ignatius (*Polyc.* 6; *Trall.* 3; *Smyrn.* 8). The church at Alexandria, according to their later reports (Jerome, *Ep.* 146; Eutychus, *Annals*, PG 111.982), was led by twelve presbyters, who chose a president as bishop out of their own number." *Encyclopedia of Early Christianity* (New York: Garland, 1988), 752.

[42]I.e., baptize persons only on the basis of a profession of faith. They also are called "Anabaptist" (re-baptize those who may have been baptized in infancy), or simply "Baptist."

[43]I.e., baptize infants.

[44]Phil. 1:1; 1 Tim. 3:8, 10, 12–13.

[45]For fuller discussion see chapter 2.

[46]John Owen, *The True Nature of a Gospel Church*, abr. and ed. John Huxtable (London: Camelot, 1947), 51.

[47]*Book of Church Order*, Presbyterian Church in America, § 8-3.

[48]Henry Webb, *Deacons: Servant Models in the Church* (Nashville: Broadman & Holman, 2001), 103.

[49]Parliament repealed the Henrican Act of Supremacy under Tudor in 1554, but passed another Act of Supremacy in 1559, making Elizabeth I "supreme governor of the church."

[50]*Book of Church Order*, § 3-1.

[51]In the Presbyterian system the elders (session) admit them to Communion. In Anglican, Lutheran, and Methodist systems they are confirmed by the laying on of hands of a bishop or minister.

[52]See other passages such as Acts 5:1–11; 13:9–11; 2 Cor 10:3, 8, 13; 1 Tim. 1:20.

[53]Owen, *The True Nature of a Gospel Church*, 113.

[54]Paige Patterson, "The Meaning of Authority in the Local Church," in *Recovering Biblical Manhood and Womanhood*, eds. John Piper and Wayne Grudem (Wheaton, Ill.: Crossway, 1991), 258.

Samuel E. Waldron

[55]*The Friberg Greek Lexicon* [CD-ROM] in *Bible Works 4* (Hermeneutika, 1999), s.v. "presbuteroj."

[56]It is interesting to note that Patterson repeatedly (and inconsistently with his own stated view) distinguishes between the pastor and the elders. He begins his chapter by telling us that when Polycarp died, the church at Smyrna "had not just suffered the loss of one of its elders; it had lost its pastor." Later on he says, "James the half brother of the Lord seems to be recognized as *the pastor* in Jerusalem." Patterson should allow the New Testament evidence to discipline his accustomed terminology.

[57]The closest the New Testament comes to such a distinction is the language of 1 Timothy 5:17 where elders who rule well are distinguished from elders who rule well but also labor in the Word and in doctrine. Clearly, however, there is

no terminological or official distinction to be found here. Both the outer circle—the elders who rule well—and the inner circle—the elders who labor in the Word—are elders. No title or terminology is used to ascribe an office or authority to the inner circle that is not also possessed by the outer circle. Some have endeavored to find a distinction between pastors and elders in the New Testament. Patterson, however, admits that no such distinction exists, and I have shown in my chapter why he is right to think so.

Chapter Four

PLURAL-ELDER CONGREGATIONALISM

PLURAL-ELDER CONGREGATIONALISM

Samuel E. Waldron

ITS DEFINITION

In this discussion of church government, I have been asked to defend *plural-elder congregationalism*. This mouthful of syllables has a clearly defined meaning within the context both of this discussion and the history of Christian debate on the subject of church government. That meaning may not, however, be immediately evident to the reader. Allow me to explain the meaning of plural-elder congregationalism through three assertions.

Congregational Church Government

Plural-elder congregationalism is, in the first place, congregational church government. Congregationalism, as it has been used historically in the Christian debates over church government, has two related, but distinct, meanings. Though a congregational form of church government has often combined both of these ideas, it is important especially for my purposes in this discussion to distinguish them. Congregationalism may refer to the independence of the local church or *independency*. It also may refer to a democratic form of government in the local church or *democracy*. It also may refer to and combine both these ideas.[1]

Congregationalism as *democracy* will be discussed below in relation to a plurality of elders leading local churches. When I refer in this first assertion to congregationalism, it is to congregationalism as designating the independence of the local church.

As *independency*, congregationalism has to do with the relation of local churches to one another. In this sense congregationalism teaches the independence (sometimes called the autonomy) of each local church. In other words, it indicates that there is no ecclesiastical government or hierarchy (in the visible church on earth) with authority over local churches. Local churches are in this limited sense independent of one another. Though independent churches have often manifested a strong *associational* impulse and have worked together in associations of local churches, even the most strongly associational congregationalist, if he or she is consistent, must carefully guard the independence of the local church.[2]

Plural-Elder Church Government

In the second place, plural-elder congregationalism is plural-elder church government. Plural-elder church government means that each local church should be led, under normal circumstances, by a plurality of elders.[3] It is clear that here I agree with my Presbyterian brother and disagree with my Baptist brother. Presbyterian churches on a local level are led by a plurality of elders. Single-elder congregationalist churches, of course, are not.

But this is not the whole story. For here we confront the problem of congregationalism (in the sense of democratic rule) versus rule by elders in the local church. Many evangelicals today have discovered in their New Testament that local churches should have (and, thus, be led by) elders. This renewed interest in elders has created a reaction against the radical, democratic form of government practiced in many evangelical churches. It is common for those who have discovered the biblical teaching about elders to say that they believe in rule by elders and not congregationalism (in the sense of democracy).

I suspect that most who say this only believe in rule by elders in comparison (or as relative) to the congregational democracy with which they have been acquainted. The rule of elders in the Reformed tradition makes the decisions of the eldership authoritative regardless of the consent of the church as a whole.[4]

James Bannerman, a respected Presbyterian author, makes clear what rule by elder has meant historically for presbyterians:

> The system of Presbyterianism requires that every proper means be employed, in the way of explanation, persuasion, and instruction, to secure the concurrence of the members in the acts and proceedings of the rulers of Christian society. But Presbyterians do not, like Independents, hold that this consent is a condition upon which the lawfulness of the acts of the office-bearers is suspended, or as much a necessary element in any judgment of the ecclesiastical body as the consent of the rulers themselves. On the contrary, the consent of the members is, upon the Presbyterian theory, a consent added to the authoritative decision of the office-bearers, not entering into it as an element necessary to its validity, without which it would be neither lawful nor binding.[5]

When I defend the leadership of a plurality of elders in the local church, I do not intend to defend the presbyterian view on this matter.

Of course, this does not mean that I am happy with the typical, democratic congregationalism of most independent churches today. Furthermore, it seems to me that a biblical appreciation of a plurality of elders in the local churches must logically and practically tend to modify and restrain the radical democratic tendencies of many evangelical churches today. Even if we reject the presbyterian version of elder rule, there is a kind of tension between a democratic view of church government and a plural-elder view of church government.[6]

Reformed or Puritan Church Government

My third defining assertion with regard to plural-elder congregationalism is that it is a Reformed or Puritan church government. Historically speaking, the main advocates of plural-elder congregationalism are firmly associated with the Reformed and Puritan traditions. These views owe much of their prominence today to the congregational and Particular Baptist elements in the Puritan movement.

The Puritan movement and Reformed tradition of which it was a part believed that the Bible provides a divinely mandated church government. Indeed, the very origin of the congregational and Particular Baptist wing of Puritanism cannot be understood apart from this. The authority and sufficiency of the Scriptures with regard to church government is emphasized in the famous *Apologeticall Narration* written by the congregational members of the Westminster Assembly in 1643:

> First, the supreame rule *without us*, was the Primitive patterne and example of the churches erected by the Apostles. Our consciences were possessed with that reverence and adoration of the fulnesse of the Scriptures, that there is therein a compleat sufficiencie, as to make the *man of God perfect*, so also to make the Churches of God perfect, (meere circumstances we except, or what rules the law of nature doth in common dictate) if the directions and examples therein delivered were fully known and followed.[7]

The Savoy Declaration of Faith and Order concludes with a detailed account in no less than thirty paragraphs of "The Institution of the Churches, and the Order Appointed in Them by Jesus Christ." John Owen in his preface to that document also asserts the complete sufficiency of the Scriptures for the government of the church:

> What we have laid down about the churches and their government, we humbly conceive to be the order which Christ has himself appointed to be observed. We have endeavoured to follow Scripture light; and those that went before us according to that rule.[8]

Such sentiments simply assert that the same *regulative principle* that guided the worship of the Puritan church also guided its order or government. That regulative principle is stated in almost identical language in each of the three great confessions of the Puritan movement: the Westminster Confession of the Presbyterians, the Savoy Declaration of the Congregationalists, and the 1689 (or Second London) Confession of the Baptists. Here is how they put their understanding of that principle:

> The acceptable way of worshipping the true God, is instituted by himself, and so limited by his own revealed will,

that he may not be worshipped according to the imagination and devices of men, nor the suggestions of Satan, under any visible representations, or any other way not prescribed in the Holy Scriptures.[9]

James Renihan in his study of the pivotal period of Particular Baptist history from 1675–1705 shows that the Particular Baptists believed that their church polity was mandated by the Scriptures. He calls this their "primitivistic impulse."[10]

My defense of plural-elder congregationalism shares this Puritan and primitivist impulse. This means that I share my Presbyterian brother's commitment to the regulative principle of the church. It means that I disagree with the traditional, Anglican rejection of the regulative principle of the church and the allowance they make for the role of human reason and authority in the construction of church government.[11] James Bannerman helpfully contrasts the Puritan doctrine and the Anglican doctrine on this matter:

> In the case of the Church of England, its doctrine in regard to Church power in the worship of God is, that it has a right to decree everything, except what is forbidden in the Word of God. In the case of our own Church, its doctrine in reference to Church power in the worship of God is, that it has a right to decree nothing, except what expressly or by implication is enjoined by the Word of God.[12]

This means that I have a profoundly different hermeneutic and approach to church government than that of the brother defending Anglicanism in this discussion.

It also means that I have a profoundly different approach to this subject than much of contemporary evangelicalism. Like the Ephesian disciples of John the Baptist who told Paul, "We have not even heard whether there is a Holy Spirit" (Acts 19:2), many evangelicals tell us by their conduct that they have not even heard whether there is a biblical church government. Without shame, many act as if they were allowed to order "the household of God, which is the church of the living God" (1 Tim. 3:15) according to their human traditions, personal tastes, and natural reason. My defense of plural-elder congregationalism is, among other things, a protest against such attitudes in evangelical churches.

ITS DISTINCTIONS

There are many variations within plural-elder congregationalism and significant differences with regard to many issues. Should elders be ordained?[13] Assuming that all (or even some of) the elders are pastors, should the elders be addressed as Pastor So-and-so (supply either a first or last name)?[14] Should elders (at least some of them) be regularly supported by the church?[15] These questions have different degrees of importance, but they are not the most critical questions for my present purpose. The two most important issues of distinction among plural-elder congregationalists have to do with the organization of the eldership and the authority of the eldership.

With regard to the organization of the eldership, the different views can be arranged on a spectrum. On the one side are those who hold a strict two-office view (elders and deacons). Here the parity or equality of the elders is carefully guarded. In this view not only do all the elders have exactly the same office, but little or no distinction between the different elders is allowed. It resists any elder being perceived as the main elder. This resistance may involve the refusal to provide any of the elders with regular, financial support. Alternatively, this resistance might involve the elders sharing equally any financial support provided by the church. Specialization in the eldership is resisted. Public preaching and teaching, other public ministries, the chairmanship of the elders, and other pastoral tasks are distributed equally or rotated among the elders in order to make certain that the parity or equality of the elders is not impaired.

At the other end of this spectrum are those who hold what approaches a three-office view of the church. In this system a distinction is made within the eldership between the teaching elder (variously called the minister, the pastor, or the senior pastor) and the rest of the elders (the ruling elders). Such an organization is very common among Presbyterians. Though the teaching elder is considered one of the elders, he also has a role in this organization that approaches a distinct office. He is the chairman of the elders. He ministers the Word as the teaching elder, while the other (ruling) elders only rarely preach or teach publicly. He is the pastor and addressed as such, but the rest of the elders are not. He is professionally trained and called from outside the church, but the rest of the eldership is composed of "lay" elders. All this being the case, the pastor carries the responsibility of giving overall leadership to the church and the elders.

I have attempted to avoid "loaded" language and to be fair in my presentation of the two ends of the spectrum. The reader, however, will probably not be surprised to learn that in my view a biblical organization of the eldership in plural-elder congregationalism lies somewhere in the middle of this spectrum. I believe that there are churches that are more or less accurately described by each of the models I have outlined above. I do not, however, have any particular churches in mind. Furthermore, I believe that most of plural-elder congregationalism practices an organization somewhere in the middle of this spectrum.

The other major issue has to do with the authority of the eldership. On this issue too there is a great deal of diversity of opinion and practice. There are those who have welded a "presbyterian view" of the rule of elders onto congregationalism (in the sense of independency). In this system the eldership appoints the officers of the church and exercises church discipline. The consent of the church is merely a desirable addition to the authoritative act of the elders in such matters. At the other end of the spectrum are those who hold that church discipline is enacted and officers are elected by the assembled church and reduce the elders to mere representatives of the assembly, administrators of the will of the church, and facilitators of group discussion.

As with the organization of the eldership, so also with the issue of its authority, I have attempted to be fair in the way I have described the two ends of the spectrum. I believe that there are churches that are more or less accurately described by each of the models I have outlined above. I do not, however, have any particular churches in mind. Furthermore, I believe most of plural-elder congregationalism practices an organization that moderates both of these extremes.

ITS DEVELOPMENT

Before I can come to the biblical defense and demonstration of the church government I have defined above, it is important to review its precedents in church history. Two periods are of particular importance to help us understand the characteristics and precedents of plural-elder congregationalism. The first is the period of the earliest post-apostolic church in the late first century and the first half of the second century. The writers of this period are known as the apostolic fathers. The second is the period of the Puritan movement in the British Isles and the American colonies from the late sixteenth through the seventeenth and even into the eighteenth century. The important writers here are the Puritan congregationalists including the Particular Baptists.

The Apostolic Fathers

The Apostolic Fathers are those writings supposed to have been written before AD 150 by the disciples of the apostles.[16] Perhaps the most important debate regarding the Apostolic Fathers has been over the issue of church government. The Anglican J. B. Lightfoot argued from the Apostolic Fathers that, though absent from the New Testament, episcopacy nevertheless had apostolic sanction. His argument is as follows. Evidence from the Apostolic Fathers attests single-bishop rule throughout the Roman province of Asia by early in the second century. John the apostle was active in Asia until the last decade of the first century. The institution of single-bishop rule must, therefore, have had the sanction of the apostle John and, thus, in this sense be apostolic.[17]

What is the evidence from the Apostolic Fathers that plays such a crucial part in this argument? It is the evidence found in Ignatius's *Seven Epistles* and, we must add, that evidence *alone*. Written possibly in 107, but no later than 116, these letters of Ignatius attest single-bishop rule in Antioch of Syria and (more to the point) in the cities of Ephesus, Tralles, Smyrna, Magnesia, and Philadelphia. To three of these cities John the apostle addressed letters in the book of Revelation. The following statement of Ignatius is representative of the view of church government found throughout his epistles:

> Now about my fellow slave Burrhus, your godly deacon, who has been richly blessed. I very much want him to stay with me. He will thus bring honor on you and the bishop. Crocus too, who is a credit both to God and to you, and who I received as a model of your love, altogether raised my spirits (May the Father of Jesus Christ

grant him a similar comfort!), as did Onesimus, Burrhus, Euplus, and Fronto. In them I saw and loved you all. May I always be glad about you, that is, if I deserve to be! It is right, then, for you to render all glory to Jesus Christ, seeing he has glorified you. Thus, united in your submission, and subject to the bishop and the presbytery, you will be real saints. . . . Yes, I had the good fortune to see you, in the persons of Damas your bishop (he's a credit to God!), and of your worthy presbyters, Bassus and Apollonius, and of my fellow slave, the deacon Zotion. I am delighted with him, because he submits to the bishop as to God's grace, and to the presbytery as to the law of Jesus Christ.[18]

Ignatius here assumes that in the local church at Ephesus there was a single bishop, several presbyters (or elders), and several deacons.

Lightfoot's argument, though problematic in other ways, gains plausibility from the Ignatian evidence. It has been subjected, however, to intense scrutiny and especially by Presbyterians anxious to show that the early churches were ruled by a plurality of elders. This scrutiny is well deserved. The astonishing fact is that there is no evidence at all for single-bishop rule of the local church in the rest of the Apostolic Fathers. It is completely absent from the other eight Apostolic Fathers mentioned above. Yet more, it is not only absent, but it is actually contradicted throughout the rest of the Apostolic Fathers by statements that indicate that churches were led by a plurality of bishops or presbyters. The two points to be observed in this evidence are that each local church is said to have a plurality of bishops and that the office of bishop and presbyter are equated.

Representative of the rest of the Apostolic Fathers are the statements made by Clement in his letter to the Corinthian church. The backdrop of this letter is a revolt in the Corinthian church that had removed their presbyters from office. Clement is writing on behalf of the church in Rome to exhort the Corinthian church to restore their former presbyters to office. As you will see, in all of this there is no mention either in Corinth or Rome of a single, supreme bishop:

Well, then, who of your number is noble, large-hearted, and full of love? Let him say: "If it is my fault that revolt, strife, and schism have arisen, I will leave, I will go away wherever you wish, and do what the congregation orders. Only let Christ's flock live in peace with their appointed presbyters. . . . They preached in country and city, and appointed their first converts, after testing them by the Spirit, to be the bishops and deacons of future believers. Nor was this any novelty, for Scripture had mentioned bishops and deacons long before. For this is what Scripture says somewhere: "I will appoint their bishops in righteousness and their deacons in faith." . . . Happy, indeed, are those presbyters who have already passed on, and who need not fear that anyone will remove them from their secure positions. But you, we observe, have removed a number of people, despite their good conduct, from a ministry they have fulfilled with honor and integrity. . . . And that is why you who are responsible for the revolt must submit to the presbyters. You must humble your hearts and be disciplined so that you repent.[19]

Also interesting because of the light it sheds on the church government at Rome from whence Clement was writing is the following quotation from the *Shepherd of Hermas*:

After that I saw a vision in my house, and that old woman came and asked me, if I had yet given the book to the presbyters. And I said that I had not. And then she said, "You have done well, for I have some words to add. But when I finish all the words, all the elect will then become acquainted with them through you. You will write therefore two books, and you will send the one to Clemens and the other to Grapte. And Clemens will send his to foreign countries, for permission has been granted to him to do so. And Grapte will admonish the widows and the orphans. But you will read the words in this city, along with the presbyters who preside over the Church."[20]

The evidence makes as clear as could be wished that the churches of Rome and Corinth did not have single bishops. Interestingly, in his letter to the Romans Ignatius did not attribute the single-bishop system to the church there.

What shall we make of all this? How shall we explain the apparent contrast between Ignatius and the rest of the apostolic fathers? It is clear from the church fathers that single-bishop rule was at a later date to hold universal sway in the ante-Nicene church. It is also admitted by Anglicans such as Lightfoot that the distinctive characteristics of episcopal church government are missing from the New Testament.[21] It is indisputable, then, that a dynamic existed in the early church that quickly developed episcopacy. Though Lightfoot attributes this development to apostolic sanction, this is not the only possible explanation. Ignatius undoubtedly was the single bishop of the large and ancient church in Antioch in Syria. It is not so clear that Ignatius was correct in attributing this system to the churches in Asia. It may be that he naively projected his fully developed single-bishop system onto churches where this system was not fully developed. Consider the proposed explanation of single-bishop rule provided by F. F. Bruce:

> One obvious consideration is that the emergence of a single leader was almost inevitable in the circumstances. Committee rule in general is weak unless there is a strong chairman. Quite often the strongest personality will become chairman in any case, and spiritual strength need not be excluded from his qualities. In practice such a man will become primus inter pares, and once his position is accepted and perpetuated, before long he will be regarded, in theory as well as in practice, as primus pure and simple. An outstanding early example of such a man who plainly acted as primus inter pares was James of Jerusalem.[22]

It may well be that the churches in Asia had *primus inter pares* (first among equals) systems and that Ignatius assumed that they were *primus* systems and that the leading elders were like himself the single bishops of the church. Such a mistake would be easy for the passionate Ignatius to make. It is also possible that Ignatius's single-minded and repeated insistence on the importance of the authority of the bishop may witness to the fact that his ideal was far from an ecclesiastical reality. F. F. Bruce asserts: "To Ignatius the monarchical episcopate is literally an idee fixe. The vehemence of Ignatius's protestations, in fact, is the plainest evidence that his view of the indispensable and supremely authoritative character of the office was far from being universally shared."[23]

What church government is, then, favored by the evidence from the Apostolic Fathers? Though the evidence may not allow dogmatism, it certainly suggests and is very consistent with plural-elder congregationalism.

In the first place, and in spite of Ignatius, the evidence suggests that the apostolic churches were led by a plurality of presbyters (elders) who were also called bishops (overseers) elected by the common suffrage of the church. The church in Corinth somehow removed (wrongly in Clement's opinion) their elders from office. He exhorts the evildoers to repent and submit to the judgment of the congregation.[24] The *Didache* confirms this congregational element in early church government by exhorting its readers to "elect for yourselves bishops and deacons who are a credit to the Lord, men who are gentle, generous, faithful, and well tried."[25] The first and fatal step away from this original system of church government and toward the monarchical episcopate of Catholicism happened when, contrary to the teaching of the New Testament, the title "bishop" was reserved for the leading presbyter in each church.

In the second place, the earliest evidence is certainly consistent with the idea of independency. Without doubt there was a strong sense of solidarity among the churches.[26] Clement manifests this sense of concern and responsibility for the church in Corinth in his letter to them. Yet Clement's concern is clearly limited to instructing, advising, and exhorting an independent church. There is no early evidence of the exercise of either a presbyterian or episcopal authority over local churches. Indeed, Lightfoot admits the independency of the earliest churches:

> Christendom had hitherto existed as a number of distinct isolated congregations, drawn in the same direction by a common faith and common sympathies, accidentally linked one with another by the personal influence and apostolic authority of their common teachers, but not bound together in a harmonious whole by any permanent external organization. Now at length this great result was brought about. The magnitude of the change effected during this period may be measured by the difference in the constitutions and conception of the Christian Church as presented in the Pastoral Epistles of St Paul and the letters of St Ignatius respectively.[27]

This is a startling admission, but even it does not go far enough. For even when we read the epistles of Ignatius, there is no evidence that a bishop possessed any authority outside his own (local) church. Similarly, there is no evidence in the Apostolic Fathers that elders possessed any but local church authority.

It is certainly true that the Apostolic Fathers manifest a church in transition to episcopacy. All the evidence, however, is consistent with the idea that the starting point of that transition and development was plural-elder congregationalism.

The Puritan Congregationalists
(Including the Particular Baptists)

Providence brought to pass a unique set of circumstances during the "Puritan Century"[28] in England. These unique circumstances resulted in the return to the visible church of the plural-elder congregationalism that was the polity of the earliest churches. What happened was this.

In most of Europe the Reformation of the sixteenth century was either persecuted into nonexistence by Roman Catholicism or resulted in the erection of Protestant or Reformed state churches. The Reformed version of these state churches was usually presbyterian in polity. The unique thing about England was that neither of these things happened. The original presbyterian convictions of the Reformed movement were never able quite to take over the Church of England. Neither, however, were they persecuted out of existence. As a result, some Puritans began to believe that neither the Episcopalians nor the Presbyterians had taken the purification of the church far enough. A whole branch of the Reformed and Puritan movement in England (and its American colonies) became congregational in their view of the local church. These congregationalists seem to have been of one mind that each local church should be independent.

About many other matters they came to disagree. Very early (in the first half of the seventeenth century) some in the Puritan congregational churches developed Baptist convictions and formed separate Particular (or Reformed) Baptist churches.[29] Differences also emerged over the relation of independent churches to the Church of England,[30] and over the issue of religious liberty.[31] Finally, and most importantly for our present purposes, there were congregationalists (known as Browne-ists after Robert Browne) who practiced a very thorough or radical form of democracy in their churches, while there were others who advocated a much stronger view of the rule of elders in the local church.[32] The many differences among the congregationalists requires that we be cautious with regard to sweeping pronouncements about their church polity that go beyond their shared independency.[33]

Congregationalism (in the sense of the independence of the local church) is, then, not really at issue with regard to Puritan congregationalism. What does need discussion is the issue of how these fathers of congregationalism believed the local church should govern itself. Two issues are involved.

First, did they believe that the local church should be led by a plurality of elders? Standing as they did in the Reformed tradition, the idea that the church should be led by a plurality of elders was their common inheritance. Shawn Wright declares:

> Every ecclesiastical entity which influenced the particular Baptists had a plurality of elders in each congregation. Plural elders was, for instance, the practice of John Calvin and the Reformed churches. More importantly, it was the practice of the Independent Congregationalists who were the forefathers of the Particular Baptists. The Presbyterians of Scotland, the divines at the Westminster Assembly, and even their theological nemeses, the General Baptists, had a plurality of elders.[34]

In the paragraph following, Wright avers that even early Particular Baptists practiced a plurality of elders.[35] Wright is correct in this summary of the situation.

The Puritan congregationalists certainly believed that each church should have, if possible, a plurality of elders. The dissenting brethren at the Westminster Assembly make this clear in their *Apologeticall Narration*.[36] John Owen remarked: "The pattern of the first churches constituted by the apostles, which it is our duty to imitate and follow as our rule, constantly expresseth and declares that *many elders* were appointed by them in every church."[37] The Savoy Declaration of Faith and Order (the confession of the English Puritan congregationalists) makes the same thing clear.[38]

The Particular Baptists also declared themselves in favor of a plurality of elders in the church. James Renihan, in a lengthy treatment of the subject of church officers, shows that there were various views of this matter, but he shows in some detail that the Particular Baptists of the late seventeenth century held with rare exception to a plurality of elders.[39] It is not surprising to discover, therefore, that the 1689 Baptist Confession suggests that each church should have a plurality of elders:

> A particular church, gathered and completely organized according to the mind of Christ, consists of officers and members; and the officers appointed by Christ to be chosen and set apart by the church (so called and gathered), for the peculiar administration of ordinances, and execution of power or duty, which he intrusts them with, or calls them to, to be continued to the end of the world, are bishops or elders, and deacons.[40]

It is true that ways of organizing this eldership varied. Many of the Puritan congregationalists organized their eldership into teaching elders and ruling elders in a very Presbyterian fashion.[41] While admitting that some Particular Baptists organized their elderships in this way, Renihan concludes: "The majority of the Particular Baptists were committed to a plurality and parity of elders in their churches."[42]

Second, what was the relationship of the authority of these elders to the power of the church as a whole? This is not an easy issue, but on this matter two impulses guided Puritan congregationalism and the Particular Baptists in the seventeenth century "in a middle way betwixt ... *Brownisme* and ... the *authoritative Presbyteriall Government*."[43]

The first impulse that guided Puritan congregationalism in all its forms was to safeguard the rights of the church to consent to the appointment of officers and to the discipline of the membership. Both the 1689 Baptist Confession[44] and the Savoy Declaration of Faith and Order adopted in 1658 by English congregationalists[45] expressly state that the election of officers requires the common suffrage of the church. The Savoy Declaration *also* requires the consent of the church for the addition of members to the church[46] and for acts of discipline.[47] The Cambridge Platform agreed upon by the messengers of New England congregationalists in 1648 requires that church officers be freely elected by the church and also teaches that churches have power to depose their officers in chapter 8, paragraphs 6 and 7. The same document in chapter 10, paragraph 5, also makes the admission and removal of officers the prerogative of the church.[48] These different documents cover the three most important wings of Puritan congregationalism.[49]

The second impulse that guided the Puritan congregationalists was their emphasis on the importance of the rule of elders in the local church. One could easily conclude from the emphasis in the formal documents of early congregationalism that they were committed to a thoroughly democratic view of church government with little real need for the rule of elders. This conclusion, however, would be quite misguided. The Cambridge Platform asserts in chapter 4, paragraph 2 that, while elders are not necessary to the very being of a local church, they are necessary to its well-being.[50] Renihan concurs on behalf of the Particular Baptists.[51] The Cambridge Platform also asserts that the government of the church is a mixed government, being first a monarchy (because of Christ the king), then a democracy (because of the power of the church), and finally an aristocracy (because of the rule of the presbytery). The *Apologeticall Narration* cites approvingly the opinions of Cartwright and Baynes who "place the power of excommunication in the Eldership of each particular church with the consent of the Church."[52] Renihan's account of how the eldership functioned in Particular Baptist churches with regard to church discipline makes clear that the elders exercised a crucial role.[53]

The thoroughly democratic congregationalism that characterizes many evangelical churches today is the unbalanced offspring of the more balanced congregationalism of a better ecclesiastical day. Without denying the power of the brotherhood, it balanced this power by means of its emphasis on a plurality of elders. The church and the eldership each exercised a role in church government that was critically necessary, even to the point that the Cambridge Platform could say that "no church act can be consummated, or perfected without the consent of both."[54] Thus, by the will of Christ, the king of the church, the church and the elders were to have distinct and interlocking roles to fulfill in the government of the local church.

ITS DEMONSTRATION

Four principles are involved in plural-elder congregationalism and must be demonstrated from the Scriptures. They are the Puritan, the Independent, the Democratic, and the Plural-elder principles.

The Puritan Principle

The Puritan principle asserts that we are given a model for church government in the Scriptures to which we are neither to add nor subtract. Deuteronomy 12:32 is, thus, applicable to church government: "Whatever I command you, you shall be careful to do; you shall not add to nor take away from it."

Along with the Puritans, I believe, however, that a distinction exists between the parts or elements of this church government and its circumstances or implementation. The 1689 Baptist Confession, in language substantially identical to the Westminster Confession and Savoy Declaration, asserts this unambiguously:

> There are some circumstances concerning the worship of God, and *government of the church*, common to human actions and societies, which are to be ordered by the light of nature and Christian prudence, according to the general rules of the Word, which are always to be observed. (italics mine)[55]

The thrust of this statement is that, though the written Word of God is sufficient to tell us how to worship God and govern the church, the circumstances and implementation of the biblical order are left to our sanctified common sense and the general principles of Scripture. Of course, they are! No book could be big enough to cover all such circumstances.

On the other hand, though the biblical model of church government obviously does not include its circumstances, the Puritan view is that God does regulate the government of his church with much more specificity than, for instance, civil government. No specific model of civil government is mandated in the Scriptures, but a clear form of church government is.[56] If the regulative principle means anything, it means that God places a special focus on the ordering of the church's worship and government.

To demonstrate the Puritan principle of church government completely would require that all the biblical arguments for the regulative principle of worship be marshaled. The limitations of the present discussion do not allow that.[57] Therefore, I will focus attention on two New Testament passages that address the issue of church government directly.

First Timothy 3:14–15 is the pivotal passage with regard to the theme of 1 Timothy. Here Paul tells Timothy why he has written:

> I am writing these things to you, hoping to come to you before long; but in case I am delayed, I write so that you will know how one ought to conduct himself in the household of God, which is the church of the living God, the pillar and support of the truth.

The significance of these verses for our purposes resides in two obvious features of the passage. First, Paul stresses the unique and glorious identity of the church. It is "the household of God, which is the church of the living God, the pillar and support of the truth." In this threefold description Paul makes clear that the church possesses a peculiar identity in the world. It, and it alone, is the "household [or house] of God." Its uniqueness resides in its peculiar association with the living God. It is the assembly or church of the living God. Thus, it has a unique and awesomely important vocation. It is "the pillar and support of the truth."

Second, Paul stresses that the church's unique identity has great, practical implications for Timothy's leadership of the church at Ephesus. "I write so that you will know how one ought to conduct himself in the household of God." This makes clear that the church identified by means of the threefold description in verse 15 comes to visible, local, and organized expression in the church at Ephesus. When we remember that this verse is telling Timothy why Paul is writing, this point is confirmed. In the preceding chapter Paul has instructed Timothy about the conduct of the assemblies of the church in Ephesus, addressing the place of prayer and of women. In chapter three itself Paul has given careful instruction about the officers of the church in Ephesus, addressing the qualifications for overseers and deacons in some detail.

From all this it is clear that the unique identity of the church requires a special conduct by Timothy and other Christians. Just as it would be outrageous to enter another man's home and without his permission begin to rearrange his furniture or discipline his children, how much more to think that we have the right to rearrange the specially arranged government of God's holy, glorious, and unique house!

The fact that there is a special, scripturally appointed government for the church is—if anything—even more clear in 2 Timothy 3:15–17:

> and that from childhood you have known the sacred writings which are able to give you the wisdom that leads to salvation through faith which is in Christ Jesus. All Scripture is inspired by God and profitable for teaching, for reproof, for correction, for training in righteousness; so that the man of God may be adequate, equipped for every good work.

This is the classic biblical assertion of the sufficiency of the Scriptures. It declares not only that the Scriptures are God-breathed (the literal meaning of "inspired by God" in verse 16), but also that the Scriptures have a multi-faceted profitability. They are profitable "for teaching, for reproof, for correction, for training in righteousness." Even having said all this, Paul does not feel that he has done justice to the sufficiency of the Scriptures. In verse 17 he adds that they make "the man of God . . . adequate, equipped for every good work." The word translated "adequate" by the NASB means according to one lexicon *qualified to perform some function* and according to another *fully qualified*. The word translated "equipped" is derived from the same root and thus conveys the same idea. The prefix attached to the root emphasizes the idea. It is variously defined to mean *fully qualified, completely adequate,* or *thoroughly prepared or furnished.*

If the description "man of God" refers to every Christian, the plain inference would certainly be that the Scriptures thoroughly equip Christians for the good work of organizing the church to the glory of God. To evade this implication would require one to defend the proposition that ordering the church is not scripturally a good work.

The fact is that the phrase "man of God" is probably *not* a reference to every Christian, but to Timothy and others like him in places of leadership among the people of God. First, this same description is used to refer to Timothy again in 1 Timothy 6:11. Second, the Old Testament uses the same term to refer to such men as Moses (Deut. 33:1; Ps. 90:1), David (2 Chron. 8:14), Elijah (2 Kings 1:9), and the prophets (1 Sam. 2:27). If the reference here is to the leader of God's people, the reference to the sufficiency of the Scriptures for ordering the life and government of the church is even clearer.

Earlier I mentioned that the Anglican argument for implied apostolic sanction for episcopacy was questionable for reasons that go beyond the historical evidence. The more basic problem with this argument is that it directly implies that the Scriptures are not sufficient to order the life of the church. It bases its view on a supposed apostolic sanction which it admits is outside the Scriptures. Worse yet, it actually presumes to alter the church government of the Bible by introducing a distinction between bishops and elders. Not only is this distinction nowhere found in the Scriptures, it is actually contradicted (as we will see below) by the evidence of Scripture.

The Puritan principle has even more important applications today. Worse than the Anglican argument is the presumption of the church growth experts who argue that a single pastor is necessary for maximum church growth.[58] To argue that a single, strong pastor nowhere mandated in the Scriptures is necessary on such pragmatic grounds is directly to imply the inadequacy of the Scriptures for the man of God and to impugn the wisdom of the God who gave the Scriptures.

Finally, the Puritan principle reminds us that the idea of the church as a monarchy is not just a nice sounding theory. The church is very really the house of God over which Christ the priest-king of his people rules through his Word (Heb. 3:6; 10:21). "The crown-rights of King Jesus in his church" take on practical meaning when we understand this. It is in the context of this principle and as its practical outworking that we must understand the meaning of the Independent, Democratic, and Plural-elder principles.

The Independent Principle

At the outset of this defense of the Independent principle, it is necessary to define carefully what it is and what it is not. I begin with what it is not. The Independent principle is not, of course, independence from Christ's authority as priest-king over the church. Neither does it mean that there is no universal church government. The church is built on the foundation of the apostles and prophets with Jesus Christ himself as the cornerstone.

Christ, the priest-king, and his apostles are universal church officers and constitute the true government of the universal church.

The Independent principle does not mean that each church is self-sufficient in its gifts and graces with no need of assistance from other local churches. In line with this reality, the Independent churches have historically manifested their sense of need for close communion with one another in many ways. The Particular Baptists frequently formed formal associations and manifested fellowship among local churches in a wide variety of ways.[59] The Puritan congregationalists of England were not hesitant to speak of meeting in occasional synods or councils.[60] The New England congregationalists probably carried these principles even further by means of their ministerial consociations, but certainly agreed with their English brethren.[61] The proceedings of these associations, consociations, synods, and councils were, of course, advisory in character. They exercised no authority or jurisdiction over the internal affairs of the local church.[62]

What, then, is the Independent principle? It may be identified negatively and positively. Negatively, it means that there is no ecclesiastical authority in the visible church on earth with jurisdiction over the local church. The local church is directly accountable to Christ and the apostles in heaven and, thus, independent of all earthly ecclesiastical authority. Positively, it means that each local church has been given sufficient authority to order its worship and discipline. In the words of chapter 26 and paragraph 7 of the 1689 Baptist Confession:

> To each of these churches thus gathered, according to his mind declared in his word, he hath given all that power and authority, which is in any way needful for their carrying on that order in worship and discipline, which he hath instituted for them to observe; with commands and rules for the due and right exerting, and executing of that power.[63]

Having clarified the meaning of the Independent principle, we are now in a position to examine its biblical basis. We will do so, first, by showing the biblical basis of the paragraph cited above from the 1689 Baptist Confession. This paragraph says five things about the authority given to the local church. Each of these five points is supported by the two major scriptural passages on exercising church discipline (Matt. 18:15–20; 1 Cor. 5:1–13, especially verses 4 and 5). No greater exercise of church power is conceivable. If the local church is competent for church discipline, then it is competent to all lesser exercises of authority. In these passages the *defined recipient* of this power is the local church. Even the local church at Corinth with all its problems possesses this power. In neither passage are the elders of the church even mentioned. On the other hand, there is repeated reference to the church and its assemblies. Its *complete sufficiency* is suggested by the mention of the keys of the kingdom in Matthew 18:18–19. In 1 Corinthians 5 this sufficiency is suggested by the assertion that in their assembly the power of the Lord Jesus was present (v. 4) and by the command to remove the wicked man in vv. 7, 13. The *origin* of this power is clearly Christ himself (Matt. 18:20; 1 Cor. 5:3–5). Christ exercises this power immediately through the local church with no indication of any mediating authority. The *specified purpose* of this power includes even the excommunication of a member of the church (Matt. 18:17; 1 Cor. 5:7, 13), but worship is also suggested by Matthew 18:20. Its *regulated execution* is clearly indicated by the detailed rules for its exercise given in Matthew 18:15–17; 1 Corinthians 5:4, 11; and 2 Corinthians 2:6–8.

Suggestive evidence for the independence of the local church comes from the letters to the seven churches of Asia in Revelation 2–3. Here the subject of church discipline is repeatedly emphasized by Christ, but each church is held solely responsible for its own members and their discipline. Christ never asserts, assumes, or implies that the other churches may exercise church discipline by intervening in another church's affairs. The entire group is not held responsible or told to act for the discipline of Laodicea. This is not to deny the responsibility one local church may have to call another to repentance for failure to exercise appropriate discipline. Remember Clement's letter to the church at Corinth. This, however, is plainly different than calling a council and executing the discipline needed through the authority of that council.[64]

More evidence for the independence of the local church may be derived from passages where elders and their authority and responsibilities are associated with particular local churches. For instance, in Acts 20:28 the elders of Ephesus (see v. 17) are told to "be on guard for yourselves and for all the flock, *among which the Holy Spirit has made you overseers*" (italics mine). Similarly, the command to the church at Thessalonica is, "But we request of you, brethren, that you appreciate those who diligently labor *among you*, and have charge *over you* in the Lord and give *you* instruction" (1 Thess. 5:12, italics mine).

Now such evidence will probably not be appreciated unless we consider the issue of the burden of proof in this matter. The Puritan principle (which presbyterians historically accept) is that there is a divinely mandated form of church government given in the Scriptures. Aside from mere circumstances, nothing is to be added to or subtracted from this form of church government. Now we have clear evidence that elders were to oversee their own flocks. We have clear evidence that local churches had authority to maintain the purity of their own assemblies. Where, however, is the warrant or precedent for elders ruling or exercising discipline in other churches? The burden of proof is on the presbyterian view, especially in light of the Puritan principle.

The key passage upon which presbyterians seek to base their view is Acts 15.[65] If this passage does not clearly support their view, they cannot make their case. Essentially, the presbyterian argument from Acts 15 rests on two points. First, the gathering in Jerusalem exercised authority over many different local churches. This point is certainly correct (Acts 15:23; 16:4). Second, the gathering in Jerusalem was a church council or synod constituted by elders representing many different local churches. It is this point which must be disputed.

It is true that "elders" were *subordinately* involved in the authoritative decision (Acts 15:23; 16:4), but so also was the whole church (15:22). Thus, if this passage supports the government of many churches by a council of elders, it also supports the government of many churches by whole congregations.[66] It is not true, however, nor can it be proven that this council was composed of the elders of many churches or even two churches. There is no evidence that even Paul and Barnabas were among "the apostles and elders" who made the decision (15:2, 4, 6, 22–23; 16:4). In fact, Acts 15:2, 4 and 16:4 specifically exclude Paul and Barnabas from the elders in view. Furthermore, absolutely no proof exists that any of the elders of the many other churches to whom the decrees were delivered were present.

For many reasons the church of Jerusalem had a unique authority in redemptive history unparalleled by any other church.

Hence, it cannot, and its elders cannot, be made an example for other later and lesser churches. (1) Chiefly, it was the church where the twelve apostles dwelt. Their influence and presence gave her official statements authority over all the churches. (2) It was the first and mother church of Christianity. (3) Its leaders (even without counting the Twelve) were the original disciples and followers of Christ. Elders such as James, the half-brother of our Lord, though not among the original twelve apostles, exercised an authority that can only be called apostolic (Gal. 2:9; 1 Cor. 15:7).

Bottom line, Acts 15 cannot sustain the burden of proof that presbyterians place upon it. It was not a gathering of the elders of many churches. It exercised authority over the churches, not for this reason, but because it had a unique place in redemptive history and because of its apostolic leadership. The independence of the local church is taught in the Scriptures. No other view has either precedent or warrant in the Scriptures.

The Democratic Principle

I use the adjective "democratic" with some hesitation. In our era, democracy as a form of government is opposed to both monarchy and aristocracy. I believe, as this chapter has already made clear, that in biblical church government democracy is qualified by the crown-rights of King Jesus in his church and also by the plural-elder principle. Thus, church democracy is not the same as popular sovereignty. Democracy in the present context is the right of the church to decide on the basis of the Bible what the will of the King is. It is not the right to vote as one pleases regardless of the will of the King.

Nevertheless, the Bible does recognize that the membership of the church has a foundational and critical role to play in the major decisions of church life. The matter in which this is most clear is corrective church discipline, including the actual putting of someone out of the church. The key texts on this subject (Matt. 18:15–20; 1 Cor. 5:1–13) have already been discussed in relation to the Independent principle.[67] The implication of the authority of the church to terminate membership is that it has the right to receive or admit new members.[68]

The right to excommunicate is so basic and important that we may infer from it that the church by its common suffrage has the right to elect its own officers. The right to elect its own officers is confirmed by the manner in which the twelve apostles led the church to elect the seven (whom I think were clearly the first deacons). Acts 6:1–7 contains the account. Here, in spite of their presence in the midst of the church, the Twelve summon the "congregation of the disciples" (v. 2) and urge them to "select from among you seven men of good reputation" (v. 3). Consequently, "the whole congregation . . . chose Stephen" and the rest of the seven (v. 5).[69] The right of the church to elect officers implies the right of the church to remove officers that disqualify themselves.

I have used the word "election," however, with reservation. To modern ears an election connotes several things which clearly deviate from the Word of God. For instance, there is no scriptural instance in which two or more men compete with each other for votes in order that one of them should be elected to office. There is no basis for the idea that election is an act of sovereign and autonomous authority or that it is the ultimate source of power in the church. Again, this idea is completely contrary to the scriptural idea. We have no biblical right to vote for whomever we please. In Acts 6, 1 Timothy 3, and Titus 1 the apostolic qualifications for office in the local church are described. The church must submit to these qualifications in the exercise of their voting privileges. They may not refuse or remove a man who is qualified. They may not retain a man who is unqualified. The term "election" is used only to epitomize what the confessions mean when they say that calling to an office in the church must be "by the common suffrage of the church itself."

A final direction in which support for the Democratic principle may be sought is in the priesthood of all believers (1 Peter 2:5, 9; Rev. 1:6; 5:10; 20:6) and the ministry that the New Testament calls them to exercise to one another (Rom. 15:14; 1 Thess. 5:12, 14). The dignity of every believer is such a pervasive emphasis of the New Testament that we would be surprised if their consent was not required in the matters discussed above. Even, therefore, without the explicit passages cited above, we might have good ground to suppose that the consent of the church was necessary in matters of the church's membership and officers.

The practical implications of the Democratic principle are many. Systems of church government that do not regard the consent of the church as necessary for the expulsion of members and the election of officers have deviated from the clear teaching of the New Testament. These systems may be an understandable reaction against the radical, democratic congregationalism typical of too many evangelical churches in our day. In the end, however, they will be found to be as susceptible to abuse as the system which they reacted against.

If the membership of the church is so critically involved in the government of the church, the importance of maintaining the purity of the church's membership cannot be underestimated. Biblical standards must be upheld for entrance into the church and continuance in the church.

Assuming this, pastors must resist the tendency to distrust the membership of the church. They must not seek to vest inordinate authority in themselves out of such mistrust. They must give credit for wisdom to a well-instructed and spiritual church.

The Plural-elder Principle

In the discussion of the distinctions within plural-elder congregationalism, I isolated two issues of primary importance: internal organization and the ecclesiastical authority of the eldership. These two issues will be the focus of this demonstration of the Plural-elder principle.

The Internal Organization of the Eldership

A comprehensive view of the internal organization of the eldership may be secured by a consideration of three matters: the plurality, the parity, and the diversity of elders.

The plurality of elders in local churches in the New Testament is not something that is doubtful.[70] We know of no church in the New Testament that had only a single elder.[71] On the other hand, we know of many churches with a plurality of elders: Jerusalem (Acts 11:30), Antioch in Syria (13:1), Lystra, Iconium, Pisidian Antioch (14:23), Ephesus (20:17), the churches of Crete (Titus 1:5), the churches of the Jewish dispersion to whom James wrote (James 5:14), probably the churches to whom Peter wrote in Pontus, Galatia, Cappadocia, Asia, and Bythinia (1 Peter 5:1–2), Philippi (Phil. 1:1), probably the churches to whom Hebrews was written (Heb. 13:7, 17, 24), and finally the unidentified church whose presbytery laid hands on Timothy (1 Tim. 4:14).

Opposed to this massive evidence for a plurality of elders, the arguments for a single elder in each church appear weak indeed.[72] James, the brother of the Lord, is sometimes cited in this regard, but we know that there was a plurality of elders in Jerusalem (Acts 11:30; 15:2; etc.). The angels of the seven churches (Rev. 1:20–3:14) are used in this way, but we know, for instance, that there was a plurality of elders in Ephesus (Acts 20:17). Some notice that in 1 Timothy 3:2 and Titus 1:7 "overseer" is singular, while in 1 Timothy 3:8 "deacons" is plural. However we are to account for this interesting fact, it cannot imply a single overseer or elder in each church. The immediate context of 1 Timothy 3:2 speaks of the *office of overseer* (v. 1), implying (what is clear from the rest of 1 Timothy) that there were a plurality of elders in the church at Ephesus (5:17). The immediate context of Titus 1:7 makes clear that elders were to be appointed in every city (v. 5).[73]

In light of the uniform and massive New Testament evidence for a plurality of elders in every local church, it is natural to ask how we should regard a church with only a single elder. Two responses to this question may be offered on the basis of the New Testament evidence. First, we may concede that a lack of a plurality of elders is not necessarily sinful. First Timothy 3:1–7 and Titus 1:5–9 absolutely require certain qualifications for the office of elder; for example, he *must be* above reproach (vv. 2 and 7, respectively). The plain assumption of these passages is that not every Christian man possesses these qualifications. Hence, it might be possible in some local churches that no men or only one man might meet those qualifications at any given time. To appoint to office someone who lacks the apostolic qualifications would be sinful. Thus, the lack of a plurality may in some rare situations actually be a result of obedience to Christ.

On the other hand, we must not allow this concession to disguise the real abnormality of a lack of plurality.[74] A plurality of elders in each local church is a matter both of apostolic precedent (Acts 14:23) and precept (Titus 1:5). The lack of a plurality of elders in any church constitutes a real deficiency in its government (Titus 1:5). To suppose that it is no problem to be without such a plurality is to impugn the wisdom of the Christ who led the apostles to appoint such a plurality in the New Testament churches.[75] Churches that lack a plurality of elders should not be complacent about the deficiency in their government. They should pray for a plurality of elders. They should use means to see a plurality raised up. If the lack is prolonged, they should seek the temporary assistance of the elders of a more fully organized church to defeat the dangers inherent in a church with only one elder.[76]

The parity of elders, as I am using it here, refers to their equality in office and authority. By advocating the parity of elders I am saying that every elder has the same authority or rule in the church. I am not saying that each elder has the same influence or power. Sheer influence and official authority are two different things in the Bible. Absalom wielded great power or influence in Israel when he rebelled against David, but David still possessed the official rule. Thus, as we shall see, parity of office may coexist with great diversity of influence.

The evidence for the parity of the elders is that the words for "elder," overseer," and "shepherd" all refer to the same office in the New Testament.[77] There is no distinction between elders and bishop in the manner of many in the early church. There is no distinction between elders and pastor in the manner of many in the modern church.

That elders and overseers are identical in the New Testament is evident in a number of passages. In Acts 20:17 Paul calls for the elders of the church. When they arrive, he refers to them as overseers (v. 28). In Titus 1:5 Paul commands that elders be appointed in every church and then proceeds to give qualifications for those elders whom he now calls overseers (v. 7). In 1 Peter 5:1–2 the elders are exhorted to exercise oversight.[78] The word used in verse 2 is the verb that means "to oversee" and comes from the same root as the word for "overseer." Even Anglicans, who would have a vested interest in finding a distinction between bishops (overseers) and elders in the New Testament, admit that it is absent there.[79]

More controversial today is the idea that shepherds (pastors) are identical with elders or overseers. The evidence is, however, compelling. First Peter 5:1–2 not only tells elders to be overseers (exercising oversight) but to shepherd (pastor) the flock of God. Acts 20:28 not only describes the elders of the church at Ephesus as overseers, it also commands them to "shepherd [or pastor] the church of God." The arguments used against the equivalence of shepherd with elder and overseer by those who desire to make a distinction between elders and shepherds only serve to illustrate the desperateness of their cause. They argue that, though the verb "to shepherd" is used of the duty of elders and overseers in Acts 20 and 1 Peter 5, the noun is not used.[80] The force of this argument is that though elders and overseers are told to shepherd the flock of God, yet they are not shepherds. This is like saying that my job is writing books, but I am not a writer. This unlikely conclusion might lead one to expect that the noun is used many times of the pastoral office in the New Testament and in ways that support a distinction between shepherds and elders. Actually, the opposite is the case. The noun "shepherd" or "pastor" is used only once of the office of shepherd in the church. That text is Ephesians 4:11 where Paul refers to the pastor-teachers that Christ has given as gifts to his church. But it also offers no contrast or distinction between pastor-teachers and elders.

Perhaps those who use this passage to teach such a distinction do so because they assume that not all elders are teachers. Because they believe that not all elders are teachers, but are rather "ruling elders," they assume that there must be a distinction in Ephesians 4:11 between pastor-teachers and the rest of the (assumedly non-teaching) elders.

Six passages are important in assessing the distinction between teaching and ruling elders. James 3:1 warns, "Let not many of you become teachers, my brethren, knowing that as such we will incur a stricter judgment." No distinction is instituted in this passage between teachers and other elders. Acts 13:1 speaks of the leadership of the church in Antioch as consisting of "prophets and teachers." Each of the leaders of the church at Antioch, then, was one who proclaimed the Word of God as a matter of gift and office. The only difference is that some were prophets and others were teachers. There is no distinction here between teachers and other elders. Romans 12:7 deals with spiritual gifts and not directly with the subject of office in the church (see vv. 3, 6). In verses 7 and 8 the apostle distinguishes the gifts of teaching, leading, and exhorting. This distinction has seemed to some to justify the idea of a distinction between a ruling elder and a teaching elder. Office and gift—as everyone must recognize—are two different things. In light of 1 Timothy 3:1–7, it is clear that every elder is required to be able to teach[81] and to rule[82] and, thus, in some measure must possess both gifts.[83] Titus 1:5–9 confirms the interpretation of 1 Timothy 3. In verses 9–11 Paul insists that the elder must hold sound doctrine and be able to use it both positively and polemically: "to exhort in sound doctrine and to refute those who contradict." Clearly, the elder-overseer-steward of Titus 1 must be a teacher.[84]

Sixth and last is 1 Timothy 5:17. It is the most important passage in the debate about teaching and ruling elders and the pastor/elder distinction. Clearly, it makes no distinction between the office of pastor and other elders.[85] Obvious features of the passage should waken us to the realization that this passage does not teach the common pastor/elder distinction. It is clear that more than one financially supported elder who labors in the Word and in doctrine is contemplated: "*those* who work hard at preaching and teaching." It is also clear that other elders who do not labor in the Word and in doctrine may be financially supported. Double honor (generous financial support) is for all who rule well. It is only *especially* for those who work hard at preaching and teaching.

Neither does 1 Timothy 5:17 make a distinction between two types or orders of elders: teaching elders and ruling elders. Its distinction is between elders who rule well and those who labor in the Word and doctrine.[86] This is not the teaching and ruling elder distinction. The passage never asserts that the only elders who teach are "those who work hard at preaching and teaching." Laboring in the Word and doctrine clearly refers to an *abundance* of labor in the work of teaching that surpasses that of even other well-ruling elders. The contrast is not between no teaching and teaching. It is between some teaching and a greater degree of teaching.[87]

The inevitable conclusion is that there is no warrant for a distinction between the office of pastor and the office of elder in the New Testament. Neither is the terminology which distinguishes teaching and ruling elders a good way of describing what the New Testament teaches with regard to the internal organization of the eldership. All elders are overseers and pastor-teachers. All elders must have the gifts of leadership and teaching.

The diversity of elders is clearly taught in the Scriptures. It is not a diversity with regard to office or authority, as we have seen, but a diversity of spiritual gift, financial support, and actual influence. In the first place, the Bible, church history, and experience show that elders may have greatly varying gifts. The New Testament emphasizes the breadth of spiritual gifts and the sovereignty of God in imparting those gifts (Rom. 12:3–8; 1 Cor. 12:4–31; Eph. 4:11; 1 Peter 4:10–11). There are several different gifts important specifically for the eldership.[88] God gives these spiritual gifts in varying degrees (Matt. 25:14–15).

The New Testament also teaches a diversity in the matter of financial support. Some elders may be supported by the church. Other elders may work at another vocation to support themselves. The key text here is, of course, 1 Timothy 5:17. Double honor in that text means generous financial support.[89] This financial support of the elders is, however, not to be indiscriminately divided among all elders. Timothy and the church at Ephesus under his leadership are to focus that financial support on the elders who rule well. Among those who rule well financial support is especially to be given to those who work hard at preaching and teaching. The measure of a man's spiritual gifts in ruling and especially teaching and preaching (as well as his experience, maturity, diligence, and godliness) is related to the matter of financial support.[90]

It is also clear that there may be great diversity in a man's actual influence. Paul labored more than all the apostles and so had a proportionately greater influence (1 Cor. 15:10). It seems clear that Peter exercised a greater influence than many of the other apostles (Matt. 16:18; Acts 1:15; 2:14, 38; 3:1).

The New Testament, then, teaches the plurality, parity, and diversity of elders in the local church. The distribution of responsibilities and ministries must be guided by each of these three principles. The diversity of gift, influence, and support must not disguise the parity of official authority belonging to each elder.[91] The parity and plurality of the elders should not suppress the implications of the diversity of elders in the distribution of the responsibilities and ministries in the church. Parity of office does not require an artificial equality in the distribution of ministry or financial support. Rather, Christ's sovereignty in giving a diversity of gifts should be acknowledged in such matters.[92]

The Ecclesiastical Authority of the Eldership

The Democratic principle discussed earlier might seem to require a purely democratic form of church government. We have seen that the Bible teaches that a church may exist without elders (Acts 14:23). We have seen that the common suffrage of the church is crucial in matters of church discipline and the election of officers.

The pure democracy apparently implied by such biblical facts and practiced by many evangelical churches today represents, however, a very one-sided view of the relevant New Testament data. It seizes upon the democratic element in New Testament church government and forgets that there are in biblical church government elements of monarchy and aristocracy as well.

The radically democratic congregationalism of the contemporary church forgets that Christ is king of the church and rules it through the Word of God and, in particular, the teaching of his apostles. This means that the logical deductions we make about church government from our experience of democracy must give way to the decrees of the King about the government of the church. The Word of God has a tendency to put things together that we in our human wisdom tend to regard as contradictory. Thus, in spite of the apparently self-sufficient democracy suggested by the facts cited in connection with the Democratic principle, the Word of God appoints that the church should have a class of ruling officers.

The New Testament teaches that the church has officers with real authority and thus supplements the democracy of the church with what the Puritans called the aristocracy of the eldership. Two things in particular manifest the real authority exercised by the eldership: the authoritative descriptions of these officers and the divine origin of these officers.

There are seven descriptions of the ruling officers of the church. Each of these descriptive names for these officers manifests the real authority they possess.

1. He is an *elder* (*presbyteros*). This is the most common name for this officer and is used in many places. In Acts 11:30 and 1 Timothy 5:17 the authority of elders is clearly implied. This name suggests that he is a member of the ruling council of the church.
2. He is an *overseer* (*episkopos*). This is the next most common name for the office (cf. 1 Peter 2:25 where it is used of Christ and translated, "guardian"). This name suggests that the elder is a watchman, guardian, and public officer sent by a higher authority to watch over his affairs.

3. He is a *shepherd* (*poimen*). The elder is frequently pictured as a shepherd of a flock of sheep (Acts 20:28; Eph. 4:11; 1 Peter 5:2).
4. The elder is several times described as a *leader* (from the verb, *hegeomai*, which sometimes means to lead or to govern; cf. Heb. 13:7, 17, 24). A related word is used of the governors sent by emperors to rule over the different provinces of their empires (1 Peter 2:14).
5. The elder is also sometimes described as a *teacher* (*didaskolos*). Elders are called pastor-teachers in Ephesians 4:11.
6. The elder is also described as a *steward* (*oikonomos*; cf. Titus 1:7). The steward is described as one whom the master puts in charge of other servants in order to provide for them in Luke 12:42 and is translated "city treasurer" in Romans 16:23.
7. The elder is also depicted as a *parent* in 1 Timothy 3:4–5.

Each of these descriptive names for the ruling office in the church designate it in one way or another as a position of authority. Several of them suggest that the authority of this ruling office is delegated from a higher authority—Christ. It is this significant implication which we must now consider.

The divine origin of true elders must also be emphasized. Acts 20:28 emphasizes this with the words "the Holy Spirit has made you overseers." Ephesians 4:11 emphasizes that pastor-teachers are gifts of Christ. Thus, the authority of true elders finds its origin in the activity of the risen Christ and the Spirit whom he has poured out on the church.

Today, elders are thought of as representatives of the church. Though they may act as its representatives, the evidence makes clear that they are not *mere* representatives. The descriptive names given to the office suggest that they have an authority far greater. Think of the names: overseer, leader or governor, and steward. And, as already noted, Acts 20:28 and Ephesians 4:11 suggest an authority not human but divine in origin. Without in any way contradicting the common suffrage of the church in electing elders, this puts their election in a new light. We now see that the church is by its common suffrage gratefully receiving a gift given it by its King! Provided that the person being considered is such a gift, the church is obliged to accept it.

The real authority of the elders over the church is very practical. The Puritan principle discussed above means, as we have seen, that a specific church government and form of worship are given the church by God. Neither the church nor its elders are permitted to alter these forms. Thus, the authority of the eldership is not a legislative power to add to the laws of God. The regulative principle of the church does not legislate the circumstances or application of church government or worship. With regard to such things, the elders have authority to arrange the circumstances of the church's life. In many cases the arrangements for such circumstances need not be brought to the church. It may, however, be wise to bring more major decisions before the church. In such cases the response of the church to its elders must be characterized by submission to its lawful rulers (1 Thess. 5:12; Heb. 13:17). Only if elders recommend something contrary to the Scriptures or that transgresses the boundaries of another human authority's jurisdiction should members of the church feel at liberty to oppose their recommendations. Of course, constructive suggestions and helpful comments should always be welcome.

The elders of the church oversee its finances. They are its stewards (Luke 12:42; Rom. 16:23) and overseers. Thus, the offering for the church in Jerusalem was brought to its elders (Acts 11:30). The deacons do not control the finances of the church. They administer them for the elders.

Even more important than these matters is the emphasis of the evidence presented on the responsibility and authority of the elders to lead the church by teaching it the Word of God.[93] This is implied especially by the descriptions of the elders as shepherds (who feed the flock), stewards (who give the other servants their rations at the proper time), and teachers (who, of course, teach). It is preeminently through this means that the eldership gives leadership to the sheep of Christ who will hear his voice!

Finally, it is clear that even in church discipline and the election of officers where the New Testament requires the voice of the church, the elders are to lead. Clearly, their authority requires them to present evidence and make recommendations in matters of church discipline. Clearly, their duty requires that they screen potential officers, recommend them to the church, and appoint them to office when elected (1 Tim. 5:22).[94]

The tenor of the New Testament's teaching regarding the ecclesiastical authority of elders is well stated by the Cambridge Platform:

> From the premisses, namely, that the ordinary powr of Government belonging only to the elders, powr of priviledg remaineth with the brotherhood, (as powr of judgment in matters of cenure, & powr of liberty, in matters of liberty:) It followth, that in an organizd Church, & right administration; all church acts, proceed after the manner of a mixt administration, so as no church act can be consummated, or perfected without the consent of both.[95]

The *consent of both* the church and its eldership (and, thus, the unity of the church) is required for every act where the church as a whole has a voice.

AN EPISCOPALIAN'S RESPONSE

Peter Toon

It is amazing to me that among those who make the claim that sacred Scripture is authoritative not only for faith and morals but also for the details of church government, there is no agreement as to precisely the church polity presented and taught by our Lord and his apostles. If the sovereign Lord had intended to make the precise details of church government part of the apostolic message, then he would have surely caused his servants to make the matter clear to all of sound mind.

Waldron belabors reasoning to find in the Bible that form of church government he thinks is the best; but, to achieve this end he has to disagree with writers and church traditions who begin from the same point as he does—i.e., that Scripture is authoritative for polity and provides such to the godly reader.

One problem that stares all of us in the face is that the godly readers (or professors with their Ph.D.'s using the most advanced exegetical tools) do not agree on what the New Testament says and how it is to be interpreted and collated. Further, it appears that most seem to find therein what they had in their minds before they began to look at the documents!

Speaking generally, I would say that all presentations of congregationalism and presbyterianism as supposedly biblically mandated are only possible given the political history of western Europe and then North America. It is inconceivable that they could have been written in, say, the fourth century, because there was not the general social and political background or the available mindset to provide the necessary conditions to produce them.

ON THE APOSTOLIC FATHERS

But let us concentrate on what Waldron says. Of the situation at the beginning of the second century, he writes: "In the first place, and in spite of Ignatius, the evidence suggests that the apostolic churches were led by a plurality of presbyters (elders) who were also called bishops (overseers) elected by the common suffrage of the church."And also: "The first and fatal step away from this original system of church government and toward the monarchical episcopate of Catholicism happened when, contrary to the teaching of the New Testament, the title 'bishop' was reserved for the leading presbyter in each church."

In response, I would say that he should not have written "in spite of Ignatius." His *Letters* are important evidence for the single bishop in one great center, Antioch, and for single bishops in other centers. The obvious prejudice of the writer is seen when he writes of the "fatal step away from this original system" (i.e., a system he has deduced from the first century evidence to equate with his preferred seventeenth-century system). The word "fatal" which is to be linked with "Catholicism" (later in the sentence) tells us where his mind is—it is in the battles between Roman Catholics and Protestants from the sixteenth century onward! He seems to think that it is not necessary to go past the writers from the very earliest part of the second century to advance his thesis. Even in dealing with the few nonbiblical authors, he pays little attention to the massive amount of patristic scholarship available.

Note also that he states that the monarchical episcopate as found in Ignatius's teaching is "contrary to the teaching of the New Testament." I ask: Was there a canon of the New Testament in the time of Ignatius of Antioch? The Canon evolved slowly and was not truly *the* Canon for another century or more. Do we know what parts of the later New Testament that Ignatius possessed? Here we have an author assuming first that the New Testament was available (seemingly as we have it) in the year AD 120 or so, then assuming that it would be studied in much the same way as it is in Protestant seminaries in North America, and then coming to conclusions on the basis of these two false premises.

Had he gone a little further into the second-century evidence, and had he used some of the tremendous amount of critical texts and scholarship on the apostolic fathers and the second-century church that has appeared since Bishop Light-foot's edition of Ignatius in 1885, then I think that he would not have been able with integrity to write what he has about this critical period—the post-apostolic period—of the church of God. He certainly could not have made the claims that he does for the church polity of that period.

Even so, he draws out of the great Dr. Lightfoot more than is reasonable to draw. He claims that the bishop admits the independency of the earliest churches in these words:

> Christendom had hitherto existed as a number of distinct isolated congregations, drawn in the same direction by a common faith and common sympathies, accidentally linked one with another by the personal influence and apostolic authority of their common teachers, but not bound together in a harmonious whole by any permanent external organization. Now at length this great result was brought about. The magnitude of the change effected during this period may be measured by the difference in the constitutions and conception of the Christian Church as presented in the Pastoral Epistles of St Paul and the letters of St Ignatius respectively.

My own reading of Lightfoot is that he does not admit any independency (in the sense of the word used by Waldron) but seeks to describe honestly the situation of a small but expanding new society, the church of God, in a hostile and difficult environment, where contact between local churches was often very difficult. Further, contra Waldron, Bishop Ignatius did not claim any authority over the churches to which he wrote as he traveled through Asia Minor on his way to Rome. In fact, no bishop in the early days claimed authority over any congregations other than those that were in his (what was later called) diocese (a city church with dependent congregations).

Waldron is right when he says: "It is certainly true that the Apostolic Fathers manifest a church in transition to episcopacy." That is all I would claim before asking readers to move into the second century and there discover that the episcopal system very soon became universal as guided by the Lord. However, Waldron is completely off the mark when he adds, "All the evidence, however, is consistent with the idea that the starting point of that transition and development was plural-elder congregationalism." In one word, such a claim is *false*!

ON THE REST OF CHURCH HISTORY

As do others, Waldron takes virtually no account of the history of the early church, not even up to the point where it formally accepted and fixed the canon of the New Testament. Had he asked the question, "How did those who were responsible for finalizing the content of the canon of the New Testament see the matter of church polity and government?" his answer would have been very different than the one he got from his study of New Testament documents within the context of the competitive supermarket of American denominations. Although he does not state this, he seems to work on the assumption that the Holy Ghost's guidance of the church as she moved into the Roman Empire (often through persecution and much tribulation) ceased about AD 120. That guidance apparently returned to some parts of the church at the end of the Middle Ages, with the Renaissance and Reformation.

The fact of the matter is exceedingly clear. The church that collected the documents that we now call the New Testament and accepted their authority as the new canon along with the older canon of the Hebrew Bible, was a church whose government was nothing like the congregational system of the writer. And further, the church that came through the great persecutions, that established the first day of the week as the day for Christian worship, that faced the exceedingly powerful heresies of Gnosticism and Arianism, and that met in council to give us the great dogmas of the Holy Trinity and the person of Christ, was not governed in the way that the writer tells us is the scriptural blueprint.

How could the councils of Nicea (325), Constantinople (381), and Chalcedon (451) have gotten right the exposition of the great verities of the Christian religion and be so out of line on church government? How is it that the powerfully scriptural minds of the Cappadocian fathers, of Chrysostom, of Augustine, and many other spiritual and pastoral giants never saw the great error of their ways when they assumed that the episcopal system is in accord with the mind of the Lord Jesus and his paraclete, the Holy Ghost?

I propose and submit that the only way that one can reasonably discern what the mind of the Lord was/is for church government is to see how those who succeeded the apostles and their successors were led by the Holy Ghost to implement church polity in the real conditions of the cities and towns of the Roman Empire during times when they were often opposed by Jew and Gentile alike and when they were living not in luxury but in poverty, persecution, and privation. If one proceeds in this manner then one comes to a clear answer—in fact all who proceed in this way come to the same answer!—the basic episcopal system. That is, there is one bishop in one church (later diocese) assisted by presbyters and deacons, and that this church (later diocese) is in fellowship with other such churches. In all cases there is a sense of apostolic succession—succession in continuing the teaching of the apostles and succession in terms of church centers and ordinations that link the apostles with their successors.

When the episcopal system was in place from the second century onward, those who thought about it and explained it assumed that it was wholly in accord with the mind of the Lord and his apostles. They were not called upon to defend it against advocates of this or that type of congregationalism or presbyterianism for there were no such polities around at that time. This is not to say that there were not varying accounts of the episcopal office and order in East and West, and within East and West; but, it is to say that the polities we know as congregationalism and presbyterianism were not then present. In fact, they didn't arrive for another thousand years or more!

ON THE SCOPE OF SCRIPTURE'S AUTHORITY

So we come back to the basic division between, on the one side, Orthodox, Roman Catholic, and Reformed Catholics (Anglicans, some Lutherans, etc.) and, the other side, those who see a blueprint in the Bible for church government. This division is the scope of the absolute authority of the Scriptures. All agree that the Bible is inspired of God and authoritative for faith and conduct, and that church government should not go against the spirit of its content. However, some (including the other contributors to this book) go further and assume that, in the same way that the Bible is authoritative in matters of faith, so it is in providing a blueprint of church organization and polity.

The difference should not be turned into a debate over the role of tradition. The very facts that the church collected and accepted some documents (from a much larger available collection) as the canon of the New Testament, submitted to the authority of that Scripture, and at the same time operated with an episcopal system of government tells us much. It was the common belief in the second and third centuries that, in fulfillment of the promises in John 14–16, the Holy Ghost had led the church into truth concerning God, Christ, and salvation, as well as order and polity. This point is critical. The bishops were seen (in certain carefully thought-out ways) as successors of the apostles and thus, as the original Twelve had done, they formed a universal college (body of clergy) by the ministry of the Holy Ghost. Hereby the unity of the church in space and time was symbolized and guaranteed—the glue to bind the body of Christ together on earth.

To make these claims and assertions is in no way to exclude sin and sinfulness from the episcopal order and system as it developed. The temptations were severe and great when the church was shown favor by Roman emperors and then made the state religion. One must not judge the episcopal system when the church has become worldly and when bishops have become princes! Such a system needed reformation—as actually happened in parts of the church in the sixteenth century. And it is in constant need of reform and renewal.

But to return to the New Testament, we find various forms of administration for the growing church of God. In some churches (e.g., Ephesus, Acts 20:17) pastoral leadership was in the hands of a college of elders under the overall authority of an apostle. In contrast, the mother church in Jerusalem had a single head in the person of James, the Lord's brother. It would have been relatively easy over the years to fuse these two forms if: (1) one of the elders in the college became by wisdom, charismatic gifts, or age the president or leader of the group, and (2) there were added to the one-leader situation a group of presbyters. In the Pastoral Epistles, *presbyteroi* are usually plural with a single *episcopos*. Probably the young churches learned by experience that one man, rather than a committee, is the best way to lead the Christian mission in the world. Ignatius of Antioch speaks strongly of what has since been called the monarchical episcopate and what he says is best understood not as a dogmatic principle but as a practical expression of the need for unity.

As the Holy Ghost led in the planting and organizing of new churches, the episcopal system became universally accepted within a century of the martyrdom of Peter. Each church (with its bishop, presbyters, and deacons) was understood as a microcosm of the whole church of God, designed to be in communion with like churches in other cities. And even though the membership of the local church elected the bishop, he was ordained by three or more bishops from other churches in order to make the point that no local church, however big, stood alone—autonomous and independent—but rather as an expression of the one, holy, catholic, and apostolic church. As that city church expanded, so it formed congregations to which the bishop sent presbyters to serve. Thus there evolved from the city church the one diocese, and the same from other city churches, each diocese in communion with the next. And when there were questions to answer and problems to solve, the bishops of the dioceses in a given region met in synod and addressed them. The most famous synod from the early centuries was at Nicea in 325, called to solve the tremendous problems caused by the spread of the Arian heresy.

To summarize, Waldron reads into the Bible a system that is first in his mind and then presents it as the biblical blueprint. Had he taken seriously the history of the early church to say AD 200 (or better, to AD 325), he would have realized just how far off the mark he is.

A PRESBYTERIAN'S RESPONSE

L. Roy Taylor

Samuel Waldron's essay on plural-elder congregationalism prompts several areas of agreement and several areas of disagreement from a presbyterian perspective. Waldron, like all the other contributors to this volume, does not maintain that one particular view and practice of church government is essential to the existence of the church, but that his view is necessary for its perfection. While I understand the Anglican argument to be essentially a historical argument, and the single-elder congregational argument (as presented in this volume) to be essentially an inferential argument or deductive argument, Waldron holds that plural-elder congregationalism is the form of church government taught in the New Testament. He says that "[t]he independence of the local church is taught in the Scriptures. No other view has either precedent or warrant in the Scriptures," and that the "*plurality of elders* in local churches in the New Testament is not something that is doubtful." He does not consider church government a matter of indifference in the New Testament. As he remarks,

> I have a profoundly different approach to this subject than much of contemporary evangelicalism. Like the Ephesian disciples of John the Baptist who told Paul, "We have not even heard whether there is a Holy Spirit" (Acts 19:2), many evangelicals tell us by their conduct that they have not even heard whether there is a biblical church government. Without shame, many act as if they were allowed to order "the household of God, which is the church of the living God" (1 Tim. 3:15) according to their human traditions,

personal tastes, and natural reason. My defense of plural-elder congregationalism is, among other things, a protest against such attitudes in evangelical churches.

Being persuaded of the biblical basis for presbyterianism, I agree with his evidence and arguments for a plurality of elders,[96] yet I respectfully disagree with the idea that the biblical pattern for churches is independence from one another. As a presbyterian, I resonate with his reference to the regulative principle of worship and its application to church government, though I think that his understanding of the regulative principle is narrower than Calvin's or that of the Westminster Assembly. One of the chief contributions of J. H. Thornwell and Robert L. Dabney, two of the leading nineteenth-century Southern Presbyterian theologians, was a reemphasis on the parity of the eldership. Therefore, being a Southern Presbyterian, I commend Waldron for his attention to the matter, though he takes the principle further than I or most Presbyterians would.

There is a spectrum of beliefs and practices in all forms of church government. Waldron lists differences within the plural-elder congregationalist perspective regarding (1) the role of the pastor (if there is to be an elder so designated), and (2) the authority of the elders vis-à-vis the congregation.

SOME PRELIMINARY MATTERS

It is necessary to remind ourselves of several preliminary matters. First, the Bible[97] gives us commandments, general principles, and historical examples of church government. But it does not give us extensive details, other than qualifications for office (Num. 11, Acts 6, 1 Tim. 3, Titus 1, and 1 Peter 5).

Second, it would not be proper to import a fully developed ecclesiastical structure into the New Testament, no matter what one's view of church government. The organization and structure of the early church was simple, not complex; rudimentary, not fully developed.

Third, the office of apostle was unique and temporary with spiritual authority and abilities not replicated in subsequent generations.

Fourth, regional assemblies of the early church were not frequent. Persecuted by Jewish, pagan, and civil authorities, the early church was widely scattered after Paul's missionary journeys throughout the Mediterranean Basin. Not until after the Edict of Milan (AD 310) legalizing Christianity and ending imperial persecution was the church free to hold frequent regional meetings. By that time an episcopacy was well under way. The first council of Nicea (AD 325) was the first general assembly the church had called since the Jerusalem council recorded in Acts 15.

Fifth, the New Testament phase of the church did not originate in a historical vacuum, but grew in the matrix of Judaism and the synagogue tradition. The Old Testament and the synagogue affected the church's forms of worship and church government. As the gospel took root within the Gentile culture, the church took on forms of worship and government adapted to that culture.

Sixth, virtually all church historians agree that an episcopacy appeared in the church by the mid-second century and developed into a more hierarchal system in subsequent centuries, culminating in the Roman Catholic papacy.

THE REGULATIVE PRINCIPLE OF WORSHIP

Waldron uses the Puritan regulative principle of worship[98] as a principle equally applicable to church government. The Westminster Confession (I–6, XX, XXI), Westminster Larger Catechism (Qq. 104–110), and Westminster Shorter Catechism (Qq. 45–52) deal with this principle, and the first of these is of particular importance in its statement:

> The whole counsel of God concerning all things necessary for His own glory, man's salvation, faith and life, is either expressly set down in Scripture, or by good and necessary consequence may be deduced from Scripture: unto which nothing at any time is to be added, whether by new revelations of the Spirit or traditions of men. Nevertheless, we acknowledge the inward illumination of the Spirit of God to be necessary for the saving understanding of such things as are revealed in the Word: and *that there are some circumstances concerning the worship of God, and government of the Church, common to human actions and societies, which are to be ordered by the light of nature, and Christian prudence, according to the general rules of the Word, which are always to be observed.* [emphasis added]

In other words, whatever is necessary for God's glory, our salvation, what we are to believe, and how we are to live is either expressly stated in Scripture or may be deduced from it. We are not to add to the Scripture either by supposed revelations of the Spirit or the traditions of men. The Holy Spirit's work in our hearts is necessary for us to understand the biblical truth of salvation. Circumstances regarding the worship of God and the government of the church, common to human activities and societies, are to be ordered by natural revelation and Christian wisdom. Of course, the general principles of the Word of God are always to be followed.

Two questions arise: (1) how does one deduce principles of worship and church government from the Bible, and (2) what is the meaning of the term "circumstances"? The regulative principle, simply put, is that *God regulates the church's worship and government through the Scriptures, that the church does not have the authority to require what the Word of God does not require.* Such a statement was an antidote to the Roman Catholic position of the church's authority to make declarations on theology, worship, and church government, without biblical warrant. It was an antidote to the Lutheran position that allowed for a very broad area of *adiaphora* (matters indifferent) in worship and church government. It was also an antidote to the Anglican position that required obedience to the Book of Common Prayer and the ecclesiastical hierarchy without due regard to matters of conscience. Certain aspects of the Bible's teachings on worship and church government are easy to discern, i.e., explicit requirements to be obeyed and prohibitions to be observed. What God says to do, we must do. What God prohibits, we must not do. It is the more general biblical principles and historical precedents which generate controversy because these may vary from culture to culture.

Some take a more restrictive view of the regulative principle and assert that one must have an explicit biblical commandment to justify a given practice in worship or church government (though even those who take the more restrictive view make some allowances for special cases). For example, some who take a more restrictive view hold to exclusive a cappella psalmody. Others who hold a more restrictive view do not receive offerings as an act of worship in the corporate services, because there is no explicit commandment in the New Testament to do so in the context of worship. Instead they have an offering box in the church foyer to receive financial offerings. Conversely, those who take a less restrictive view of the regulative principle of worship allow for hymns as well as psalms because there is a biblical "warrant" or principle of worshiping God through singing; they allow financial offerings as part of a corporate worship service because there is a biblical principle of worshiping God through giving. Those who hold a more restrictive view of "circumstances" of worship are concerned with small matters such as the times of Lord's Day services; those with a less restrictive view are not so concerned. Waldron takes a more restrictive view on the application of the regulative principle to church government than I, particularly in regard to the role of the pastor.

THE PLURALITY OF ELDERS

Waldron gives ample evidence to establish the plurality of elders in a local congregration not only in the New Testament but, with the exception of Ignatius, in eight of the nine major sources of the Apostolic Fathers. He holds that the terms "elder" (*presbyteros*) and "bishop" (*episkopos*) are used as synonyms in the New Testament. Though I agree with all this, I respectfully disagree with his view on plurality of elders on basically two points: (1) the authority of the elders and (2) the role of the pastor.

The Authority of Elders

In his chapter, Waldron takes a mediating position between elders having no authority and their being only advisory. He clearly demonstrates that elders rule, guide, teach, and direct, that they do not merely advise. Their authority is not absolute in that they are elected by the congregation and may be recalled. Nevertheless, he insists that the congregation must vote to ratify the elders' decisions on disciplinary cases. Here is an example of where our differences on the regulative principle come into play. Waldron understands Matthew 18:15–20 to require an action of the congregation, evidently because there is no explicit statement that the elders handle matters of discipline. However, presbyterians (and *some* plural-elder congregationalists as well) hold that the elders may decide disciplinary cases because (1) the organization of the church was to be developed though the ministry of the apostles following the Old Testament origin of the office of elder (Num. 11), (2) the organization of the church at that point (while Christ was on earth) was simple and rudimentary, (3) the office of elder, as it developed in the New Testament, was one of spiritual authority and leadership,[99] and (4) the church followed the synagogue practices in several respects in form of worship and government (discipline was handled in the synagogue by the elders, not the congregation). Therefore, presbyterians and some plural-elder congregationalists take our Lord's command "tell it to the church" (Matt. 18:17) to mean "take the matter to the leadership (elders) of the church" rather than "take the matter to a congregational meeting." Obviously, the presbyterian argument is deductive, a good and necessary inference, and not at all simplistic. Nevertheless, I believe it is valid.

The Parity of Elders

When Waldron describes the parity of elders, I agree with much of what he has to say, though I would not go so far as to say that there is no such thing as a distinctive role of pastor, *primus inter pares* (first among equals) among the plurality of elders. Waldron is willing to accept a view that one elder may be the first among equals, yet because of his restrictive view of the regulative principle, he does not want the leading elder to have any title that would distinguish him from the other elders because he does not see an explicit biblical commandment to do so:

> The distinction between this elder and the other elders must always be a *de facto* and not a *de jure* distinction. It must be a distinction, in other words, of influence and not of office. This means that no terminological distinction may be reserved for this elder. He must not be called the bishop, the pastor, the minister, or the senior pastor in contrast to the rest of the elders or the rest of the pastors.

However, our other Baptist brother, Patterson, has pointed out that the Anabaptist Schleitheim Confession of 1527, the Congregationalist Savoy Declaration of 1658, the London Baptist Confession of 1644, the Second London Baptist Confession of 1648, the Somerset Baptist Confession of 1656, and the Philadelphia Baptist Confession of 1688 speak of the office of pastor. Moreover, it is the long-standing practice in Congregational and Baptist communions that pastors are ordinarily the leaders who administer baptism and the Lord's Supper.

INDEPENDENCY

My primary disagreement with what both of our Baptist brothers have maintained is with their position that the churches of the New Testament were independent (autonomous) and therefore that churches today should be independent.[100] I believe that the churches of the New Testament were interdependent, not independent, and that connectionalism is a biblical principle to be followed today. I maintain that position for two reasons: (1) the witness of the New Testament, and (2) the doctrine of the church.

The Witness of the New Testament

The churches of the New Testament were geographically separated. Transportation and communication were difficult compared to modern times, not to mention that much of the church was poor and could not afford to travel. As noted earlier, the organizational structure of the church was simple and rudimentary, and persecution made a large regional gathering dangerous and ill-advised. That is why the Acts 15 record of the council of Jerusalem is of particular importance. If the church of the New Testament was simply a confederation of independent local churches, the council of Jerusalem could not have settled a theological issue (must Gentiles be circumcised to be saved?), nor would their decision have any binding effect on all the churches.

It is true that there is no reason to believe that elders from the churches of Cyprus and Asia Minor which Paul and Barnabas had established on the first missionary journey attended the council of Jerusalem. I would also grant that elders from the churches of Phoenicia and Samaria attending the council (vv. 3–4) is an inference (though a reasonable one). However, the fact remains that the decisions (*dogmata*) of the council of Jerusalem were ecclesiastical decrees of an authoritative assembly, not just pious advice of a convention of confederated churches. The council deputed Paul and Barnabas to deliver the decrees to the churches (vv. 22–29) in Antioch, Syria, and Cilicia. Later, Paul, Silas, and Timothy delivered the decrees to the churches of Derbe, Lystra, and others so that the decrees might be obeyed (16:4). If the early churches of the New Testament were independent, why would the council issue such decrees? Waldron explains the force of the decrees on the basis of the uniqueness of the Jerusalem mother church. However, once one concedes this, the argument for independency is lost, for the very essence of independency is that no local church or synod of churches has any authority in matters of theology and discipline over another. Whether the church of Jerusalem had a "unique authority" over the churches or whether it was a synodical authority, the fact remains it was an authority contrary to congregationalism/independency.

The Church Universal

The final point of issue with independency relates to the doctrine of the church universal. The church universal is a precious doctrine of the Scripture.[101] Paul describes the church most fully in his epistle to the Ephesians, as the bride of Christ, the body of Christ. The biblical images of the church are those of unity in spite of its diversity, of oneness in spite of its imperfections. Throughout the centuries, the church has recognized herself as unique—one, holy, catholic,[102] and apostolic. While independency fits well with rugged American individualism and the entrepreneurial spirit, it is the least suitable form of church government to express the universality and oneness of the church.

A SINGLE-ELDER CONGREGATIONALIST'S RESPONSE

Paige Patterson

Sam Waldron's elucidation of plural-elder congregationalism is both thorough and persuasive. He demonstrates familiarity with historical sources and logic, but builds his case where he should—on the exposition of Holy Scripture. The differences between Waldron's view and my own are few and small, although, I think, not insignificant. Areas of agreement abound and those areas will constitute the initial section of this response.

AREAS OF AGREEMENT

The Autonomy of the Local Church

Unlike many who advocate the ministry of multiple elders in a church, Waldron endorses the autonomy of each Christian assembly and even insists that the elders of a church are to be selected by the church as a whole. In his view, the local church is vested with ultimate human authority, thus denying this authority to elders or to a primary level of pastors known as bishops. In fact, Waldron argues cogently and correctly that pastors, elders, and bishops are indistinguishable in both identity and general function. He properly concludes that the earliest church had but two offices, elders and deacons, a conclusion warranted by the elaboration of qualifications of those chosen thus to serve in 1 Timothy 3:1–13.

Concerning the congregationalism of the earliest churches, Waldron finds that this pattern, rather conclusively outlined in Scripture, is carried over into the earliest post-apostolic Christian literature. In one of the finest sections of his chapter, he assesses the evidence of Clement of Rome, Polycarp, the *Didache*, the Epistle to Diognetus, the Epistle of Barnabas, the Shepherd of Hermas, Pseudo-Second Clement, the fragments of Papias, and the various letters of Ignatius, to show that with the exception of Ignatius, the early writings betray no development of hierarchy or even the authority of one bishop or church over another. He further demonstrates that even the evidence gleaned from Ignatius is ambivalent.

Waldron believes that the case for a presbyterian form of church government has to be made based on Acts 15 or else give way to congregational polity. I not only concur with that analysis but join Waldron in finding the presbyterian case unconvincing. He points out that local churches are urged to undertake church discipline. He further argues that if local assemblies are competent to judge such serious matters, they must be seen as competent in others also.

The Church Not a Pure Democracy

At this point special attention regarding a limitation of congregational church government is in order. Waldron is appropriately concerned that congregationalism not be construed as "rugged individualism" but rather as an assembly of believers determined to seek the mind of the Spirit and the will of Christ. And I might add that the congregationalism of the New Testament does not encourage anyone to voice any opinion he has or vote any way he wishes. The church is not, strictly speaking, a democracy. Christ rules as sovereign over the church, and the object of "churchcraft" is to discover Christ's will and purpose and to fulfill that on the earth.

The Number and Authority of Elders in New Testament Churches

Regarding the elders themselves, Waldron says that the churches of the New Testament period most often had a plurality of elders, although he recognizes that some had none. The recognition that some had none seems to suggest that some might have had only one. While I have no trouble in allowing for this possibility, I confess that I do not know the basis for the conclusion that most first-century churches had multiple elders. Clearly, only a small number of the churches in Macedonia, Italy, Asia Minor, Syria, and Roman Palestine are even mentioned in Scripture. Any evidence suggesting that "most"of those mentioned had multiple elders is not clear to me. If so, however, no element of faith or practice is thereby violated; so I will not contest this conclusion.

Further, Waldron notes that elders did exercise great authority in the New Testament churches. Surely he is correct. It seems to me impossible to read anything else into Hebrews 13:7–17 or 1 Timothy 5:17. This "rule," whether the *hegeomai* of Hebrews or the *proestetes* of 1 Timothy, represents a strong exercise of decisive leadership. In congregational polity, the church selects its elders precisely because they are judged to be men of God; and having selected the elders, the congregation follows them as godly authorities. The exception to this is also clearly outlined in 1 Timothy 5 where elders who are "sinning" are to be publicly "rebuke[d] in the presence of all" (v. 20)—language that lends significant evidence for congregationalism.

If I have read Waldron correctly, he and I agree that Christ is sovereign over the church, mediating that sovereignty through the minds and hearts of believer-priests by means of the Holy Spirit who indwells each believer-priest. Furthermore, to each assembly God provides an elder or elders called of God and selected by the church to assist the church in understanding God's will and purpose and in accomplishing all tasks of Christ thus assigned. In all of this, I agree.

AN AREA OF DISAGREEMENT: THE NECESSITY OF THE PLURALITY AND PARITY OF ELDERS

Where I differ with Waldron is primarily regarding the necessity or even the essential desirability of multiple elders. In addition, I contest his insistence upon the "parity" of elders. If by "parity" he means that eldership is without rank and that the congregation recognizes all elders as ministers of Christ, then I agree. There is even a sense in which the same can be said of every believer in the church. But, if by parity Waldron means that a decisive leader did not emerge in most of the churches, then I think he is on shaky ground both historically and sociologically. Although I disagree with Peter Toon's Anglicanism, here he may be of help. I think Toon might note that even if Ignatius's form of church government was not universal in the second century, Ignatius's letters as well as the other sources Waldron cited seem to suggest a very prominent elder in each of the cities and/or churches. Nor is there any evidence in the New Testament to contradict this practice. Sociologically, to have clear leaders is the normal state of affairs. Democracies with elected leaders and monarchies prove workable while oligarchy is always condemned to struggle. Neither is the case in Scripture any different where God raises up a judge, a prophet, an apostle, etc. to lead in a particular place and time. Surely biblical evidence points to a rather decisive leadership role for James, the Lord's brother in the Jerusalem congregation (Acts 15:13–21; Gal. 1:19). John's position in Ephesus seems also to be something more than being just one of the elders.

Furthermore, in the contemporary church the idea of parity among elders is advocated more often than it is practiced. In fact, in discussing Ignatius, Waldron admits that the churches of Asia may have had a system of *primus inter pares* (first among equals), which Ignatius mistook for regional bishops. This "first among equals" is precisely what generally emerges in congregations with multiple elders today. This testifies to the innate difficulty of "shared leadership" or any approaches where all elders are perceived as equal.

In this regard, Waldron is somewhat overly enamored with the pattern of ecclesiology established by Particular Baptists with a strong Reformed bent. Large numbers of Baptists, Anabaptists, and other free church traditions rejected the Reformed emphasis in church government and boasted single elders or a leading elder among several. What Waldron also fails to mention is that this same result of one decisive pastor-leader often was observable even in some Particular Baptist churches. Also, a century and a half ago Spurgeon, strongly influenced by Reformed soteriology, had nevertheless opted for the pattern of a single pastor-leader, although other elders served with him. They were not equals in anyone's estimation.

Even if Waldron could establish that the ideal circumstance for a New Testament church is that of multiple elders, he cannot, on the basis of the New Testament, demonstrate that these had parity in the local assembly. As I acknowledge in my chapter, I cannot show for certain that they did not have parity. We, therefore, in candor are reduced to snippets of evidence and to a general pattern of God's call of individual leaders for the people across the centuries. Here is a place where dogmatism may profitably be avoided.

Finally, in insisting that the ideal pattern is that of multiple elders, Waldron presents an impressive list of churches mentioned in the New Testament, which, according to him, had multiple elders. A number of these are suspect. When "elders" are mentioned for multiple cities—as for example on Crete (Titus 1:5) or for Lystra, Iconium, and Psidian Antioch—the burden of proof falls on Waldron to show that the plural in the text requires multiple elders in *each* city. Could it not also be read as appointing elders so that each city has at least one? Of course, I agree that the larger churches such as Jerusalem, Syrian Antioch, and Ephesus had multiple elders (although not parity). But this actually makes my point. Why should a new congregation of ten to twenty or even forty people have multiple elders? How could they support their ministries? Is it not far more probable that every church needed an elder; and, as the congregation grew, they added as many as needed to care for the flocks?

In conclusion, I wish to affirm once and again my broad agreement with Waldron. I find his arguments for the necessity of multiple elders in every situation of doubtful validity, but I have no strong objections to the view. Our major difference is on the idea of "elder parity," a view which in my persuasion is virtually void of New Testament mandate or precedent. Beyond that, I rejoice in his perspective of Christ as the sovereign of the church, with congregational government under the clear leadership of an elder(s) as the modus operandi of local churches.

Chapter 4: Plural-Elder Congregationalism Notes

Samuel E. Waldron

[1]This distinction is not original with me. Bannerman in his classic presentation of presbyterian church polity distinguishes the congregational principle (by which he means the democratic) and the independent principle in independent church polity: James Bannerman, *The Church of Christ* (London: Banner of Truth, 1974), 1:v. Cf. also the comments on this distinction of James Renihan, *The Practical Ecclesiology of the English Particular Baptists, 1675–1705: The Doctrine of the Church in the Second London Baptist Confession as Implemented in the Subscribing Churches* (Ph.D. diss., Trinity Evangelical Divinity School, 1997), 129.

[2]The 1689 Baptist Confession, perhaps historically the most influential confession of independent churches, illustrates this clearly (chapter 26, paragraphs 14 and 15).

[3]As I will argue below, a plurality of elders in the local church is not so obligatory according to the Scriptures as to necessarily involve sin if it does not exist. This is why I have qualified my statement with the words, *under normal circumstances*. Of course, though sin is not necessarily involved, the lack of plurality is a deficiency that for both biblical and practical reasons must be seriously addressed.

[4]The exception to this rule is that often elders are elected by the church. After this election, however, the elders' decisions are decisive in church discipline and other matters.

[5]Bannerman, *The Church of Christ*, 2:300–301. But see Wayne Grudem, *Systematic Theology* (Grand Rapids: Zondervan, 1994), 925; and Louis Berkhof, *Systematic Theology* (Grand Rapids: Eerdmans, 1941), 587–90. Grudem asserts that presbyterian churches elect their own elders. It is true that Berkhof not only allows that "both the officers and the ordinary members of the church have a part" in the calling of the ordinary officers of the church, but even speaks of "the relative autonomy of the local church." As an independent I welcome Berkhof's statements. His treatment in my opinion contains major concessions to congregationalism and compromises the real principles of the historic, presbyterian system.

[6]Shawn Wright, "Authority, the Congregation, and Elders: The Struggle for Biblical Rule among the Particular Baptists" (paper presented to Dr. Timothy George in partial fulfillment of the requirements for a university study course, Beeson Divinity School), 1997. In this paper Wright traces the decline of a plurality of elders to four factors, the most important of which he says was "the fear that having a plurality of elders would remove the authority from the congregation" (pp. 19–20, 30). Whether Wright is correct or not, it cannot be denied that there is a problem or tension here that needs to be addressed by those from a congregational background who wish to hold a plurality of elders. Cf. also Greg Wills's essay in *Polity*, ed. Mark Dever (Center for Church Reform, 2001), 34.

[7]Thomas Goodwin, Philip Nye, Sidrach Simpson, Jeremiah Burroughes, William Bridge, *An Apologeticall Narration Humbly Submitted to the Honourable Houses of Parliament*, ed. Robert S. Paul (Boston: United Church Press, 1963), 9.

[8]The Savoy Declaration of Faith and Order (1658) (London: Evangelical Press, 1971), 4.

[9]This is chapter 21:1 in the Westminster and 22:1 in the Savoy and 1689.

[10]Renihan, *The Practical Ecclesiology of the English Particular Baptists*, xvi-xvii. Here is what he says: "At the root of particular Baptist ecclesiology was keen primitivistic impulse. T. L. Underwood has identified this as 'the emphasis in faith and practice on the first, earliest pattern as described in the New Testament that entailed efforts to re-create or imitate such a form in the present.' Throughout this investigation, it will be evident that the Baptists sought relentlessly to apply this principle to their doctrine and practice. It was the impetus behind the development of believer's baptism, the practice of immersion, the order and government of the church, the roles of officers, the various aspects of worship and the outworking of inter-church relationships. . . .The pattern was found in the New Testament, and the responsibility to replicate it was paramount in the congregations of saints."

[11]Bannerman, *The Church of Christ*, 1:339. The twentieth of the Church of England's Thirty-Nine Articles states: "The Church hath power to decree rites or ceremonies and authority in the controversies of the Faith. And yet it is not lawful for the Church to ordain anything contrary to God's Word written."

[12]Bannerman, *The Church of Christ*, 1:339–40.

[13]My view is that elders should be installed into their office in a local church by means of the laying on of the hands of the existing eldership of the church and that in this sense they should be ordained.

[14]It is in my opinion biblically appropriate to express respect in the way we address others and especially those in authority over us. Since elders do have authority over us, it is proper on appropriate occasions (not always and on every occasion) to address elders as *Pastor John* or *Pastor Smith*.

[15]This is an important issue, but the vast majority (though not all) of plural-elder congregationalists agree that at least some elders should be regularly supported. Cf. especially 1 Cor. 9:14; Gal. 6:6; 1 Tim. 5:17.

[16]A ninefold classification may be used to identify the writings usually classed as the Apostolic Fathers. Not all were actually written by the person named in the title. What follows is a list of those writings together with the standard dating and assessment of each. Clement of Rome's *Epistle to the Corinthians* is thought to be genuine (authored by the biblical Clement) and written about AD 97. Ignatius's *Seven Epistles (to the Ephesians, Magnesians, Trallians, Romans, Philadelphians, Smyrnans, and Polycarp)* are thought to be genuine in their shorter versions and were probably written in the year 107. Polycarp's *Epistle to the Philippians* is associated with *The Martyrdom of Polycarp* and is regarded as genuine and was written in the year 156. The *Didache,* also known as *The Teaching of the Twelve Apostles,* was not written by the twelve apostles, but was probably the work of an editor around the year 150 who was working with sources dating from the year 100 or earlier. *The Epistle to Diognetus* has an unknown author and may have been written about the year 129. *The Epistle of Barnabas* was not written by the biblical Barnabas but dates from about the year 131. *The Shepherd of Hermas* was not the production of the biblical Hermas, but

was written about the year 145 in Rome. *Pseudo-Second Clement* was not written by the biblical Clement and dates from about the year 140. The *Fragments of Papias* are quotations from the lost five-volume work of the early disciple Papias which is dated about the year 125. These quotations are found in Eusebius of Caesarea's church history (written about the year 324).

[17]J. B. Lightfoot, *St. Paul's Epistle to the Philippians* (Peabody, Mass.: Hendrickson Publishers, 1987), 202.

[18]Ignatius, *Epistle to the Ephesians*, 2:2; *Early Christian Fathers*, trans. and ed. Cyril C. Richardson (New York: Macmillan, 1970), 88.

[19]*Clement's Epistle to the Corinthians*, chapters 54, 42, 44, 57; *Early Christian Fathers*, trans. and ed. Cyril C. Richardson, 68, 62, 63, 64, 69.

[20]*Shepherd of Hermas*, Vis 2, ch. 4. Cf. also Vis 3, Sim. 9, ch. 27. *Ante-Nicene Fathers*, ed. Alexander Roberts and James Donaldson (New York: Scribner's Sons, 1905), 2:12.

[21]Lightfoot, *St. Paul's Epistle to the Philippians*, 193–201.

[22]F. F. Bruce, *The Spreading Flame* (Grand Rapids: Eerdmans, 1961), 206.

[23]Bruce, *The Spreading Flame*, 203–4. Cf. also Thomas M. Lindsay, *The Church and the Ministry in the Early Centuries* (Minneapolis: James Family Publishing, 1977), 204. Lindsay remarks: "During the last decades of the second and throughout the third century the conception of Ignatius, to him perhaps only a devout dream, dominated the whole Church, or at least a great part of it.... Compare Ramsay, *The Church in the Roman Empire*, pp. 370–71, where he says that Ignatius is not an historian describing facts but a preacher giving advice; and adds that he does not find in Ignatius proof that bishops were regarded as ex-officio supreme, that his language is quite consistent with the view that the respect actually paid to the bishop in each community depended on his individual character, and that his reiteration of the principle of the authority of the bishop, which came to him as a revelation, makes it evident that he did not find his ideal in actual existence."

[24]*Clement's Epistle to the Corinthians*, chapter 54; *Early Christian Fathers*, trans. and ed. Cyril C. Richardson, 68. The key words are: "Well, then, who of your number is noble, large-hearted, and full of love? Let him say: 'If it is my fault that revolt, strife, and schism have arisen, I will leave, I will go away wherever you wish, and do what the congregation orders. Only let Christ's flock live in peace with their appointed presbyters.'"

[25]*Didache*, ch. 15; *Early Christian Fathers*, trans. and ed. Cyril C. Richardson, 178.

[26]With the development of single bishop rule in the local church, the churches eventually moved away from independency and in the direction of diocesan episcopacy (in which many churches were ruled by a single bishop).

[27]Lightfoot, *St. Paul's Epistle to the Philippians*, 202.

[28]Sydney Ahlstrom, *A Religious History of the American People* (New Haven: Yale University Press, 1972), 90. Ahlstrom makes the "Puritan Century" to be the period from the accession of Elizabeth to the Restoration of Charles II.

[29]Renihan, *The Practical Ecclesiology of the English Particular Baptists*, 1–15.

[30]Perry Miller, *Orthodoxy in Massachusetts (1630–1650)* (Boston: Beacon Press, 1959), 53–101.

[31] Miller, *Orthodoxy in Massachusetts (1630–1650)*, 263–313.

[32] Goodwin et al., *Apologeticall Narration*, 8–14, 23–24.

[33] The authors of *Apologeticall Narration* also dislike the term, "Independencie" (cf. page 23), but this simply manifests its pejorative connotation in their day. Editor Robert S. Paul argues in his comments on this document that the term "congregational" was adopted at an early stage to describe their form of church government. Goodwin et al., 65–66.

[34] Wright, "Authority, the Congregation, and Elders: The Struggle for Biblical Rule among the Particular Baptists," 15–16.

[35] Wright, 15–16.

[36] Goodwin et al., *Apologeticall Narration*, 8–14.

[37] John Owen, *The Works of John Owen*, ed. William H. Goold (Edinburgh: Banner of Truth, 1968), 16:113.

[38] The Savoy Declaration of Faith and Order, 44–45. Note particularly paragraphs 8–12 of "The Institution of Churches, and the Order Appointed in Them by Jesus Christ."

[39] Renihan, *The Practical Ecclesiology of the English Particular Baptists*, 177–230.

[40] This is chapter 26, paragraph 8 of the Second London Baptist Confession of Faith of 1689.

[41] The Savoy Declaration of Faith and Order, 44–45. Note particularly paragraphs 9–12. With this compare the Cambridge Platform, chapters 6–7: Creeds and Platforms of Congregationalism, 210–14.

[42] Renihan, *The Practical Ecclesiology of the English Particular Baptists*, 205.

[43] Goodwin et al., *Apologeticall Narration*, 24.

[44] In chapter 26, paragraph 9.

[45] In paragraphs 9, 11, and 12 of the Order appended to the Declaration of Faith.

[46] In paragraph 17 of the Savoy's Platform of Church of Order.

[47] In paragraph 19 of the Savoy's Platform of Church of Order. Cf. also Goodwin et al., *Apologeticall Narration*, 46–47.

[48] Creeds and Platforms of Congregationalism, ed. Williston Walker (Philadelphia: Pilgrim, 1960), 194–237.

[49] Renihan, *The Practical Ecclesiology of the English Particular Baptists*, 128–76. Though the 1689 Baptist Confession provides a briefer account of the necessity of the consent of the church, there is no reason to think that there is any substantial difference in its views from that of the Cambridge Platform. In fact, Renihan has shown that the practice of those churches that subscribed the 1689 Baptist Confession was substantially the same in these respects.

[50] Creeds and Platforms of Congregationalism, 210.

[51] Renihan, *The Practical Ecclesiology of the English Particular Baptists*, 182.

[52] Goodwin et al., *Apologeticall Narration*, 12–13.

[53] Renihan, *The Practical Ecclesiology of the English Particular Baptists*, 154–56, 209–11, 216.

[54] Creeds and Platforms of Congregationalism, 220.

[55] This is chapter 1, paragraph 6 in each of the Confessions mentioned.

[56]I know that I am disagreeing with some theologians. I certainly am not denying that principles of civil righteousness are revealed in the Scriptures that impact our thinking about civil government. I am saying that the Scriptures nowhere require either a monarchy, an oligarchy, or a democracy. Nowhere is permission given to refuse subjection to the "wrong" form of civil government. Cf. Romans 13:1–7.

[57]Let me recommend my more lengthy treatments of that subject, *A Modern Exposition of the 1689 Baptist Confession of Faith* (Darlington, England: Evangelical Press, 1999), 267–71; and *The Regulative Principle of the Church* (Quezon City, Philippines: Wisdom Publications, 1995). The latter is available from Truth for Eternity Ministries in Grand Rapids, Michigan.

[58]Grudem, *Systematic Theology*, 929, 931. To his credit Grudem sees the unbiblical character of this argument.

[59]Renihan, *The Practical Ecclesiology of the English Particular Baptists*, 313–50. Note The 1689 Baptist Confession, chapter 26, paragraphs 14–15.

[60]Savoy Declaration of Faith and Order, 47–48. (Paragraphs 25–27 of the *Order*.)

[61]Creeds and Platforms of Congregationalism, 229–34. (Chapters 15–16 of the Cambridge Platform.)

[62]Note the plain statements of this in the references given in the previous three footnotes.

[63]Compare the more detailed, but substantially identical statement in the Savoy Declaration of Faith and Order, 43. (Paragraphs 4–6 of the Order.)

[64]Poh Boon Sing makes an interesting argument for the independence of the local church from the fact that there are seven lampstands (representing seven distinct churches) and not one lampstand with seven branches (as in the Old Testament tabernacle). *The Keys of the Kingdom* (Kuala Lumpur, Malaysia: Good News Enterprise, 1995), 59–61. John Cotton also argues for the independence of the local church from this passage. *John Cotton on the Churches of New England*, ed. Larzer Ziff (Cambridge, Mass.: Harvard University Press, 1968), 148–49.

[65]Bannerman, *The Church of Christ*, 2:325–26. Grudem (*Systematic Theology*, 926–27) confirms the importance of this passage to presbyterians.

[66]As Grudem points out (*Systematic Theology*, 926–27). It is likely that the elders and the whole church are mentioned to emphasize that not just the apostles but the entire church repudiated the teaching of those who had troubled the Gentile churches (Acts 15:24).

[67]Second Corinthians 2:6 should not, however, be forgotten in this regard. It confirms the democratic principle in 1 Corinthians 5 by speaking of the "punishment which was inflicted by the majority."

[68]This may be the implication of Acts 9:26. I do not see it to be necessary that an actual vote of the church be taken on this matter. In a larger church this may become unwieldy. The consent of the church may be obtained by a public announcement of the application for church membership to which no objection is made.

[69]Acts 14:23's reference to the stretching out of hands is often cited as an example of the popular election of elders. I doubt if that is the meaning of the text

at all. I think it refers to the laying on of hands by the apostles in ordination and not the lifting of hands by the church in election. Whether I am right or not, it certainly is not clear enough to be cited as a proof text in the present connection.

[70]My use of the biblical evidence here assumes what I have already argued in my treatment of the Independent principle. Thus, for instance, I assume that the church in Ephesus was really just one local church. Of course, if there were many congregations in Ephesus that were all part of one (proto-presbyterian) city church, it might be theorized that each of the individual congregations had only one elder. Grudem is, of course, correct to note that such a theory still suffers from a complete lack of evidence for it in the New Testament (*Systematic Theology*, 912).

[71]Of course, we do know of churches without any elders at all (Acts 14:23). Hence, I agree with the idea that elders are not necessary to the being, but only to the well-being, of the church. The reason, of course, that these churches lacked elders is that they had just been planted and were not fully organized. It is noteworthy that, when they were organized, a plurality of elders were appointed in each church by the apostles: "they … appointed elders for them in every church."

[72]Here I express my debt to Grudem who identifies and refutes the major arguments for single elders in his *Systematic Theology*, 928–32.

[73]Some argue that the pattern of a plurality of elders was only due to the large size of the local churches in view. This argument fails because it admits that a pattern is biblical at least in some cases. More importantly, it fails because it lacks any biblical support. How do its advocates know that this was the reason for the pattern of plurality in the New Testament? Where is a single text to support the theory?

[74]Biblically speaking, it is necessary to speak of the abnormality of a lone elder. In the Bible elders are almost by definition plural. What I mean is that an elder is always part of a council or presbytery. We have seen the evidence for this in the local church. In the Bible we also read, however, of the elders of Israel (Ex. 3:16 and many other times), the elders of a city (Ruth 4:2 and many other times), the twenty-four elders in heaven (Rev. 4:10 and several other times in the book of Revelation), and the Sanhedrin is called the presbytery of the Jews (Luke 22:6; Acts 22:5).

[75]Of course, I am not denying that a merciful God may grant peace, good government, and blessing to a church that through ignorance or lack of gift does not possess a plurality of elders.

[76]The dangers are anarchy (the abuse of the elder) or tyranny (the abuse of the church).

[77]To avoid confusion, I must make clear that there are three Greek words used for this office (*presbyteros*, *episkopos*, and *poimen*). In the older English these words were translated respectively: presbyter, bishop, and pastor. The same words are often in more modern English translated: elder, overseer, and shepherd. Thus the designations, shepherd and pastor, overseer and bishop, and elder and presbyter, are simply the newer and older translations of the same three Greek words. All in my opinion refer to the same office in the church.

[78]The verb is *episkopeo*.

[79]Lightfoot, *Epistle to the Philippians*, 95.

80Poh Boon Sing, *The Keys of the Kingdom*, 166–67.

81First Timothy 3:2 contains the same root used in Romans 12:7.

82First Timothy 3:4–5 contains the same root used in Romans 12:8.

83First Timothy 3:1–7 requires that elders be "able to teach." The single Greek word translated "able to teach" is used elsewhere in the New Testament only in 2 Timothy 2:24. It is derived from the same root as the word for "teacher" in Ephesians 4:11 and is variously defined as "skillful in teaching" and "pertaining to being able to teach." The parallel use in 2 Timothy 2:24 seems to emphasize that "the servant of the Lord" must have the proper spirit of a teacher and be patient, gentle, and irenic when wronged and opposed. The description of "the servant of the Lord" as one who is able to teach is significant for our study. We suppose that it will be generally admitted that the servant of the Lord describes someone who, whatever in addition he may be, is certainly a pastor or minister of God's Word. The use of "able to teach" to describe such a one strengthens the conclusion that no distinction is to be made between the ordinary elder or overseer of 1 Timothy 3:1–7 and the pastor-teacher of 2 Timothy 2:24.

84Confirming this conclusion is the use of the term "steward." This term as it is elsewhere used in the New Testament clearly describes one who is charged to feed the people of God with instruction in the Word of God (Luke 12:42; 1 Cor. 4:1, 2; 1 Peter 4:10).

85This terminological distinction is absent from the passage. True, we may be used to calling the elder of the church who works hard at preaching and teaching *pastor* and calling the other overseers *elders*. We may all too easily read that understanding into this passage, but there is utterly no justification for that distinction in the passage itself.

86Actually, there is another distinction implied. It is a distinction between all the elders and the elders who rule well. Thus, we may distinguish in 1 Timothy 5:17 three concentric circles. The outer ring encompasses all the elders. The second ring encompasses all the elders who rule well. The innermost ring are the elders who rule well and who work hard at preaching and teaching.

87Other plain implications of this passage are important for a biblical view of the eldership. First Timothy 5:17 does not say that all elders must work hard at preaching and teaching. It allows for elders who may work for their living at something else. This disallows the interpretation that would make all elders full-time preachers. The passage does say that the priority of the church in terms of supporting elders must be on "those who work hard at preaching and teaching." This certainly teaches the primacy of the proclamation of the Word in the leadership of the church. Finally, the passage does assume that there are different degrees of the gifts of leading and teaching within the eldership and that these different degrees of gift may lead to differences of functions or roles within the eldership and to differences of financial support. See the treatment of the diversity of elders to follow.

88Romans 12:7–8 names the gifts of teaching, exhorting, and leading. First Corinthians 12:28 mentions the gifts of teaching and administration. First Peter 4:11 mentions the gift of speaking.

[89]Double honor in the context of 1 Timothy 5:17 is to be contrasted with the honor given to widows. Without any doubt this honor for widows consists in financial support (1 Tim. 5:3–4, 8, 16). Widows are, then, to be honored, while well-ruling elders are to be given double honor—the generous financial support necessary to comfortably support a man with a wife and children. The financial character of this honor is confirmed by verse 18. Here Paul cites the same Old Testament text that he used in 1 Corinthians 9:9 to teach that ministers of the gospel should live of the gospel or be generously, financially supported. He also cites a saying of the Lord that in both Matthew 10:10 and Luke 10:7 had to do with the financial support of those who preach the gospel.

[90]Of course, in some cases the church may be unable to do all it should with regard to the financial support of elders. In such cases the priorities set by 1 Timothy 5:17 should govern the distribution of financial support to elders.

[91]Within the ranks of those who like myself hold the plurality and parity of the elders, the "leading elder" view has developed. This view argues that it is reasonable and biblical to believe that one man will emerge to become the primary leader of the eldership. It is usually assumed that this man will be the main preacher and the chairman of the elders. In support of this, the examples of primary leaders such as Moses and Joshua in the Old Testament and Peter and James in the New Testament are cited. The example of the angels of the seven churches is also sometimes cited. The angel is assumed to be the primary leader or leading elder. I do not agree with some of the arguments brought forward to support this view. I am particularly troubled by the use of the seven angels of the seven churches to support the primary leader. For those who believe in the plurality and parity of elders, using this passage to support a primary leader view would prove far too much. If this use of the passage is proper, then it strongly tends to the view that there must be a primary leader in every church. It would also strongly imply that he should be terminologically distinguished from the other elders by being called the angel-elder. Such an interpretation of the passage would introduce an important element into the government of the church missing from the rest of the New Testament. It would do all this on the basis of a figurative reference in the book of Revelation. The violations of biblical hermeneutics in this should be obvious. It interprets plain passages on the basis of uncertain and figurative ones. Other interpetations much more consistent with the rest of the New Testament are available. The angels may be the human messengers that carried John's letters to each church. The Greek word for "angel" may also be translated "messenger." Alternatively, it may refer to the "guardian angel" of each church (cf. Grudem, *Systematic Theology*, 930–31). Yet, in light of what the New Testament teaches about the diversity of elders, I am prepared to accept a qualified version of this view. A leading elder may emerge as a kind of first among equals (*primus inter pares*) in the eldership. Within certain boundaries, this does not violate the plurality and parity of the elders. Some of those boundaries are as follows. The distinction between this elder and the other elders must always be a *de facto* and not a *de jure* distinction. It must be a distinction, in other words, of influence and not of office. This means that no terminological distinction may be reserved for this

elder. He must not be called the bishop, the pastor, the minister, or the senior pastor in contrast to the rest of the elders or the rest of the pastors. This would be to take a small but serious step away from the teaching of the Bible, as the history of the early church bears out. Likewise, it should not be taught that there must be a leading elder in every eldership. The emergence of a primary leader, while admitted to be permissible and occasional, must not be made mandatory or universal in the absence of biblical warrant. Practically speaking, the other elders must feel that they are the peer of the leading elder in office (if not in influence). Both the leading elder and the other elders must feel and act as if the leading elder is under the pastoral oversight of the other elders, just as all the other elders are.

[92]Of course, this does not mean that the best preacher should do all the preaching or receive all the financial support. The New Testament also teaches the value of multiple ministry in the church and the importance of developing gifts in the eldership and in the church. The principle of maximum edification (1 Cor. 14:1–26) does not mean that the one who is generally regarded as the best preacher or teacher should do all the preaching and teaching. A different voice may occasionally be of more edification than a greater gift.

[93]Once again this suggests the difficulty from a biblical perspective of *ruling elders* who do not teach.

[94]At least some of the Puritan congregationalists treated ordination as not essential to appointment to office in the church (Walker, Creeds and Platforms of Congregationalism, 215–16). It seems to me, however, that a case could be made that ordination by the eldership is the last step in the biblical appointment of officers and that it is a qualification for the office that the eldership may withhold on biblical grounds (1 Tim. 5:22).

[95]Creeds and Platforms of Congregationalism, 220.

L. Roy Taylor

[96]Though I believe he diminishes the authority of elders somewhat and I think that his perspective on the role of a pastor as first among equals is inadequate.

[97]The reader will note that I said the "Bible," not just the New Testament, because the Old Testament is the origin of the office of elders (Num. 11), and such office was developed in the synagogue setting before its continuance in the New Testament phase of the church.

[98]The term "regulative principle of worship" is a term that arose after the Westminster Assembly (1643–48) had produced the Westminster Confession and Catechisms. The term itself is nowhere explicitly stated in the *Westminster Standards*, but the concept is certainly there.

[99]As Waldron has ably shown.

[100]They use the term "independent" to mean "self-governing." The Southern Baptist Convention is the largest Protestant denomination in America. Its churches are autonomous but are associated together in a denomination to accomplish a common mission. Other churches are independent in that they are not associated with a denomination.

[101]The Westminster Confession of Faith, Ch. XXV, says,

1.   The catholic or universal Church, which is invisible, consists of the whole number of the elect, that have been, are, or shall be gathered into one, under Christ the Head thereof; and is the spouse, the body, the fullness of Him that filleth all in all.

2.   The visible Church, which is also catholic or universal under the Gospel (not confined to one nation, as before under the law), consists of all those throughout the world that profess the true religion; and of their children: and is the kingdom of the Lord Jesus Christ, the house and family of God, out of which there is no ordinary possibility of salvation.

3.   Unto this catholic visible Church Christ hath given the ministry, oracles, and ordinances of God, for the gathering and perfecting of the saints, in this life, to the end of the world: and doth, by His own presence and Spirit, according to His promise, make them effectual thereunto.

4.   This catholic Church hath been sometimes more, sometimes less visible. And particular Churches, which are members thereof, are more or less pure, according as the doctrine of the Gospel is taught and embraced, ordinances administered, and public worship performed more or less purely in them.

5.   The purest Churches under heaven are subject both to mixture and error; and some have so degenerated as to become no Churches of Christ, but synagogues of Satan. Nevertheless, there shall be always a Church on earth to worship God according to His will.

6.   There is no other head of the Church but the Lord Jesus Christ. Nor can the Pope of Rome, in any sense, be head thereof.

[102]Universal, transcending all barriers, of race, gender, social standing, political persuasion, economic status, geography, etc.

Chapter Five

CLOSING REMARKS

AN EPISCOPALIAN'S CLOSING REMARKS

Peter Toon

Instead of responding to specific contributions of the three distinguished writers, I shall address certain basic positions which all three hold or appear to hold. I think they are misplaced and that they contribute to the disagreements among them as well as, in my estimation, to the existence of a vast array of denominations within the American supermarket of religions (check any big-city Yellow Pages to see what I mean). That is because they work on the assumption that we can go to the Bible, see therein a clearly revealed pattern or plan of church government, then import it into the present situation of a nation that prides itself on variety and freedom of religion, thus keeping the "supermarket" open with brisk business.

It is not that I do not take seriously the exegesis of particular parts of the gospel and epistles; it is not that I do not take seriously the attempt to produce what we may call a biblical theology (in contrast to a systematic theology); and it is not that I do not realize that many worthy persons of great piety and ability have labored on the assumption that there is a blueprint for church government and polity in the sacred Scriptures. It is that I think that little will be achieved by my responding to individual pieces of exegesis. There is value in looking at the details, but only when the whole picture is in focus. Thus, my concern is with the general paradigm or mind-set with which we approach the reading and use of the canon of the Old and New Testaments in this particular enterprise. Further, on the basis of John 17 I see a clear goal before us all to be unified as Christians, and I cannot imagine this being possible without the episcopate as the living glue.

CLARITY

All three gentlemen appear to hold that the sacred Scriptures—the canon of the Old and New Testaments—present, offer, and teach a doctrine of church polity and church government as clear to behold as the identity of Jesus as the Messiah or as the one mediator between God and man. If this is their basic starting point, then why do they not all agree as to what that clear government and polity is? Why do they agree only in thinking that there is a blueprint but that the others have got it wrong?

I spent a good deal of time some years ago studying and writing on the English and American Puritans, among whom were Presbyterians and Congregationalists as well as Episcopalians. Many of the Presbyterians believed in a divine-right form of presbyterian church government and many of the independents/Congregationalists/ Baptists believed in a divine-right congregationalism. They were willing to suffer and die for what they took to be the clear teaching of the Bible, but yet they disagreed among themselves. And their disagreement was a major one because the actual differences between the Presbyterian Way and the Congregational Way are of large proportions.

In the situation then and now, might I suggest that a person already has something in mind when he goes searching the books of the New Testament. And that something has some part in determining what he finds and then defends. So often the claim of *sola scriptura* is in reality this: the Bible as interpreted by me, or by my group, or by the leaders of my group, or by a small part of the whole church during one specific period of history and in a certain cultural context, or by my denomination, or by this or that school of thought. Let us not misunderstand. The Bible is and must be the full and final authority for the church of God. However, not only is the Bible written in languages that few of us know, but we read and interpret it in given contexts with our own particular mind-sets shaped by all kinds of forces.

The classic Anglican Way speaks of *one* canon of Scripture in which are contained *two* Testaments, whose basic content is summarized and confessed in *three* Creeds (Apostles', Nicene, and Athanasian), whose dogma concerning the identity of the Trinity and the person of Jesus the Christ is set forth in the first *four* ecumenical councils (325, 381, 431, and 451), and whose developed liturgy, canon law, and church polity are seen in the first *five* centuries of its growth. Thus the historic episcopate is not an isolated phenomenon but part of a whole reality that we may call "the catholic faith."

In the light of all this, certain questions arise, such as: why was the basic episcopal polity and government of the church not seriously challenged until the sixteenth century? Let us be swift to admit that before AD 1500 the excesses, errors, and pollutions that had become attached to the basic threefold order of bishop, presbyter, and deacon were often exposed, and reforms were attempted and pursued. But let us also recognize that there was no obvious and serious exposition of congregationalism or presbyterianism, as the supposed divinely revealed form of church government/polity, until the effects of the Renaissance and of nationalism began to be felt in Europe and until the Bible was translated into a variety of languages and its pages were open for all to read and interpret.

Now to accept that congregationalism and presbyterianism only came on the scene in any meaningful sense in the sixteenth century, and, further, to claim that either one is clearly set forth in Holy Scripture for the right-minded to see is also implicitly to make several other claims, such as:

1. That the church had been blind in this matter for sixteen centuries.
2. That Christ the Lord of the church had allowed the church to be blind for so long.
3. That there is in the Reformation period a great development of doctrine, a development so great as to require the total dismemberment of the visible church on earth and its being put back together with a different "body."

If the shape, structure, and content of church government are so obviously clear in the New Testament, then there is a massive judgment over the centuries against the church—upon its pastors, teachers, and guides—for actually failing to see it. Worse still, for their thinking, teaching, and confessing that the Episcopal Way is that which is pleasing unto almighty God, being brought into being by his providential guidance.

EXISTENCE THROUGH SPACE AND TIME

Another matter to bear in mind is that the church of God has existed through space and time not only from the exaltation of Christ but before that, as the people of Israel under the Mosaic covenant. In fact, it is most important that we confess that the church is one, holy, apostolic, and catholic. Further, it is important that these marks or attributes of the church be taken as referring to the life, worship, and witness of the one people of God through time/history and in all places/space. So, the catholicity of the church refers to its being present through history in the whole world as well as (the redeemed) in heaven—the church militant and triumphant.

Now one reason why the episcopal polity can reasonably be seen as God's appointment is that it has the capacity to reflect the unity and catholicity of the visible church of God through space and time. The ordination and consecration of bishops by other bishops in historical succession and in communion with their brethren across space in other places is a clear sign of the unity and catholicity of the church. It demonstrates that the apostolic faith, with the Scriptures that contain it, are preserved and guarded for each generation. Not only are the actual faith (summarized in the creeds) and the text of Scripture passed along but so too are Scripture's interpretation and understanding. The latter, which we may call tradition, is of course reformable, and should be renewed and reformed regularly for the good of the whole visible church. Further, episcopal polity itself is reformable. For example, the excessive development of the role and power of the bishopric of Rome after the collapse of the western part of the Roman Empire is in principle reformable, even if it seems impossible right now to contemplate (especially when the pope is probably the most well known and popular man in the world!).

Now with the best will in the world it is difficult to imagine how other systems and polities could function as well as the episcopal one. Of course, if we think of the church as essentially and really only one when considered as invisible (that is, as known only from the bird's-eye view of heaven), then it is not crucial that the polity on earth be the means of maintaining and symbolizing its unity and catholicity. What matters on earth is that a given polity ensure the possibility that individual persons have a direct personal relationship to God through Christ and thus membership in that which in its true reality is only known and seen by God. But if we insist that there is a divinely given form of church polity in the New Testament, then that polity will surely be of such a nature and have such characteristics that it will naturally and efficiently portray the unity and catholicity as well as the apostolicity of the church of God. Neither presbyterianism nor congregationalism have this capacity for both cannot by their nature efficiently and obviously highlight that the church exists as one through space and time until the Lord returns in power and glory to judge the living and the dead.

Yet, if we look through the eyes of modern individualism (which originated about the time of the Protestant Reformation), we will see the local church as merely an efficient way of presenting the gospel so as to enable individuals to have individual relationships with Jesus and in him with God the Father, and thus be members of the church invisible, and the true elect of God. In that case, modern forms of congregationalism and presbyterianism will be more attractive than the historic and classical episcopal government of the church on earth.

THE CANON OF THE NEW TESTAMENT

What finally persuaded me—in the years that I studied Puritanism and Calvinism—of the givenness of the episcopal polity as a gift from the Lord of the church were two parallel developments that took place in the church of the second and third centuries.

First, there was the process whereby a variety of books claiming apostolic authorship or superintendence was received by the church after their content was tested and discerned over many years and in most places. Eventually, these books were agreed upon as the canon of the New Testament, which was itself added to the canon of the Old Testament. The church agreed on the canon of Scripture and those in charge of this process (in terms of presiding) were bishops.

Second, there was the process whereby from different starting points (in terms of the governing and leadership of local churches in the cities of the Empire) there arose over the years agreement as to the right polity of the church and the right form of ordained ministry. So not only did the church have the high privilege and awesome duty to serve the living Word of God, the Lord Jesus Christ, by collecting and authorizing the written Word of God but also to reveal the Threefold Ministry of bishop, presbyter, and deacon as ordained of God to rule and guide the visible church on earth.

In this period of the church, when her members were often persecuted and many became martyrs—and when she obviously read the Old Testament and (what we now call) the New Testament with fervor and commitment—why is it that she did not see either congregationalism or presbyterianism if they are so clearly set forth therein? As far as I know, the move from the flexible polity of the apostolic period, through various forms of episcopal/presbyterial government in the city churches of the Empire, to the full episcopal polity that at last emerged was without major hitches or debates. In fact, to suggest that there were is wholly to misunderstand the developing polity of the church of God in this important, formative period. Thus, I submit that it is of great importance that we recognize that the church which was so zealous to preserve and collect the documents of the new covenant was also zealous to preserve what the same people took to be the continuance of the apostolic faith and leadership through the persons of bishops, duly chosen and consecrated.

RELATION TO CONTEXT

Of course, it is true that the administration of the church, as she grew through evangelization and missionary endeavor, made use of the existing order within the Roman Empire. It made good sense to have major bishoprics in major cities and to develop the diocese as a basic unit over which a bishop had pastoral care. However, the basic Threefold Ministry is separate from this administrative procedure and can exist and function in wholly different situations and circumstances. So, in the missionary thrust into the world outside the Roman Empire, the historic episcopate adapted to local need and circumstances.

It is difficult to think of either presbyterianism or congregationalism existing before the time when they came into being (the sixteenth century), even as it is difficult to think of the kind of Baptists that exist in the United States as Southern Baptists before the nineteenth century. The reason for these assertions is that the Western world had to reach a certain stage of political development, including the beginnings of the assertion of what we now call human rights, in order for these polities to make sense, have an appeal, and thus to (as it were all of a sudden) actually appear as present in the Bible (now open to all to read).

In contrast, the episcopal system is much more flexible in terms of not being dependent upon the development of human, social, and political consciousness. It can function well under all forms of human government and in an ethos of highly developed theories of human rights as well as under a dictatorship. This testifies to its being produced under the providential guidance of God. Yet, as we have noted, the fact that it is of God's appointment does not mean that it is exempted from the influence of the world, the flesh, and the devil. In fact, it is open to be more corruptible than other polities because it has further to fall! On the other hand, as was stated at the beginning, the Lord Jesus prayed and prays still for the unity of his people on earth, and this visible unity will only be possible if the church is governed in an episcopal way. For this way alone has the potential and capability to hold together in a dynamic way millions of people from different cultures.

The episcopal polity does not mean that there is no place for shared ministries, for local ordained ministry, and for "lay" ministry. While certain specific leadership roles and duties are certainly reserved to the bishop, many varied and important ministries at the local, diocesan, and national levels are open to presbyters, deacons, and the nonordained. In fact, one can say that all the benefits claimed for both the congregational and presbyterian systems can be experienced richly within a properly functioning episcopal system, because local and district lay leadership is necessary to the right functioning of episcopal polity.

CONCLUSION

As the chief pastor, teacher, administrator of the sacraments, and imposer of discipline, the bishop is an authentic and necessary part of what—in terms of historical evidence—is Christianity and the church of God. For many centuries the entire church on earth was led by bishops, and even since the sixteenth century to this day the majority of the church's membership is bishop-led.

Unless we are thinking wholly individualistically, then Christianity as a historical religion has always included bishops.

In what is often called the Chicago-Lambeth Quadrilateral of 1888, the Lambeth conference of Anglican bishops set forth what they saw as the basis for the reunion of the churches. The four essentials were the Scriptures, the creeds, the gospel sacraments, and the historic episcopate "locally adapted in the methods of its administration to the varying needs of the nations and peoples called of God into the unity of his church."

Those who advocate other forms of church government fail to take the clear evidence of centuries of clear testimony into account. This is usually because they are reacting to what they call Romanism or popery, or because they have a wrong view of *sola scriptura*, and/or the implications of stating that the Bible is the final authority for all matters of faith and conduct. The canon of Scripture did not drop down from heaven, as it were, wrapped in golden paper and containing within the parcel the one and only correct interpretation of its holy content. It emerged in historical circumstances and within a church that already possessed what it knew to be the gospel and sound teaching, which may be called tradition. Thus, with the emergence of the canon of Scripture there existed and developed a sense of its central message.

A final word. I have been describing the episcopal system as it ought to be and can be; but yet I realize that it has often been, and is today, in some places weak or corrupted. I can only say that the church is in the world to serve the world and to be there for the world, but it is not to be of the world! And what applies to the church applies to its divinely ordained Ministry!

A PRESBYTERIAN'S CLOSING REMARKS

L. Roy Taylor

A SURREJOINDER TO TOON

Presbyterianism has never been popular in England. Episcopacy and monarchy were seen as necessary to each other, as evinced by the terse statement "no bishop, no king." Even in the days of the Protectorate under Cromwell, though the English parliament adopted the Westminster Confession of Faith, it never adopted the Form of Government, a document advocating presbyterian polity, advanced by the Westminster Assembly. Dr. Toon's emphatic critique of presbyterian polity[1] is essentially a historical argument with overtones of Anglican disdain for things presbyterian.[2]

Toon's major criticism is that I do not recognize that episcopacy developed under the providence of God in space and time. As a Calvinist I believe that *everything* that happens is within the providence of God. That does *not* mean that God directly causes everything to happen that occurs; that is fatalism. Our understanding is that (1) some things God directly causes; (2) some things God allows to happen; (3) some things God keeps from happening; (4) some evil God limits in its extent; (5) but God uses all things eventually to accomplish his will. My Anglican brother seems exercised that I will not agree that because episcopacy developed early in the life of the church, that God *caused* episcopacy to become its polity. No, I do not accept the argument that just because a belief or practice developed in the church (in this instance episcopacy) over a period of time, that God directed it thus. There were a number of beliefs and practices that arose early in church history and were embellished in the medieval era that Protestant Reformers later repudiated.[3] Surely Dr. Toon would not use the same line of reasoning that God must have directed the church to believe and teach matters later regarded as heresies simply because they appeared early in the life of the church, at least in rudimentary form. Using similar reasoning one could argue that since the idea of Petrine supremacy appeared in the patristic era and the Roman papacy later developed, it must have been God's ideal design for the church.

The Roman Catholic Church and the Eastern Orthodox churches hold that the church herself is infallible. This leads to some rather strained attempts to reconcile some apparently contradictory statements made by church councils. Protestants do not believe that the church is infallible. Presbyterians ,[4] Lutherans,[5] and Protestants in general understand that some synods and councils have erred. The Anglican tradition likewise recognizes this to be true.[6] Indeed, Anglicans do not necessarily hold to the teaching of all seven ecumenical councils, but only to the first four, as Toon has pointed out elsewhere.[7] As an Anglican, Toon would not argue for an infallible church. Yet his insistence on the necessity for one who holds to presbyterian polity to accept episcopacy because that is what the church taught and practiced from the mid-second century through the early sixteenth century appears to flirt with the idea of an infallible church on the issue of polity.

Toon offers several alleged proofs of episcopacy (and thereby alleged refutations of presbyterianism) that seem to me to be *non sequiturs*. First, he argues that the early church councils that approved the canon of Scripture and early creeds were councils of bishops, and therefore proves episcopacy. A Presbyterian could similarly argue that since the Synod of La Rochelle (1571), the Reformed Synod of Emden (1571), the Synod of Dort (1619), and the Westminster Assembly (1643–48) were Presbyterian councils in an era when the church was blessed by God (i.e., the Reformation), that such providential circumstance proves the principle of presbyterian polity. Second, he argues that my conceding that episcopacy prevailed for more than fourteen centuries also proves that God directed episcopal polity. As

I see it, such a concession is simply an objective recognition of historical fact; it is not agreeing that episcopacy was the divine intention. Third, he argues that one who holds to presbyterian polity may not legitimately appeal to the writings of the Fathers since episcopacy appeared so early in the church and many of the Fathers were bishops. But one need not agree with another in every particular to benefit from his insights. For example, Anglicans do not accept John Calvin's polity, yet much of the Thirty-Nine Articles of Religion are consistent with Calvin's theology. In the same manner, one need not hold to episcopacy to benefit from a bishop's writings. The post-biblical writer whom Calvin[8] most frequently quoted in the *Institutes* was Augustine, bishop of Hippo.

There are also several misunderstandings Toon appears to have regarding my argument for presbyterian polity. First, he seems to think that I maintain that there was one, standard, extensively developed polity in the church from the time of the apostles until the incipient episcopacy of the mid-second century. Due to slowness of communication and the geographical dispersion of the churches coupled with the local cultural influences of each church, I think that variations existed within a general framework. Moreover, I argued a position that the Bible teaches *general principles,* not exhaustive details of polity.

Second, he is under the impression that I would base a theology of ministry solely upon the Old Testament office of elder. The primary purpose of my chapter was to argue for a representative-connectional (presbyterian) church government, not to explain fully the office of minister of the Word. A cursory look at Reformed confessions of faith, books of church order, and theological works on ecclesiology will reveal that in some respects the new covenant minister of the Word is similar to the prophets, declaring the Word of God by expounding the Scriptures; in some respects the minister is similar to a priest representing the people to God and God to the people, but without sacerdotalism.

Third, Toon seems to believe that I was saying that the transition from early presbyterian polity to episcopacy in the second century means that "the church was going down the broad way that leads to perdition rather than seeking to walk in the narrow way that leads to life." I do not think that it was a sin for ministers to serve within a hierarchy of what became the Threefold Ministry.[9] I believe, as I delineated, that circumstantial reasons explain why the patristic church developed into episcopacy.[10]

Toon characterizes my argument for presbyterianism as essentially a biblical argument and one not shaped by the post-apostolic history of the church. In that respect he is accurate. We disagree, however, as to how one interprets the history of the church regarding the development of an episcopal hierarchy. As one considers a basis for a greater unity in the church, presbyterians could agree to the patristic consensus of one canon of Scripture, two testaments, three creeds,[11] and the first four undisputed ecumenical councils. But we could not accept the necessity of the episcopacy that had developed by the end of five centuries, as our Anglican friends consider essential.

A SURREJOINDER TO PATTERSON

Dr. Patterson agrees with much of what I advocated, namely that historical circumstances primarily account for the rise of episcopacy, that the New Testament uses the terms "bishop" and "elder" synonymously,[12] that no one form of church government guarantees the maintenance of theological orthodoxy, and that the "no-creed-but-Christ" claim is simplistic. However, there are many points of disagreement, some based on misunderstandings.

Miscellaneous Clarifications and Responses

He asks for some clarification on the matter of apostolic succession. In my primary chapter, I sought to distinguish between a more physical view of apostolic succession through a supposedly unbroken chain of ordination of bishops who theoretically could trace their ordinations back to the apostles[13] and a spiritual succession of faithful ministers who follow the teaching and practices of the apostles. In the latter view, apostolic succession is not limited to the "historic episcopate." On the matter of Landmarkism, I do not believe I stated that Landmarkism is or ever has been the majority view among Baptists.

Evidently Patterson believes that presbyterian church government is a hindrance to missions, judging from his suggestion that "denominational bureaucracies of the type Taylor advocates are seldom an asset to world mission endeavors." It would be well to note that it was not until the twentieth century that Baptists in America fielded more missionaries than American Presbyterians (though Presbyterians were fewer in number).[14]

Patterson avers that I misunderstand congregationalism. I stated that, "On the other end of the continuum, congregational government in its purest form is found in smaller congregations. As congregations grow, it becomes impractical to have the congregation vote on minute details of church ministry operations." I indicated that, practically speaking, there must be some delegation of decision-making authority as congregations grow, either through a *de facto* presbyterianism or a *de facto* episcopal government. I did not say that congregationalism requires that the congregation vote on every item. Theoretically that could be the case, but practically it is virtually impossible.

Patterson argues that both presbyterianism and episcopacy are, by nature, bureaucratic and that bureaucracies are "seldom efficient and often self-serving." Just as I argued that no form of church government absolutely guarantees the maintenance of theological integrity, I also argue that any system of church government may develop into a bureaucracy. Surely Patterson would not argue that his own congregationally governed denomination, the largest Protestant denomination in the USA, is free of denominational bureaucracy! Patterson argues, "The burden of proof for the necessity of abandoning congregationalism that seems often present in the New Testament still rests upon the advocates of elder rule and presbyterianism." That assumes (1) that one may only use the New Testament in determining church government, and (2) that the New Testament advocates congregationalism, both of which I have disproved in my primary chapter.

Patterson seems to think that I do not hold the Scripture to be the final authority in determining the form of church government for the church today because I said that "most Christians would turn first to the Bible. But there are other factors to consider as well, such as common sense, culture, Christian wisdom, local circumstances, biblical precedents and general biblical principles, not just biblical commands and prohibitions." At no point, however, did I or would I place extrabiblical factors above or equal to the Bible. Insofar as I know, no serious scholar claims that there is a *highly developed, complex* system of church governance in the Bible. Each system's advocates use more than biblical commands and prohibitions alone to seek to establish an argument. Moreover, many of the practices we use to coordinate ministry in local churches, regional denominational ministry, and national denominational ministry are based on Scripture in a rudimentary form, but are fully embellished by the use of the other factors we have mentioned. Other matters, though not explicitly derived from the Bible, are not contrary to the Bible and we may use them.[15] All branches of the church have developed such traditions. The intimation that advocates of presbyterian church government place ecclesiastical tradition on par with or above the Scriptures is simply factually incorrect.

Continuity and Discontinuity Between the Testaments

Patterson objects to my using the principle of biblical interpretation of emphasizing certain continuities between the Old Testament and the New Testament particularly in relation to ecclesiology. It is on the basis of the Reformed view that the continuity of the church spans both testaments that I began my discussion of polity with the Old Testament. The issue of continuity and discontinuity of the Old and New Testaments affects not only church polity and the sacraments,[16] but the nature of the church itself. Is the New Testament church a separate entity from Old Testament Israel? Virtually all major systems of Christian theology recognize that there are both similarities and differences between the Old and New Testaments. But the respective systems place varying degrees of emphasis on the continuities as distinguished from the discontinuities. Eastern Orthodoxy and Roman Catholicism place great emphasis on the continuities and little on the discontinuities and, as a result, have a priesthood and a sacrificial view of the Eucharist. At the other end of the theological continuum are those who are heir to the sixteenth-century Anabaptists (non-dispensational Baptists according to Patterson) or heir to nineteenth-century dispensationalism[17] who place great emphasis on the discontinuities. Between those two polar positions are the Anglicans, Lutherans, and the Reformed or Presbyterians.[18] Evidently, Patterson leans toward the dispensational position, judging from his statement that, "The church is the bride of Christ, and it seems doubtful to me that this distinction [between Old Testament Israel and the New Testament church] will be lost even in eternity," which appears to be reminiscent of the Scofield–Chafer position that Israel will spend eternity on the new earth and the church will spend eternity in the new heaven.

The relationship of Old Testament Israel and the New Testament church is so significant and complex that it warrants more extensive discussion than the scope of this book allows.[19] Because it has a direct bearing on the issue of church polity, in my primary chapter I briefly outlined why presbyterians believe that the church is composed of God's people of both the Old and New Testament eras (see p. 76).[20]

In addition, the unity of the church from the Old Testament to the New Testament is demonstrated by the New Testament's claim that Old Testament statements about Israel are fulfilled in the New Testament. For example, when Peter preached on the Day of Pentecost (see Acts 2, particularly vv. 14–40), he described the outpouring of the Holy Spirit as a direct fulfillment of the prophecy of Joel 2:28–32.[21] Peter offered no nuanced interpretation of Joel's prophecy that would separate Israel and the church. And at the council of Jerusalem (Acts 15), when the apostles debated whether Gentile believers need to be circumcised to keep the ceremonial law, the issue was settled by an appeal to Amos 9:11–12. Apparently James saw no problem with the conversion of the Gentiles being a fulfillment of Amos's prophecy.[22]

Patterson places much of his argument on Paul's statement regarding the church as "mystery" (Eph. 3:1–7). He states, "Further, believers make up 'the body of Christ,' an idea unknown and unforeseen in the Old Testament (1 Cor. 6:19; Rev. 21:9)." He later qualifies that statement a bit by saying, "But, by the same token, the church is a mystery of God anticipated in the Old Testament only by references to a coming 'new covenant,' promises of a Messiah, and the vision of an era of Gentile responsiveness to God (Jer. 31:27–40; Isa. 9:1–3)." All Christians agree that the Bible describes the church as a "mystery." The issue is the meaning of the term "mystery." Was it a concept entirely hidden from the Old Testament prophets, something totally unknown by them, something new and unique to Paul? Or could it be that a "mystery" was a truth only partially revealed in the Old Testament through various hints and clues, not explained until the fuller revelation of the New Testament?[23] Patterson objects to my appeal to the continuity of the church from the Old Testament to the New Testament when discussing polity. But what we really have is a basic disagreement over the relationship between the Old and New Testaments, principles of biblical interpretation, and resultant differences between doctrines of the church.

A SURREJOINDER TO WALDRON

Plural-elder congregationalism is similar to presbyterianism in that both views of ecclesiastical polity hold that (1) the Bible teaches that there should be a plurality of elders as the spiritual leaders of a local congregation, that the pastor is not the only elder,[24] and (2) that the office of deacon is one of mercy ministry, sympathy, and service, not one of spiritual oversight.[25] Moreover, the Reformed family of churches extends beyond Presbyterian churches to include others who hold to a Reformed soteriology, but not necessarily presbyterian church government and a covenantal view of the sacraments.

The Continuity of the Church in the Old and New Testaments

Waldron objects to my view of the continuity and discontinuity between the Old Testament and New Testament phases of the church. As a Baptist he *must* do so in order to reject the connection the New Testament makes in Colossians 2:11–12 between the Old Testament sign of the covenant (circumcision) and the New Testament sign of the covenant (baptism). Waldron does not advance the dispensational view of the church, as did Patterson. Instead, in expressing his view, he quotes from the 1689 Baptist Confession that was based, to a very large extent, on the Westminster Confession.[26] While Patterson sees the church as an exclusively New Testament entity unknown to and unforeseen by the Old Testament prophets,[27] Waldron places his emphasis on the differences between the old covenant and the new covenant. Waldron states, "The Old Testament church was a physical nation. The New Testament church is a spiritual nation." I would not dispute that statement altogether, but I would qualify it somewhat. In the Old Testament, the church (if we define it as the elect persons) existed *before* the calling of Abraham and the birth of the nation Israel. Moreover, in the Old Testament phase of the church, there were people who were part of the covenant nation of Israel (visible church) who were not regenerate and therefore not part of the true people of God (invisible church). Paul made that quite clear in Romans 2:28–29. There are also similar statements to that effect in the Old Testament.[28] We understand that part of the Old Testament law, the civil law, related to the unique theocracy of Israel[29] and that the New Testament does not require the establishment of a theocratic state. Under the Old Testament theocracy, church discipline and civil penalties were intertwined,[30] which is assuredly not the case in the New Testament.[31] The New Testament places a stronger emphasis on the spiritual aspects of the covenant. In short, there are certainly discontinuities between the Old Testament and the New Testament, but the distinctions are not as simplistic and airtight as Waldron seems to indicate.

Both Waldron and Patterson give great weight to Christ's promise in Matthew 16:18 being in the future tense: "I *will* build my church." For Patterson, it is a proof text for the church's being a uniquely New Testament entity, unrelated to the Old Testament believers. For Waldron, who holds to unity of the church spanning both testaments, Matthew 16:18 indicates, "The drastic discontinuity between the nature and polity of the old church and the new church is behind Jesus' use of the future tense in his first recorded mention of the church." I respectfully disagree with Patterson's and Waldron's exegesis. My explanation of Matthew 16:18 is simply that Jesus was reiterating the principle set forth in many places in the Bible, under numerous similes, metaphors, and other figures of speech, namely, that Christ and the gospel, through the church, will eventually triumph in this world over Satan and all his forces.[32]

I appreciate Waldron's comment that "information about elders in the Old Testament may be helpful in understanding what the New Testament teaches." I would go further to say that the New Testament's statements about elders should be interpreted in light of the Old Testament's teaching on the subject. Church polity is like other doctrines, introduced in the Old Testament and more clearly and completely developed in the

New Testament. But that does not mean we only *optionally* consider the Old Testament data.[33]

The Distinction Between Teaching and Ruling Elders

Waldron questions my view of there being two types of elders, namely ruling elders and teaching elders. In response, first, I point out that we are not talking about two entirely separate and unrelated categories. Second, I remind the reader that the office of elder originated in the Old Testament (see Num. 11) with the seventy elders sharing the burden of spiritual leadership with Moses. Third, I have no objection to Waldron's using three concentric circles, not just two, to describe the role of all elders.[34] Fourth, Waldron is concerned that a presbyterian distinction between ruling elders and teaching elders "*implies*" [emphasis added] the distinction between clergy and laity." Presbyterians, however, have *never* taught the type of clericalism that one finds in Roman Catholic, Eastern Orthodox, and Anglo Catholic circles. Moreover, most Baptists still prefer that, *ordinarily*, a minister (rather than a ruling elder or deacon) administer baptism and communion. Fifth, Waldron is concerned about my reference to teaching elders as "pastors." Just as all elders teach in various ways, but some are more gifted in teaching, the same principle applies to shepherding. All elders are to be involved in various ways in shepherding the flock; some elders are particularly gifted and called to the pastoral function. Sixth, Waldron is disquieted that I supposedly cite only three texts[35] to justify a distinction between ruling elders and teaching elders. I believe that the Old Testament bases for the office of elder and synagogue tradition also have bearing on the issue. I believe we all agree that the biblical data on polity is not as extensive as on other matters, such as the deity of Christ. Moreover, given the divine inspiration and final authority of the Bible, how many proof texts does one need to establish a point? Would not even one be sufficient?

The Representative and Connectional Nature of Presbyterian Polity

Waldron lists only two major objections to presbyterian polity: (1) "New Testament polity is not strictly and legally representative," and (2) New Testament church polity is not strictly and legally connectional." I note, and trust that readers will note, that Waldron speaks of "New Testament church polity" not "biblical church polity." I have already extensively addressed the issue of using both testaments in developing church polity. Notice also that Waldron qualifies both objections with the words "*not strictly*" [emphasis added], indicating that he cannot completely object to my assertion that biblical polity is representative and connectional.

Waldron cites two major texts that deal with church discipline (Matt. 18:15–20 and 2 Cor. 5:1–13) to support his view that the congregation, not the elders representing the congregation, is to practice church discipline. Frankly, at first glance, those two texts may appear to militate against the presbyterian position. Regarding both texts, I agree with most commentators and church historians that church polity in the New Testament is in embryonic form. I would add that there are certain clear, though nascent, principles in the New Testament. I understand Matthew 18:15–20 in light of the embryonic form of church polity at that point. I interpret that text in light of the Old Testament office of elder and the synagogue tradition of elders handling spiritual discipline. Moreover, there are occasions in Scripture where a figure of speech called a synecdoche is used (a part is used for the whole or the whole used for the part).[36] Matthew 18:15–20 may be a synecdoche; "tell it to the church" may mean to have the church's spiritual leaders (the elders) handle disciplinary cases.[37] Concerning the 2 Corinthians passage, Waldron (who holds that *ideally* a local church should have a plurality of elders) states, "The elders of the church in Corinth are never mentioned in this letter. Indeed from the contents of this epistle itself it remains uncertain whether this church even as yet had elders." Though it was Paul's practice to ordain elders in every church (Acts 14:23), and though there may have been elders in Corinth without their being specifically mentioned, I concede that in the church at Corinth, at the point of Paul's writing his epistles to them, "it remains uncertain whether this church *even as yet* [emphasis added] had elders." Both Matthew 18 and 2 Corinthians 5 bring us back to the hermeneutical issue of the relationship of the Old and New Testaments.

Waldron's second major objection is "New Testament church polity is not strictly and legally connectional." As his major proof, he offers his understanding of Acts 15, the council of Jerusalem. Essentially he offers two arguments to substantiate his qualified statement. First, after conceding that the council's elders shared authority with the apostles, he explains this was a unique presbyterial authority because the Jerusalem church was the mother church and because the troublemakers who insisted on circumcision of Gentile believers may have been from the Jerusalem church. It is significant that Waldron concedes that elders shared authority together, and that they shared authority even with the apostles. If congregationalism (whether single-elder or plural-elder) is the teaching of the New Testament, then no church, not even the Jerusalem mother church, may have any authority over any other church such as Antioch or the family of churches Paul and Barnabas had planted on the first missionary journey.

Second, Waldron concedes that the theological decision of the council was a binding confessional standard on all churches as Acts 15:23, 30 clearly indicates. He turns the question from *whether* there was a binding confessional standard to *why* there was a binding confessional standard. His explanation again is to state that the Jerusalem church was unique because the apostles were in it and perhaps because the Jerusalem elders had some sort of unique authority due to their association with the apostles. But changing the question to *why* it was binding may not simply dismiss the undeniable fact *that* it was binding, which thus negates any claim to congregational theological autonomy. Waldron sees the council of Jerusalem as "a unique, redemptive-historical event" without any force of precedent. I see it as an authoritative paradigm for church polity.

A SINGLE-ELDER CONGREGATIONALIST'S CLOSING REMARKS

Paige Patterson

A SURREJOINDER TO TOON

Peter Toon's response to my chapter supporting single-elder congregationalism is both enlightening and disappointing. Inadvertently, I am certain, he totally misrepresents my position, based not on what I say but rather upon his own suppositions. Toon alleges that I have "virtually no interest in the history of the one, holy, catholic, and apostolic church from the end of the first century until the early decades of the sixteenth century." This conclusion is erroneous on at least two counts and possibly three, and finally fails as an argument.

First, as an interested student of the history of theology, I personally have digested, as heavily as the temporal demands of my assignment allow, the perspectives of theologians and ecclesiastical movements in every area of church history. In fact, I have studied especially the dissenting movements within Christianity, many of which predate the sixteenth century. Some of Toon's claims make me wonder whether he has availed himself of this rich, but lesser known, history of God's people. Peter Chelcicky, for example, led a radical separatist movement in Bohemia at the close of the fourteenth century and the beginning of the fifteenth century. His emphasis on biblical authority and doctrine obviously precedes the Reformation.

Second, interest in the "one, holy, catholic, and apostolic church" would not necessitate agreement with all the views endorsed by the theologians of that era. Hopefully, Toon would endorse Augustine's Christology but reject his astrological sentiments. As for me, I applaud the efforts of many in the patristic church to assess the New Testament teaching on the Trinity but reject the unbiblical development of virtually defining the church based on its clergy.

Third, depending upon what Toon means by "one, holy, catholic, and apostolic church," the level of my interest is indeed affected. If he means the fellowship of all true, twice-born, regenerate children of God, then I am very interested in what they think, whenever they lived. On the other hand, if he references the developing hierarchy of a connectional church in ways distinct from the New Testament, then I still, as an aspiring scholar, have interest, but admittedly far less than I have for the Scriptures and the practices revealed therein.

Finally, this whole line of reasoning fails because it does not address the issue. The issue is not what men have said, however clever, but rather: has God spoken? If God has said something on a subject, it does not seem to me that his followers have the liberty to do otherwise. Since I believe that the development of ecclesiastical government violated New Testament practice, the question of "interest" in the first five centuries is of only relative importance.

On a second point, Toon alleges that I do not believe in the providential oversight of God in the early church. He claims that I "ignore or pass by the decrees of church councils." Of course, this is not the case, but hopefully Toon himself does not embrace every action of all the church councils in the first five centuries. But Toon cannot have his cake and eat it also. God's providence cannot be implicated in decisions to develop ideas or forms that contradict New Testament precedent and commandment.

Next, Toon pronounces me "poor," an allegation to which I readily admit. However, Toon's concern for me is that having cut myself off "from the grace of God revealed in the saints of those years," I am "left with a half-empty basket when it could be full." To this I only need to suggest that it is better to have a half basket full of revelation of God, which is true, than to have a full basket of the "revelations" of saints, some of which are in error.

Although Toon admits that he can point to no sentence or paragraph in my chapter to sustain his conclusion, he, undeterred by this limitation, suggests that I am using the pragmatic principles of the supermarket in formulating my views. Whether or not I have made my case based on the Scriptures is for the reader to determine. But to charge that my view is based on some principle other than those found in the source I claim as my authority is unworthy of a scholar of Toon's ability.

Toon complains, "It is difficult to argue with someone like Patterson who enters the debate ruling out the major evidence concerning the case." But a scholar of Toon's erudition surely encounters no difficulty with me. Rather his problem in the debate is that which he inadvertently confesses in this complaint. Ostensibly, by appealing to the Bible alone, i.e., to the Word of God, I am "ruling out *the major evidence* concerning the case" (italics mine). Here, in a nutshell, is the whole issue between Toon and me. If the "major evidence" to be filtered belongs to the developing church of the first five centuries, then Toon may well be able to make his case. If, however, the Bible alone is the "major source" for the determination of our ecclesiology, then his case is hopelessly lost. Virtual admission of this is found when he notes that "nothing would be achieved by my offering alternative readings of the New Testament evidence (verses and the like) for episcopal polity—that is, offering a differing exegesis and interpretation." Once again, the issue for Toon is not the exegesis of the Scriptures but rather the developing doctrine of the church across five centuries.

Other reasons for this lack of concern for the scriptural formation of ecclesiology is made lucid in note 35 of his critique. Toon writes:

> Today, it is generally argued by episcopalians that the New Testament evidence, read alone and without the context of the early church, wherein the books of the New Testament were read and collected, contains *no* blueprint for a later, specific form of polity. This is because the apostolic age is one of expansion and development and the results of this work of the Lord are only seen in a settled form in say AD 150 or 200.

While I too have stressed the fluid nature of the developing churches of the New Testament period, moving from the absolute authority of Christ to the somewhat diminished authority of the apostles (except when writing under divine inspiration) to the further diminished authority of the pastor and, where applicable, the other elders, to the empowerment of the congregation, such a situation does not necessitate developments in ecclesiology from a later period that violate New Testament principles.

Perhaps Toon's most unfortunate error occurs in his discussion of the origins of congregationalism. He says:

> Furthermore, the sixteenth and seventeenth centuries saw a massive reaction to much of what the medieval church had stood for and taught. In such reaction the danger was (and the reality became) that the baby was thrown out with the bathwater. The Bible was read without reference to the way it had been understood by the church which authorized the Canon, making it possible to set aside God's providential guidance and rule of his church over the preceding fifteen centuries. Nothing really mattered between AD 100 and 1520!

The concern of the Reformers initially was to reform the church, calling it back to a more biblical base for its theology and practice. When Rome was unresponsive and Luther was excommunicated, the Reformers were faced with the inevitabilities of establishing the various church expressions of the Reformation, including, oddly enough, the Anglican Church. At no point was Luther, himself an Augustinian monk, uninterested in church life and thought between 100 and 1520. The Anabaptists, on the other hand, were in the strictest sense, restorationists rather than reformers, believing that what is largely corrupt is unreformable. Yet even they, biblicists though they were, sometimes cited the church fathers, demonstrating both awareness and interest.

On the other hand, Toon needs to revisit the famous incident at Leipzig in 1519 when noted Catholic debater John Eck accused Luther of being a Hussite. Up until this pregnant moment, Luther apparently still held to conciliar authority even though he rejected papal authority. Reading Hus, Luther discovered the inadequacy of conciliar authority and abandoned it in favor of the now renowned *sola scriptura*. It seems to me unfortunate that Peter Toon, a Protestant, finds himself in more agreement with Eck than with Luther. After all, one cannot have it both ways.

"There is no trace of any clear evidence for what in modern times has been called congregationalism until well into the sixteenth century." This is Toon's avowal, which demonstrates once again his unfamiliarity with the history of dissent.

Toon concludes that "Patterson's arguments are only convincing to those who blot from their minds, memories, and evaluation the real evidence: that episcopal polity was the polity of the church of God from earliest times to the sixteenth century and has been since then, right until the present day, the polity of the greatest part numerically and geographically of the fractured church of God." Maybe so. On the other hand, perhaps many shall be discovered for whom tradition as authority is too bad to be true. Maybe there are lovers of freedom and the free church who still prefer to hear from and govern themselves according to the Word of God. I pray so.

A SURREJOINDER TO TAYLOR

Roy Taylor's response to my chapter represents a kind, fair, carefully considered evaluation of my free church position from the perspective of a presbyterian. While respecting his tradition, few will find it unusual that we do not agree on much in ecclesiology.

The earliest records of the New Testament church reveal the following. In Acts 1, immediately after the ascension of Jesus, the disciples returned to the Upper Room. The Holy Spirit through Luke wrote the unusual words, "The number of names was about a hundred and twenty" (v. 15), suggesting a possible list of names composing membership. Peter reminded this assembled group, that must at least be considered the incipient church, that Judas had fallen, thus fulfilling Scripture (vv. 16–20). Then, apparently the entire body sought God's face and rendered their judgment, choosing Matthias as Judas's replacement. The congregation made the decision!

In Acts 6, the Twelve again faced a problem and they "summoned the multitude of the disciples" (v. 2), explained the situation, and then the church chose the seven (v. 5). Here again the whole assembly of believers seems to assume responsibility.

Previously I have argued that the fluid state of affairs which existed in the apostolic era regarding authority in the churches existed precisely because the apostles were still alive and active among the churches. This reality constituted a transitional stage from the absolute authority of Jesus to the less pervasive apostolic authority of the post-ascension church, leading ultimately to the authority of the believers themselves in the local churches in the post-apostolic age. If this is an accurate depiction, then the two events chronicled above are even more remarkable in that the Twelve do neither of these important tasks without the solicitation of the entire church.

If anyone had the knowledge, power, and authority to make these decisions about the replacement of Judas and the selection of the seven, surely the twelve apostles could have claimed that authority! Instead, what rather clearly unfolds in this early phase of congregationalism was quite consistent with the theology of the individual believer-priests, each possessing the permanent indwelling of the Holy Spirit (John 14:17).

Governance in the church should develop from a theological understanding of Christ, salvation, and the purpose and nature of the believing community. While important Old Testament concepts are retained in the new order, the church is, nonetheless, a new order. As a part of that new order, the priesthood of the few has been replaced by the priesthood of all true believers, and this alone constitutes a radical departure with extensive ramifications in the life and governance of churches.

Regarding the role of elders and deacons in those assemblies, Taylor did not accurately represent my position. For example, he insists that I posit the pastor as usually the only elder in the local church. In fact, I argue to the contrary that any local assembly which experienced growth would soon, of necessity, have multiple elders. I also argued, to borrow a phrase from Sam Waldron, for a *primary*-elder congregationalism, recognizing the leadership role of the teaching elder in this arrangement. However, no mandate for multiple elders in a given congregation is distinguishable in the New Testament.

Second, Taylor suggests that in many Baptist churches, deacons have a role of spiritual leadership, not just mercy ministry. This I certainly never denied, although I did suggest the physical ministries of the church as the primary role of the deacons (Acts 6:1–6). Furthermore, the unfortunate practice in many Baptist churches of creating a governing "board" of deacons is no more commendable than episcopacy or elder rule except that at least more of the church would usually be involved in the decision-making process.

In any case, the practice of a few or many individual Baptist congregations is not the standard for faith and worship. The New Testament must remain supreme in this regard. Interestingly, Taylor acknowledges that "in the late first and early second centuries, the deaconate was a lay ministry of mercy. As the episcopal system began to develop in the second century, the office of deacon became an entry-level clergy position." Thus, Taylor has signaled both the state of affairs in the early church as well as the unfortunate drift toward episcopacy. The presbyterian approach is a halfway house on the road from New Testament ecclesiology to episcopacy.

A major response of Taylor to my theological basis for congregationalism is to grasp firmly the obvious, namely, that the indwelling Holy Spirit in each member of a body of believers scarcely ensures right decisions. I agree for two reasons. Some in the gathered church may not really be regenerate (1 John 2:19). If these have a predominant voice, the church will often be in error and in some cases even fail. Furthermore, even Spirit-indwelt believers are not yet glorified and may often allow pride, desire for power, etc. to triumph over the witness of the Spirit.

That acknowledged, one may be forgiven for asking how exactly is episcopal or presbyterial rule either different or an improvement? Surely, the historical landscape is just as littered with the failures of episcopal bishops and presbyterian elders as of congregational misfires.

In fact, the debacle of the episcopacy's recent recognition of gay bishops, while many more biblically centered and spiritually committed in the church watch helplessly the drift of the Anglican church, should be proof enough. Congregational churches can also make such mistakes, but when they do, they do not take all others with them in their heresy.

But Taylor would correctly resist by saying that his plea is for the elder rule of presbyterianism, not for episcopacy. But what about all of the saintly Presbyterians who find themselves marooned in the Presbyterian Church U.S.A.? Of course, Presbyterians can and did create a new denomination, the Presbyterian Church of America, but the older one, still with many godly parishioners, holds its individual congregations in captivity.

Since, therefore, all systems are subject to fallible and fallen men, I would rather bank on a system that has its roots set firmly in the regenerative action of the Holy Spirit who indwells each twice-born believer, making of the group together a "holy priesthood" exercising all the rights and responsibilities incumbent upon a New Testament priesthood. Furthermore, just because I do know the carnage of ecclesiastical fallibility, I believe I will continue with the New Testament concept of autonomous congregations (note again the apostle Paul pleading with the church at Corinth to do right rather than ordering them to act [1 Cor. 5:1–5]), working separately but voluntarily cooperating together for the work of the kingdom. That way, if the ship takes on water in one compartment, it will not sink the whole.

Finally, regarding "elders," I fear that Taylor makes several mistakes. Appeal to the seventy elders in the Old Testament is only valid if Reformed ecclesiology is adopted which sees the Jewish nation as the "church" in the Old Testament. Obviously, I view the church as a mystery, made known in Christ, and in any event, totally distinct from Israel, the people of God under the old covenant. There is indebtedness to the old order on the part of the church, but there is much that is new, not the least of which is the priesthood of the believers.

Taylor also continues to assume, without offering convincing evidence, that the earliest churches all had a plurality of elders. As I have demonstrated elsewhere, the texts he cites (e.g., Titus 1:5) can just as easily and, I might add, under the circumstances more likely be understood to mandate at least one elder for each of the several congregations on the island of Crete.

Concerning the uses of the terms *proistemi* and *hegeomoi*, Taylor seems not to have done his lexical homework. A look at the *Liddell-Scott Greek Lexicon*, or any substantial lexicon of Koine Greek will be sufficient to establish that, like most words, both *proistemi* and *hegeomoi* have a range of meanings from strong concepts like "rule" to less demanding ones like "care for" or "give aid." Reicke, for example, writing on *proistemi* in the *Theological Dictionary of the New Testament*, remarks that most New Testament uses of the word apparently have the sense of "lead."[38] Büchsel comes to a similar conclusion regarding *hegemoi*.[39]

While I join Taylor in finding a stronger sense of both terms (particularly *hegemoi*) than that advocated by Reicke or Büchsel, I do not think it possible on this basis to establish a presbyterian form of church government. Furthermore, Taylor's appeal on this issue will do more to assist Toon in his argument for episcopacy than it will to help presbyterianism.

Finally, I conclude concerning both the theology of the nature of salvation and the purpose of the church, that the precedent of emerging congregationalism in the New Testament, and the history of the church all testify eloquently to the wisdom of primary-elder congregationalism. Though all systems may be abused, primary-elder congregationalism offers freedom, authority, and responsibility all marvelously knit together under one Lord.

A SURREJOINDER TO WALDRON

May I begin by expressing my appreciation for Sam Waldron's response to my chapter. The two of us are actually much closer to one another than would be the case with either Toon or Taylor. For this reason I was surprised at the length and vociferousness of his response. Nevertheless, I am happy for the opportunity to clarify one matter and to sustain my argument further in certain other ways.

First, a word of clarification needs to be offered regarding my assignment in this volume. Waldron mistakenly says, "As noted previously, it is gratifying to see that Patterson has given up any attempt to defend *single-elder congregationalism*. He has chosen rather to defend *primary-elder congregationalism*. In so far as this reflects movement toward *plural-elder congregationalism*, this is, from my perspective, encouraging."

Waldron here falsely assumes that there has been some alteration in my position. This is understandable in that the editor may not have made it clear to him what I took to be my assignment in this book. I have no problem with multiple elders in a congregation when necessary. Clearly churches in the New Testament era often had more than one elder. It was my agreement with the editor that I could support single-elder congregationalism only if it was understood to denominate what Waldron calls primary-elder congregationalism. Therefore, Waldron's hope that I have changed is destined to disappointment, and he will be sad to learn that I remain quite unconvinced by his arguments. However, I do approve of his designation of "primary-elder congregationalism" and thank him for the appropriate nomenclature.

Essentially Waldron has three problems with my position. First, he assails my position as being held on "purely pragmatic grounds." To prove this point he makes the mistake of assuming that every appearance of the word "elder" in the plural ("elders") constitutes overwhelming evidence of plurality of elders in every congregation. In this regard he cites Acts 11:30; 13:1; 14:23; 20:17; Titus 1:5; James 5:14; 1 Peter 5:1–2; Philippians 1:1; Hebrews 13:7, 17, 24; and 1 Timothy 4:14. But these references do not achieve what Waldron hopes. Acts 11:30 and Acts 20:17 have in view the churches in Jerusalem and Ephesus—large churches, which, as I also have argued, would need a plurality of elders. Acts 12:1, 1 Peter 5:1–2, Philippians 1:1, and Hebrews 13:7, 17, 24 do not even mention elders as such, referencing "teachers" in the first case, "overseers" in Philippians, and "leaders" in the remaining references. However, I would probably agree with Waldron that elders are in view. At Philippi the church was likely large enough to necessitate multiple elders, but uncertainty about who is being addressed in Hebrews and James opens just as much the possibility that the plural "elders" accords to the plurality of churches addressed and not to the number of elders in any given congregation. This is surely the case in Acts 14:23 where Iconium, Lystra, and Derbe are all in view, and in Titus 1:5 where new churches on the island of Crete needed an elder for each of these congregations. First Peter 5:1–2 seems to be even more a case of this paradigm given Peter's extensive audience of saints living in Pontus, Galatia, Cappadocia, Asia, and Bithynia (1 Peter 1:1). That there is a message from Peter, a "fellow-elder," to elders in these areas makes perfect sense. Given the way Peter uses the title of himself suggests that even 1 Timothy 4:14 and the "laying on of the hands of the elders" does not require multiple elders in just one assembly.

The point I wish to make is brought to bear clearly when Waldron states: "Biblically speaking, it is *necessary* to speak of the abnormality of a lone elder" (italics mine). My question is simple. Where does the Bible say this? Again he says, "The New Testament teaches that it is *abnormal* and *deficient* for the church to have one elder" (italics mine). Where does the New Testament say this? How on earth can one get the idea of *deficiency* from the fact that Iconium, Lystra, Derbe, or various churches in Crete had only one elder? This classic example suggests eisegesis—reading into a text what you want it to say. What is *deficient* would be for a church to have no elder at all. This situation is, among other things, what Titus was to correct in Crete.

Waldron's second stated difference is really just the reversal of his first problem. He wishes to dispute the normative character of a single, primary elder. He wonders why the issue is so important to me if there are "simply no commandments" on the issue. First, it is important to me precisely because some want to make plurality of elders mandatory when there is no such command. Waldron is exhibiting the trait that makes this position an issue for me. Even if it could be demonstrated that all the churches in the New Testament era boasted multiple elders (which it emphatically cannot) that would still be less than a mandate. The church is told to evangelize, teach, baptize, etc., but never in the same fashion to have more than one elder. I have attempted to evaluate the practice in the New Testament, admitting that we are lacking a clear mandate from the Scriptures. Waldron might want to consider greater hermeneutical humility in his own claims.

Although a less significant matter, I was disappointed in Waldron's response to my appeal to the angel passages in Revelation 2–3. All four of the possible alternative interpretations are advocated by some. But Waldron, being a good student of the New Testament himself, knows that these views are weaker than the one I advocated and are never argued very convincingly.

Finally, Waldron thinks that multiple elders "may tend to deliver the church from becoming marked by the foibles and idiosyncrasies of one talented leader." The oversight here concerns the greater difficulty of overcoming the foibles and idiosyncrasies of a committee (ruling elders) than that of overcoming the failures of one man. Besides, this responsibility in congregationalism belongs to the church as a whole and not to a regulative body of elders.

Waldron's last concern is what he refers to as "the advisory nature of pastoral authority," which he supposes that I hold. Here I may have misled Waldron by what I said. So may I clarify my position by saying that I too believe in the "authority" of the elder or pastor. The injunctions of Hebrews 13:7, 17 for the saints of God *to remember* and even *to obey* those who have rule over them are clear enough. But there is nothing here or elsewhere in the New Testament to take away the ultimate responsibility of the entire congregation. The church as a whole, involving as it does a "kingdom of priests," is to seek the mind of the Spirit and follow the lordship of Christ. The pastor's "authority" is based on moral ascendancy. He is not a king or a governor. He is a spiritual leader and teacher. Having proven himself to be a genuine man of God, the church will hear him gladly if the congregation is spiritually determined. If the church is not spiritually motivated, no amount of authority vested in an elder will change that.

Waldron supposes that he defeats my point about the major leadership of one pastor-elder by citing the Lord's appointment of twelve apostles. First, it should be observed that the apostles were not the elders of a single church as far as we know. Even if they were viewed as the initial elders of the Jerusalem congregation, I am afraid that Waldron only demonstrates the point I am making. Surely it is obvious that James, John, and Peter, particularly John and Peter, achieved a leadership role more significant than the others. And even then, Peter is subject to the rebuke of Paul who was not even one of the Twelve (Gal. 2:11ff.)

In conclusion, let me simply restate my understanding in response to Waldron's concerns. I am a committed congregationalist, not a quasi-congregationalist. The principles of the indwelling of the Holy Spirit in every true believer and the priesthood of the believers provide the theological basis for establishing congregationalism and, further, the autonomy of each congregation. No convictional authority transcending the local congregation is observable, much less mandated, in the New Testament.

Absences of specific New Testament commandments concerning the number of elders appropriate to a congregation should generate careful humility in the claims of the interpreter. What does seem to emerge rather clearly from the Bible is that the Lord intended his churches to have both deacons (no number specified) and pastors (elders, bishops—also with no number specified). I can only conclude that the determination of the number of such deacons and pastors depended largely upon the need for such. Furthermore, the pattern of God's activity throughout the Bible as well as the continuing pattern in church history of God's raising up primary individuals as decisive leaders points to a teaching-elder (a pastor) in every congregation who carries on his shoulders responsibility for the church under the ultimate authority of Christ through the saints of the autonomous congregation. There is no more *abnormality* or *deficiency* in a local church with only one elder than in a church with only one deacon. If *ministry* is the issue, one can minister as surely as many.

A PLURAL-ELDER CONGREGATIONALIST'S CLOSING REMARKS

Samuel E. Waldron

The responses in this volume to my chapter have generally been both thoughtful and kind. Before I walk back onto the playing field of debate in the rest of my conclusion, I want to offer each of my theological opponents a kind of written handshake and thank-you for a hard-fought, but fairly played ecclesiastical match. Having reiterated my great respect for each of them as Christians and churchmen, in the rest of this conclusion I will attempt one more time to make clear why they are wrong (!) in the various disagreements they have expressed with the position I have defended.

A SURREJOINDER TO TOON

Most of what I might wish to say in rejoinder to Toon's response to me was already said in my response to his chapter. I refer the reader to that response and to the relevant parts of my chapter. In particular note my comments about the regulative principle, early tradition, how early tradition at points contradicts the New Testament, the recognition of the Canon, and the divine authority of the Lord's Day.

On Various Misunderstandings of What I Said

Toon seems to think that I believe that Ignatius and other early bishops claimed authority over the churches to which they wrote. Actually, I said the opposite: "For even when we read the epistles of Ignatius, there is no evidence that a bishop possesses any authority outside his own (local) church."

Toon objects to my statement that Ignatius's teaching is "contrary to the teaching of the New Testament." He thinks this statement anachronistic and asks:

> Was there a canon of the New Testament in the time of Ignatius of Antioch? The Canon evolved slowly and was not truly *the* Canon for another century or more. Do we know what parts of the later New Testament that Ignatius possessed? Here we have an author assuming first that the New Testament was available (seemingly as we have it) in the year AD 120 or so, then assuming that it would be studied in much the same way as it is in Protestant seminaries in North America, and then coming to conclusions on the basis of these two false premises.

Whether he knows it or not, Toon has significantly misrepresented what I was saying in the place from which he cites my words. Here is what I said: "The first and fatal step away from this original system of church government and toward the monarchical episcopate of Catholicism happened when, *contrary to the teaching of the New Testament*, the title 'bishop' was reserved for the leading presbyter in each church."

First, I never said Ignatius had the whole New Testament in the form that we have it. I do not believe he did. Second, I reject the view of the recognition of the Canon assumed by Toon. Consult my response to his chapter.

Third, all this is irrelevant to my simple point. The New Testament beyond any shadow of a doubt teaches that the offices of elder and bishop are equivalent. When anyone (including Ignatius) teaches contrary to this by distinguishing the two offices, they contradict the teaching of the New Testament. How else can it be said? This assertion assumes neither that Ignatius had the Canon as we have it, nor that it was studied in exactly the same way that it is studied in Protestant seminaries in North America. It does assume the authority, clarity, and sufficiency of the Scriptures!

On Why Christians Disagree

Toon thinks that the disagreements among genuine Christians about church polity show that the scope of the Scriptures does not include the issue of church polity: "If the sovereign Lord had intended to make the precise details of church government part of the apostolic message, then he would have surely caused his servants to make the matter clear to all of sound mind." This is a conclusion that has seemed reasonable to other Christians beside Toon—and on other issues! Let us test it.

People disagree on the issue of whether Calvinism or Arminianism properly understands the teaching of Scripture on salvation. Does Toon wish to say that this issue is also not decided by Scripture? I doubt it. I also doubt that he wishes to say that either Calvinists or Arminians are not Christians. I doubt that he wants to say that one party or another is not *of sound mind.* So true Christians of sound mind disagree, but Toon still thinks, I assume, that the issue is clear in Scripture. In fact, I assume that Toon thinks that many issues are clearly revealed in Scripture about which Christians of sound mind disagree. So also church polity may be clear in Scripture, even if Christians disagree about the matter!

The fact is that sin has intellectual consequences (Rom. 1:21; Eph. 4:17–19). Even Christians have remaining sin (1 John 1:6–2:2). Even in Christians, therefore, sin has intellectual consequences. Because I admit that the issue of church polity is not so central to biblical revelation as certain other doctrines, it is easy for me to see how even very holy Anglicans (with remaining sin) can be wrong on this issue. Plural-elder congregationalists are not necessarily and in general holier than Anglicans. Christians are subject to the subtle, noetic effects of sin and must test everything in light of the Word of God. Since our remaining sin may blind us to aspects of divine revelation, the fact that we disagree does not mean that divine revelation is obscure.

On the Fallibility of Early Church History

Toon appeals again and again to early church history. I have no wish to depreciate the study of church history. Far be it from me! On the contrary, having taught church history for many years, I am well aware of the many benefits of a thorough understanding of church history. Toon appeals to church history on this issue, however, with the air of a man playing the high trump in a card game. The unwary may conclude from this that, at least when we come to the earliest periods of church history, we find a pure church free from the corruptions of later periods. I have already warned the reader against accepting this tantalizing assumption, but perhaps a few illustrations will reveal how treacherous is the premise upon which Toon has built his view. The following illustrations are taken from this earliest period of the post-apostolic church, the apostolic fathers.

Let it be said that the apostolic fathers were consciously intent on preserving, both doctrinally and practically, apostolic Christianity. In spite of this, however, instances of amazing declension from the level of New Testament revelation were multiplied. Sincerity is no substitute for truth.

Clement of Rome's letter to the Corinthians was written probably around AD 97. This letter most closely parallels the thought of apostolic literature of any of the apostolic fathers. Even here, however, the contrast with the apostles is apparent. Without any sense of absurdity, Clement appeals to the story of the phoenix in proof of the resurrection.

> Let us consider, dear friends, how the Master continually points out to us that there will be a future resurrection. Of this he made the Lord Jesus Christ the first fruits by raising him from the dead. . . .
>
> Let us note the remarkable token which comes from the East, from the neighborhood, that is, of Arabia. There is a bird which is called a phoenix. It is the only one of its kind and lives five hundred years. When the time for its departure and death draws near, it makes a burial nest for itself from frankincense, myrrh and other spices; and when the time is up, it gets into it and dies. From its decaying flesh a worm is produced, which is nourished by the secretions of the dead creature and grows wings. When it is full-fledged, it takes up the burial nest containing the bones of its predecessor, and manages to carry them all the way from Arabia to the Egyptian city called Heliopolis. And in broad daylight, so that everyone can see, it lights at the altar of the sun and puts them down there, and so starts home again. The priests then look up their dated records

and discover it has come after a lapse of five hundred years. Shall we, then, imagine that it is something great and surprising if the Creator of the universe raises up those who have served him in holiness and in the assurance born of a good faith, when he uses a mere bird to illustrate the greatness of his promise? For he says somewhere: "And you shall raise me up and I shall give you thanks"; and, "I lay down and slept: I rose up because you are with me." And again Job says, "And you will make this flesh of mine, which has endured all this, to rise up."[40]

Another example of the early decline from apostolic Christianity may be found in the *Didache,* commonly known as *The Teaching of the Twelve Apostles*, various parts of which are dated between the years 80 and 120. The *Didache* unconsciously manifests an externalism often associated with legalism. Referring to Jesus' warning in the Gospels not to fast as the hypocrites do (Matt. 6:16; Luke 18:12), it remarks, "Your fasts must not be identical with those of the hypocrites. They fast on Mondays and Thursdays; but you should fast on Wednesdays and Fridays."[41]

Ignatius (writing either in 107 or 116) illustrates the extravagant language that later gave rise to false doctrine regarding the Lord's Supper:

> At these meetings you should heed the bishop and presbytery attentively, and break one loaf, which is the medicine of immortality, and the antidote which wards off death but yields continuous life in union with Jesus Christ.[42]

These examples are from three of the earliest and most trustworthy writings of the apostolic fathers. Examples of this sort and much worse could be multiplied in later writings, even in the second century. My point is that the unwary must not think that all is as wonderful with the early church as Toon's argument makes it appear.

A SURREJOINDER TO TAYLOR

I am not surprised to find that Taylor expresses a number of areas of agreement with and appreciation for my chapter, given that we share a deep respect for the Reformed tradition. For this I thank him.

On the Regulative Principle

One thing for which Taylor expresses appreciation is my embrace of the regulative principle of worship and its application to church government. He considers, however, that I may embrace the regulative principle a little too tightly and with a little too much enthusiasm. Thus, he remarks in a number of places that I take a more restrictive view of the regulative principle than he, Calvin, or the Westminster Confession. I certainly am aware that the regulative principle has not infrequently been used to justify a reactionary conservatism when it comes to worship. I do not think that I embrace views typical of such reactionary conservatism.[43]

On the other hand, it is interesting to me that Taylor does not appear to give a very strong presentation of the regulative principle himself. The one part of the Westminster Confession that Taylor cites on this issue is the qualifying statement in 1:6. When he gives his own rendition of the regulative principle, it seems rather weak compared to the confession. He says: "God regulates the church's worship and government through the Scriptures, that the church does not have the authority to require what the Word of God does not require." This is true as far as it goes, but compare the statement of the regulative principle in the Westminster Confession (21:1):

> But the acceptable way of worshipping the true God, is instituted by himself, and so limited by his own revealed will, that he may not be worshipped according to the imagination and devices of men, nor the suggestions of Satan, under any visible representations, or any other way not prescribed in the Holy Scriptures.

It seems clear to me that Taylor's statement is weak as compared to that of his own confession.

On the Distinction between Pastors and Elders

One place at which Taylor thinks I illustrate my more restrictive view of the regulative principle is in regard to the role of the pastor. On the one hand, it is certainly true that my view of the regulative principle does enable me to see this matter quite clearly. On the other hand, one does not need to have a "restrictive view" or any other kind of view of the regulative

principle to see my point. Take the Scriptures simply as normative and one sees that they equate the offices of elder and pastor. Simple submission to the Scriptures, then, requires us to
refrain from distinguishing the two.[44]

If Taylor's view of the regulative principle is so broad as to
allow him to distinguish elders and pastors where the Scriptures
do not, then why is it not also broad enough to allow him to distinguish elders and bishops? What is the difference? Of course,
no presbyterian can or will accept such a distinction. The essence
of their age-old polemic against episcopalianism is that elders and
bishops occupy the same office. It seems to me that Taylor must
accept that elders and pastors are equivalent or give up presbyterianism. For on the same ground that he distinguishes elders
and pastors, episcopalians may distinguish elders and bishops.

On the Authority of Elders

I want to clear up some confusion about my position on the
authority of elders that results from this statement of Taylor:
"Waldron takes a mediating position between elders having no
authority and their being only advisory." Taylor is right when he
describes my position on this matter as mediating, but not correct in describing the two positions that I hope to mediate. My
view is rather this. The positions that elders have no authority
and that their authority is only advisory seem to me to be substantially the same. They constitute one end of the spectrum. The
other end of the spectrum is presbyterianism in which elders are
viewed as constituting the church with power, for instance, even
to excommunicate without the consent of the church. These are
the two "extremes" that I attempt to mediate in my position.

On Presbyterian Connectionalism

I have nothing to add to my argument against presbyterian
connectionalism here. If the reader has any questions about the
significance of what is said here, I urge that he or she consult the
argument for independency in my chapter and my argument
against presbyterian connectionalism in my response to Taylor.

In his response to me, however, Taylor makes a claim that
seems to miss the entire point of my argument. To assure myself

that the reader does not miss the point, I will respond to his claim. Here is what Taylor says:

> However, once one concedes this [the church of Jerusalem's unique authority over the whole church], the argument for independency is lost, for the very essence of independency is that no local church or synod of churches has any authority in matters of theology and discipline over another. Whether the church of Jerusalem had a "unique authority" over the churches or whether it was a synodical authority, the fact remains it was an authority contrary to congregationalism/independency.

I think not! My point is that the Jerusalem church (primarily because of the presence of living apostles) exercised an authority over the whole church. This authority was unique to and limited by the peculiar realities of the apostolic age. With the passing of that foundational and transitional period, the unique authority of both living apostles on earth and the transitional importance of the mother church in Jerusalem passed away. The authority of the Jerusalem council was real, but apostolic, and so limited to the apostolic period of church history. It creates no precedent or model for authoritative councils on earth today.

One further word of explanation may be appropriate. Independents like myself do not hold the absolute independence of the local church. Rather, we emphatically affirm the authority of Christ and his apostles over local churches. Through Christ's Spirit and the apostolic Scriptures a real authority is exercised over local churches. Independents only argue that the local church is free from any higher authority *on earth today.* We do not argue that local churches were independent of the apostolic authority on earth during the apostolic period.

A SURREJOINDER TO PATTERSON

On the Plurality of Elders

In his generally appreciative response to my chapter, Patterson seeks to cast doubt on the evidence I brought forward for the normative character of a plurality of elders in each local church. Before I address one or two particulars in Patterson's response to me on the subject of plurality of elders, it is important to remind the reader of exactly what I said on the issue. First, I pointed out that there is no example in the New Testament of a local church with only one elder. Second, I pointed out a lengthy list of churches in the New Testament that clearly or probably possessed a plurality of elders. Third, in my response to Patterson's chapter, I noted that the very idea of an elder throughout the Scriptures implies the idea of a ruling council composed of several elders. To speak of a one-man eldership is to speak of a one-man council—an oddity and abnormality that should shortly be rectified. Patterson in his response asks, "Why should a new congregation of ten to twenty or even forty people have multiple elders?" The answer is simply that even small churches need ruling councils. Contrary to contemporary church practice, these councils should be composed, not of deacons, but of elders.

Here we come to an exegetical matter that Patterson raises to me when he writes: "When 'elders' are mentioned for multiple cities—as for example on Crete (Titus 1:5) or for Lystra, Iconium, and Pisidian Antioch—the burden of proof falls on Waldron to show that the plural in the text requires multiple elders in *each* city." Since I have cited these examples in proving my position, there is a sense in which Patterson is right to say that the burden of proof falls on me. However, there is another sense in which Patterson is incorrect. My case is cumulative. I have cited a great deal of other evidence (summarized above) that is not dependent on the exegesis of Acts 14:23 and Titus 1:5. In fact, to some extent, the case is actually the reverse. The interpretation of Acts 14:23 and Titus 1:5 partly depends on this other evidence. The facts that (1) we know of no other church in the New Testament with only one elder, (2) all the others (where we have any evidence) had a plurality of elders, and (3) the very idea of an elder (as we have noticed) implies a council of elders must surely influence the interpretation of Acts 14:23 and Titus 1:5. In such a case, the presumption surely should be that we should simply accept the most natural meaning of the text. That most natural meaning is that a plurality of elders was appointed in every church (Acts 14:23) or in every city (Titus 1:5).[45]

Patterson also asks, "How could they support their ministries?" Here I must remind the reader that I have argued that not all elders need be supported financially by the church. There is a legitimate diversity in this and in other respects. I insist on equality of *office*—not on equality of support. Here, however, we approach the other matter that I want to discuss in light of Patterson's response to me.

On the Parity of Elders

With respect to the issue of the parity of elders, I can only hope that the reader will understand me better than Patterson has. Since this lack of understanding may be my own fault, let me attempt to restate more clearly the main points that I made in my chapter and my response to Patterson.

First, I have not denied that significant diversity among elders in the same church may exist consistent with true parity. I have made an important distinction between authority and influence. Patterson notes my comments on the *primus inter pares* (first among equals) system that seems to have existed in some churches in the earliest period after the apostles. I have no problem with an elder who is first among equals *as long as the others are really equal.* One may be first in influence and usefulness, as long as the others are his peers in office and authority. Thus, I admit that, for instance, Spurgeon's elders were not his equals, but I insist that, though they could not have been his equals in usefulness, they should have been his equals in office and authority. If they had been, the church Spurgeon led might have fared better after his premature death.

Second, Patterson has in my judgment never assailed the exegetical basis of my insistence on parity. He admits that elder, shepherd, and overseer describe one and the same office in the New Testament. If all elders (presbyters) are also shepherds (pastors) and overseers (bishops), then all may be called by those titles. All also have the same office and, therefore, the same authority of the office. If Patterson is to disprove parity of office—and parity of office is all that I am insisting upon—he must prove either that these titles do not refer to the same office, or he must prove that certain elders possess another office in addition to that of elder-shepherd-overseer. Until he can prove one of these things, he has no right to resist the clear, biblical evidence for parity. In my judgment he cannot prove, and has not attempted to prove, either.

On the 1689 Baptist Confession

Taylor and Patterson both seem to think that the 1689 Baptist Confession (also known as the Second London Baptist Confession and later—when adopted and slightly revised in North America—as the Philadelphia Baptist Confession) supports a distinction between pastors and elders. This matter is not so clear as they assume. The relevant statements are found in the extended treatment in the chapter on the doctrine of the church. Here are the relevant statements found in Chapter 26:8–11. I have italicized the relevant phraseology.

8. A particular church, gathered and completely organized according to the mind of Christ, consists of officers and members; and the officers appointed by Christ to be chosen and set apart by the church (so called and gathered), for the peculiar administration of ordinances, and execution of power or duty, which he intrusts them with, or calls them to, to be continued to the end of the world, are *bishops or elders*, and deacons.

9. The way appointed by Christ for the calling of any person, fitted and gifted by the Holy Spirit, unto *the office of bishop or elder* in a church, is, that he be chosen thereunto by the common suffrage of the church itself; and solemnly set apart by fasting and prayer, with imposition of hands of *the eldership of the church*, if there be any before constituted therein; and of a deacon that he be chosen by the like suffrage, and set apart by prayer, and the like imposition of hands.

10. *The work of pastors* being constantly to attend the service of Christ, in his churches, in the ministry of the word and prayer, with watching for their souls, as they that must give an account to Him; it is incumbent on the churches to whom they minister, not only to give them all due respect, but also to communicate to them of all their good things according to their ability, so as they may have a comfortable supply, without being themselves entangled in secular affairs; and may also be capable of exercising hospitality towards others; and this is required by

the law of nature, and by the express order of our Lord Jesus, who hath ordained that they that preach the Gospel should live of the Gospel.

11.   Although it be incumbent on *the bishops or pastors of the churches*, to be instant in preaching the word, by way of office, yet the work of preaching the word is not so peculiarly confined to them but that others also gifted and fitted by the Holy Spirit for it, and approved and called by the church, may and ought to perform it.

When these paragraphs are examined carefully, it turns out that no distinction between pastors and elders is to be found in them. Paragraph 8 seems to equate bishops and elders. Paragraph 9 similarly equates bishops and elders and speaks of the eldership of the church ordaining additional elders. Paragraph 10 speaks of the importance of pastors being supported, but says nothing of their relation to bishops and elders. Paragraph 11 seems to equate bishops and pastors. While perfect clarity may not be attainable, there is certainly nothing like a clear distinction between pastors and elders made in these paragraphs. The evidence in fact inclines in the opposite direction with paragraphs 8 and 9 appearing to equate elders and bishops and paragraph 11 seeming to equate bishops and pastors. Thus, it seems that elders equal bishops who equal pastors.

CONCLUSION

I stated my deepest heart concern for the evangelical reader in chapter 4 of this book. It remains my deepest concern today.

I have a profoundly different approach to this subject than much of contemporary evangelicalism. Like the Ephesian disciples of John the Baptist who told Paul, "We have not even heard whether there is a Holy Spirit" (Acts 19:2), many evangelicals tell us by their conduct that they have not even heard whether there is a biblical church government. Without shame, many act as if they were allowed to order "the house of God, which is the church of the living God" (1 Tim. 3:15) according to their human traditions, personal tastes, and natural reason. My defense of plural-elder congregationalism is, among other things, a protest against such attitudes in evangelical churches.

Although I hope that I have made a convincing case for the details of my position, my deepest hope is that the reader will be convinced that there is a biblical church government and that he or she has a solemn duty to honor it.

Chapter 5: Closing Remarks Notes

L. Roy Taylor

[1]Note his frequent use of exclamation points in his response.

[2]See Peter Toon, *Puritans and Calvinism* (Swengel, Pa.: Reiner Publications, 1973).

[3]See chapter 1, note 28.

[4]"All synods and councils, since the apostles' time, whether general or particular, may err; and many have erred." Westminster Confession of Faith, XXXI, 3.

[5]Augsburg Confession, Article XXII.

[6]Thirty-Nine Articles of Religion, Article XIX, adopted by the Church of England and the Protestant Episcopal Church in the United States of America. See also The Irish Articles of Religion, Article 78, Irish Episcopal Church, 1615.

[7]Peter Toon, *Yesterday, Today and Forever* (Swedesboro, N.J.: Preservation Press, 1996), 191.

[8]Calvin reintroduced presbyterian polity to the church in the Reformation.

[9]Some of my English ancestors served within the episcopal ministry of the Church of England. I do not regard them as "heretics."

[10]These were (1) the persecution factor, (2) the geographical-political factor, and (3) the efficiency factor. I will also concede, as Toon advocates, that as the church patterned its ministry more after the Old Testament priesthood, it developed a hierarchy.

[11]Apostles' Creed, Nicene Creed, Athanasian Creed.

[12]In the early church, Gentiles would more easily understand "bishop" and the Jews would more easily understand the term "elder."

[13]Advocated by the Eastern Orthodox churches, the Roman Catholic Church, and some Anglicans.

[14]I suggest that the reason for decline in the number of Presbyterian missionaries was due to theological decline, not to church polity. This writer's denomination, the Presbyterian Church in America, sends one missionary for every five hundred of its communicant members. A denomination with an evangelical theology does not find a presbyterian church government to be a hindrance to missions. Compare to the present ratio of members to missionaries in the Southern Baptist Convention which is now approximately one missionary for every four thousand members.

[15]Some examples are the use of parliamentary procedure in conducting church business meetings (a British and North American tradition), the use of committees, boards, and agencies, etc. Southern Baptists are noted not only for their zeal for evangelism but also for the size and complexity of their denominational organizations. It is doubtful that Baptists would feel obligated to cite biblical proof text for each minute detail of denominational operations.

[16]Patterson notes, "The sometimes devastating results of improperly distinguishing between Israel and the church can properly be observed in the tendency to equate New Testament baptism with circumcision and, therefore, with the determination to baptize infants." Note that Paul equates baptism with circumcision (Col. 2:11–12).

[17]Systematized by English Plymouth Brethren, most notably John Nelson Darby, and popularized in America through the *Scofield Reference Bible*, Lewis S. Chafer's *Systematic Theology*, the writings of faculty from Dallas Theological Seminary, and the Bible institute/college movement.

[18]Calvin saw five basic differences between the testaments. First, in the Old Testament God used material blessing as the visible evidence of his blessing, grace, mercy, and favor in order to prompt his people to trust, obey, and worship him. In the New Testament there is little emphasis at all on material blessings. Second, in the Old Testament, God used symbols, types, and figures (sometimes rather cryptically) to reveal his attributes and covenant. In the New Testament the ceremonial law with all its symbolic prefigures of the Messiah has been fulfilled in the once-for-all-time death and resurrection of Christ and the bloody covenant signs of the previous era (Passover and circumcision) have been superceded by the Lord's Supper and baptism. Third, in both testaments there are emphases on law and gospel, death and life, external form and inward reality, literal and spiritual, ceremonial and experiential, condemnation and deliverance, temporal blessings and eternal life. The Old Testament places a stronger emphasis on the former, whereas the New Testament places a stronger emphasis on the latter. Fourth, because the New Testament is a fuller revelation of the grace of God, the New Testament sounds more clearly the message of spiritual freedom versus bondage, of hope and assurance versus uncertainty. Fifth, and most significantly, in the Old Testament God's grace was shown primarily and almost exclusively to national Israel and through her prophets. But in the New Testament, there is an effusion of grace upon the Gentiles, to all nations of the earth. See John Calvin, *Institutes of the Christian Religion*, trans. Ford Lewis Battles, 2 vols. (Philadelphia: Westminster Press, 1960), 1:429, 430, 450, 453, 456, 458, 460, 461.

[19]For an extensive discussion see Oswald T. Allis, *Prophecy and the Church: An Examination of the Claim of Dispensationalists That the Christian Church Is a Mystery Parenthesis Which Interrupts the Fulfillment to Israel of the Kingdom Prophecies of the Old Testament* (Philadelphia: Presbyterian and Reformed, 1972).

[20]The Westminster Confession of Faith states, "The catholic or universal Church, which is invisible, consists of the whole number of the elect, that have been, are, or shall be gathered into one, under Christ the Head thereof; and is the spouse, the body, the fullness of Him that filleth all in all. The visible Church, which is also catholic or universal under the Gospel (not confined to one nation, as before under the law), consists of all those throughout the world that profess the true religion; and of their children: and is the kingdom of the Lord Jesus Christ, the house and family of God, out of which there is no ordinary possibility of salvation" (XXV, 1, 2). See also chapter 2, note 12.

[21]See also Isa. 40:5; 66:23; Pss. 65:2; 145:21.

[22]Additionally, Peter in his first epistle quotes three Old Testament statements about Israel being fulfilled in the church [Lev. 19:2 (1 Peter 1:15); Hos. 2:23 (1 Peter 2:2–10); Ex. 19:5–6 (1 Peter 2:9)]. In 2 Corinthians 6:16, Paul links together a chain of Old Testament passages, originally descriptive of Israel, as being fulfilled in their highest sense in the church (Lev. 26:11ff; Ezek. 37:26ff; Jer. 24:7). In Romans 9:24, Paul speaks of God's presently calling Gentiles as

well as Jews to himself through the gospel. As proof Paul quotes Hosea 2:23 and Isaiah 1:9 which were originally addressed to Old Testament Israel. At the end of his epistles Paul frequently closes with a benediction. As he blessed the churches of Galatia composed of both Jewish and Gentile believers (Gal. 6:15), he calls upon the Lord to grant mercy and peace upon the church, "the Israel of God." But Paul's most lengthy discussion on the continuity of believers from the Old Testament is Galatians 3, in which he draws a direct connection between Old Testament believers within ethnic Israel and New Testament believers when he discusses the Abrahamic covenant. Paul emphasizes that God preached the gospel to Abraham in the Abrahamic covenant, foreseeing the day when God would justify the Gentiles by faith in Abraham's promised seed, the Lord Jesus Christ (Gal. 3:7–9). Gentile believers in Christ are recipients of the covenant promises and blessings given through Abraham (Gal. 3:9, 14, 22, 29). Indeed Gentiles believers in Christ are sons of Abraham (Gal. 3:7, 14, 29)! See also Romans 4:16, where Paul says unequivocally to Jewish and Gentile Christians alike that Abraham is the father of us all.

[23]The conversion of the Gentiles was predicted several times in the prophets (Hos. 1:10; 2:23; 12:22; Joel 2:28–32; Amos 9:11–12; Isa. 2:2, 3; 11:10; 45:22; 49:6–8; 52:15; 53:11; 60:1–5; Jer. 31:31–34; Dan. 7:27) and the psalms (Pss. 2:8; 22:27; 47:2–8; 72:7–11, 17; 86:9; 110:1; 117:1), and is a fulfillment of the covenant of grace given through Abraham (Rom. 4:13–25; Gal. 3:5–29). The term "mystery" is used twenty-nine times in the New Testament, most often by Paul. For example, he uses it to refer to Christ (Col. 2:2, 4:3; 1 Tim. 3:16). All Christians agree that there are numerous references to Christ in the Old Testament both in prophecies and types, but the fuller explanation of the Trinity, the two advents, Christ's divine and human natures, and his present intercessory ministry are explained in the New Testament. In the same way, the concept of the church as the people of God, both believing Jews and Gentiles, is set forth in the Old Testament, but the *details* and the *fuller implications* of that truth are revealed in the New Testament. As Paul explicitly states, "This mystery is that the Gentiles are fellow heirs, members of the same body, and partakers of the promise in Christ Jesus through the gospel" (Eph. 3:6). The mystery is that Gentiles are heirs to the covenant promises given through the prophets, that believing Jews and Gentiles are part of the same body (cf. Rom. 11:13–24) and beneficiaries of the covenant promises fulfilled in Christ. There was great animosity between the Jews and the Gentiles. Part of the mystery is that Christ unites the two in peace (Eph. 2:14–16), removing the animosity. In fact, Paul uses several analogies to describe the benefits of the gospel to the Gentiles (vv. 11–22) and their equal standing with Jewish Christians before he uses the term "mystery" to refer to the church in chapter 3.

[24]In single-elder congregationalism, ministers are the only elders. In episcopal church government, the ministers (or priests) are the only elders. In neither system are there any ruling elders, or lay elders.

[25]In single-elder congregationalism, deacons are the spiritual administrative leaders of the church. In an episcopal system, deacon is an entry-level clergy position to a three-level clergy of deacon, presbyter (priest), and bishop.

[26]Both confessions affirm one covenant of grace spanning both testaments, and one people of God, the elect of both testaments united into the invisible church. A Reformed Baptist could affirm the 1689 Baptist Confession affirming one covenant of grace and one people of God, whereas a dispensationalist Baptist could not. In this instance, the 1689 Baptist Confession, 26:1 is a quotation of the Westminster Confession, 25:1 with only slight alterations.

[27]See my surrejoiner to Patterson for my refutation of the dispensational view of the church.

[28]Deut. 10:16; 30:6; Jer. 4:4.

[29]"To them also, as a body politic, He gave sundry judicial laws, which expired together with the state of that people; not obliging any other now, further than the general equity thereof may require." Westminster Confession of Faith, 19:4.

[30]The death penalty was in effect in the Old Testament theocracy for adultery, blasphemy, Sabbath breaking, etc. (Lev. 20:10, 11, 15, 16; 18:22; 20:13; 24:11–14; Ex. 35:2; Num. 15:32–36; Deut. 13:1–10).

[31]Jesus did not urge the stoning of the woman caught in adultery (John 7:53–8:11) and Paul urged the excommunication of the Corinthian adulterer, not his execution (1 Cor. 5:1–13).

[32]Gen. 3:15; 12:1–3; 15:5–6 (Rom. 4:3; Gal. 3:6); Pss. 2:8; 22:27; 110:1; Hos. 1:10; 2:23; Joel 2:28–32; Amos 9:10–12; Isa. 2:2–3; 11:10; 25:6–12; 45:22; 49:6–8; 52:15; 53:11; 60:1–5; Dan. 2:44–45; 7:13–14, 27; Matt. 13:31, 33; 22:1–14; Mark 4:26–29, 30–34; Luke 13:6–9, 18, 20; Rev. 5:9; 19:7–10.

[33]The issue of the continuity of the church from the Old Testament to the New Testament and the relationship of continuities and discontinuities from the Old Testament to the New Testament are important in a number of matters, particularly on the issues of sacraments and polity. Concerning the former, this is why Patterson (a dispensationalist) and Waldron (who is Reformed) as Baptists must both object to my position, since the principles of one covenant of grace and one people of God spanning both testaments form the basis for the Reformed and Covenantal view of baptism that includes infants of believers, just as circumcision was the covenant sign administered to children of believers in the Old Testament. The focus of this volume is on polity so I devote my reply primarily to polity.

[34]Waldron states, "There are three concentric circles of elders (all qualified elders, the elders who rule well, and those who work hard at preaching and teaching) and not just two types of elders." All elders teach in certain ways (by godly example, one-to-one discipleship, ministry to small groups of believers, ministry to larger groups, or, in some cases formal preaching/teaching in the context of public worship).

[35]1 Cor. 12:28; Rom. 12:8; 1 Tim. 5:17.

[36]For example, Judg. 12:7; Mic. 4:3; Isa. 2:4; Joel 3:10.

[37]Hebrews 13:17 would reinforce such a view. "Shepherding" (Acts 20:28; 1 Peter 5:1–2), which is the duty of all elders under both plural-elder congregationalism and presbyterianism, includes not only instruction in the Word, discipleship, encouragement, etc., but spiritual discipline of the flock as well.

Paige Patterson

[38]*Theological Dictionary of the New Testament*, Vol. VI, 701.

[39]*Theological Dictionary of the New Testament*, Vol II, 907.

Samuel E. Waldron

[40]Clement of Rome's *Epistle to the Corinthians*, chapters 24–26. Cf. Cyril C. Richardson, *Early Christian Fathers* (New York: Collier Books, Macmillan, 1970), 55–56.

[41]*Didache* 8:1; Richardson, *Early Christian Fathers*, 174.

[42]Ignatius, *To the Ephesians*, 20:2; Richardson, *Early Christian Fathers*, 93.

[43]Taylor mentions two illustrations of such conservatism: exclusive *a cappella* psalmody and the refusal to receive offerings during worship. Just so the record is clear, I reject exclusive psalmody and believe that the reception of offerings during worship is mandated by Scripture.

[44]The evidence for the equivalence of the office of pastor and elder is expounded at length in both my chapter and my response to Taylor's chapter.

[45]Notice how the singular church is juxtaposed with the plural elders in Acts 14:23 (*kat ekklesian presbyterous*) and how the singular city is juxtaposed with the plural elders in Titus 1:5 in an identical construction (*kata polin presbyterous*).

CONCLUSION

Steven B. Cowan

Who runs the church? Is the government of the visible church primarily in the hands of a hierarchy of priests and bishops? Or is it in the hands of an elected assembly of elders? Or is it governed by a team of pastor/elders? Or one strong pastor? Or by the deacons or the congregation? These have been the central questions of this book.

As the reader no doubt knows by now, the contributors to this volume are sharply divided on these questions. This should come as no surprise. Christians have been divided on the subject of church polity for at least five hundred years. This division has persisted, as I pointed out in the introduction, because Christians typically have seen the question of church government as vitally relevant to the *bene esse* of the church. The health and vitality of the body of Christ has been perceived to depend, in part, on how the government of the church is structured. On this point, all of the contributors to this volume are united. We do not think that the question of church polity is a question that Christians may safely ignore or trivialize. The practical consequences of decisions related to church government are too far-reaching, too affective in the lives of the saints, to be treated as a minor issue.

It is our hope that the readers of this book will be convinced of the importance of this topic if nothing else—convinced enough to carefully consider and evaluate the arguments presented herein both for and against each position represented. And convinced enough to engage in further serious study of church government. It is also our hope, in this same connection, that more Christian scholars (who have for so long ignored this subject) will do more research and writing on it. The church universal can only benefit from such renewed focus.

With this hope in mind, I wish to conclude this book by outlining in more detail the key questions that have arisen in the course of discussion, those questions that readers must answer if they are to reach their own conclusions regarding church government. I list these questions in a more or less descending order of relevance (that is, answers to subsequent questions in the list may depend on answers to prior questions).

1. *Must we follow the regulative principle in addressing the subject of church government?* That is, must we adhere to the rule that our views on church government are strictly limited to what the biblical data allow? Or, are we free to supplement and/or revise the biblical data on church polity using reason, common sense, church tradition, etc.?

2. *To what extent may church tradition, especially the tradition from the first five centuries of church history, influence our views on church government?* Are the theological views of the church fathers to be considered normative or authoritative on this matter?

3. *Are there biblical or theological grounds for connectionalism?* That is, are there good reasons to think that there should be an ecclesiastical structure beyond the local church, whether episcopal or presbyterian in nature? Or, are there grounds for affirming the autonomy of the local church?

4. *Who are the officers of the local church?* Are there pastors/elders who lead the church? Are there priests/rectors? Should the church have deacons? May there be other church officers such as associate pastors, youth ministers, etc.?

5. *Must there be a plurality of pastors/elders?* Are there biblical or theological grounds for insisting that a fully organized local church must be led by multiple elders? Or, is it sufficient that a church have only one elder?

6. *In churches that have multiple pastors/elders, may official distinctions be made between them?* That is, may teaching elders be distinguished from ruling elders (presbyterianism), or may senior pastors be distinguished from other pastors (associate pastors, youth pastors, etc.) considered subordinate (both presbyterian-

ism and single-elder congregationalism)? Or, is there parity of office among plural elders (plural-elder congregationalism)?

7. *What authority do pastors/elders have in the local church?* Is their authority absolute? Are they accountable to the congregation or to officers outside the local church? How should pastors be chosen? How may pastors be disciplined or removed from office?

8. *What is the role of the deacons in the local church?* Do they have any governing authority? What is their relationship to the pastors/elders? What is their function within the church?

9. *Is there a biblical or theological basis for the episcopate?* That is, what if any grounds are there for the office of bishop distinct from and superior to the office of pastor? Should there be a hierarchical ecclesiastical structure beyond the local church?

10. *Is there a biblical or theological basis for a representative form of government beyond the local church?* That is, do we have grounds for the establishment of church assemblies consisting of leaders from multiple churches who make policy for all those represented?

These are the major questions that must be answered in the debate over church government. May the Holy Spirit illumine and guide you as you seek to discern God's will in this matter.

DISCUSSION AND REFLECTION QUESTIONS

CHAPTER 1: EPISCOPALIANISM

1. What practical significance might there be in the differences Toon notes between the "Anglican Way" and other forms of episcopalianism such as the "Roman Catholic Way"?
2. Toon says, "It is difficult to believe that Almighty God ... would have allowed the church in its formative years ... to go so seriously wrong as to make a major mistake in terms of its general polity and church government." Do you agree? Why or why not?
3. Toon claims that the historical episcopate is the best means to set forth the continuity and unity of the universal church. Why does he think this? Do you agree? Why or why not?
4. What do you think are the most significant weaknesses in Toon's defense of episcopal church government as raised by the other authors?

CHAPTER 2: PRESBYTERIANISM

1. Taylor grants that, in addition to the Bible, other factors like common sense, culture, Christian wisdom, and local circumstances may play a role in determining some details of church government. What might be some specific ways in which these other factors would be relevant?
2. How does Acts 15 support the presbyterian system of government according to Taylor? Do you find his case convincing? Why or why not?

3. What are presbyterianism's practical benefits? Are there any significant weaknesses that Taylor overlooks?
4. What do you think are the most significant weaknesses in Taylor's defense of presbyterian church government as raised by the other authors?

CHAPTER 3: SINGLE-ELDER CONGREGATIONALISM

1. What does Patterson think is the relevance of the priesthood of all believers to the issue of church government? Do you agree with his assessment? Why or why not?
2. How does Patterson respond to the apparent "enigma" of biblical texts that may be interpreted to support other forms of church government? Does his response satisfy you? Why or why not?
3. Why does Patterson believe that in every New Testament church there was always one elder/pastor who was the primary leader? Do you agree? Why or why not?
4. What do you think are the most significant weaknesses in Patterson's defense of single-elder congregationalism as raised by the other authors?

CHAPTER 4: PLURAL-ELDER CONGREGATIONALISM

1. Waldron argues that the testimony of the apostolic fathers favors plural-elder congregationalism. What role, if any, does this argument play in the case for plural-elder congregationalism?
2. Much of Waldron's case depends upon the Puritan (regulative) principle. Do you agree with this principle? Why or why not?
3. Waldron says that the "lack of a plurality of elders in any church constitutes a real deficiency in its government." Do you agree? Why or why not?
4. What do you think are the most significant weaknesses in Waldron's defense of plural-elder congregationalism as raised by the other authors?

CHAPTER 5: CLOSING REMARKS

1. Toon argues that episcopal polity is correct because those in the ancient church who presided over the recognition of the Canon saw no conflict between biblical teaching and episcopal polity. Do you find this argument persuasive? Why or why not?
2. Much of Taylor's defense of presbyterian polity depends on his view of the continuity between the Old and New Testaments. Has he adequately defended this view? Why or why not?
3. Patterson is accused by other authors of holding his single-elder view on purely pragmatic grounds. Do you think he has adequately responded to this charge? Why or why not?
4. Someone might object to Waldron's view on the parity of elders by saying, "You can't run a church by committee—someone has to be in charge!" Could Waldron respond to this objection? If so, how?

ABOUT THE CONTRIBUTORS

Dr. Steven B. Cowan is associate director of the Apologetics Resource Center in Birmingham, Alabama. He earned his Ph.D. in philosophy from the University of Arkansas. He is an adjunct professor at Southeastern Bible College, Birmingham Theological Seminary, and New Orleans Baptist Theological Seminary. Dr. Cowan served for eight years as pastor of a Southern Baptist church. He is the author of numerous articles in the areas of philosophy, apologetics, and theology, and was the general editor of the Counterpoints book *Five Views on Apologetics.*

Dr. Paige Patterson is president of Southwestern Baptist Theological Seminary in Fort Worth, Texas. He earned his Th.M. and Th.D. degrees in theology at New Orleans Baptist Theological Seminary. He has pastored numerous Baptist churches and twice served as president of the Southern Baptist Convention. For seventeen years, Dr. Patterson served as president of Criswell College in Dallas, Texas, and for eleven years as president of Southeastern Baptist Theological Seminary, Wake Forest, North Carolina.

Dr. L. Roy Taylor is the stated clerk/coordinator of administration of the General Assembly of the Presbyterian Church in America. He earned the M.Div. from Grace Theological Seminary and the D.Min. from Fuller Theological Seminary. Dr. Taylor served as a PCA pastor for sixteen years, and has been professor of practical theology at Reformed Theological Seminary for ten years.

The Reverend Dr. Peter Toon was ordained deacon and priest in the Church of England in 1973–74. He is a member of Christ Church, Oxford, and has the Doctor of Philosophy from Oxford University. He is the author of more than twenty books and hundreds of articles and essays. In January 2002, Dr. Toon became rector of Christ Church, Biddulph Moor, Diocese of Lichfield, in the Church of England, after serving in the American

Episcopal Church for eleven years as a professor and as president of the Prayer Book Society.

Mr. Samuel E. Waldron is currently a Ph.D. candidate in systematic theology at the Southern Baptist Theological Seminary. He has earned the Th.M. from Grand Rapids Baptist Seminary. Mr. Waldron has been a pastor of the Reformed Baptist Church of Grand Rapids since 1977. He is also the author of numerous books and pamphlets including *The Modern Exposition of the 1689 Baptist Confession, In Defense of Parity: A Presentation of the Parity or Equality of Elders in the New Testament,* and *The End Times Made Simple*.

SCRIPTURE INDEX

SUBJECT INDEX